《金砖国家国别与合作研究》 总主编：董洪川
　　　　　　　　　　　　　　副总主编：刘玉梅

BRICS Studies

金砖国家
国别与合作研究

第二辑

蒲公英 / 游涵·主编

Brazil
Russia
India
China
South Africa

时事出版社
北京

《金砖国家国别与合作研究》编委会

总　主　编：董洪川
副总主编：刘玉梅

编委会委员：（按姓氏拼音为序）
　　　　　　谌华侨　刘梦茹　龙兴春　孟利君　段孟洁
　　　　　　蒲公英　严功军　游　涵　张　庆　朱天祥

学术顾问：（按姓氏拼音为序）
蔡春林　（广东工业大学）
陈　才　（西南科技大学）
程　晶　（湖北大学）
崔　铮　（辽宁大学）
邓瑞平　（西南大学）
江时学　（上海大学）
蓝庆新　（对外经贸大学）
林跃勤　（中国社会科学院）
卢　静　（外交学院）
王　磊　（北京师范大学）
徐　薇　（浙江师范大学）
徐秀军　（中国社会科学院）
杨　娜　（南开大学）
张淑兰　（山东大学）

卷首语

四川外国语大学金砖国家研究院成立于2013年5月，是重庆市人民政府外事侨务办公室与四川外国语大学协商共建的应用研究型机构。如今，金砖国家研究院既是中联部金砖国家智库合作中方理事会的理事单位（四川外国语大学为副理事长单位），又是教育部国别和区域研究备案中心，同时还是重庆"走出去"战略与金砖国家研究省级2011协同创新中心的牵头单位。在学校提出创建高水平应用研究型外国语大学目标的新背景下，金砖国家研究院将继续努力在应用研究和社会服务方面做出相应的贡献。

经过多年的实践和探索，研究院已正式将人文交流确定为川外金砖国家研究的主攻方向。这不仅有利于发挥学校外国语言文学学科的传统优势，而且有助于外语学科与其他人文社会学科的融合发展。目前，研究院借助学校英语、俄语、葡萄牙语、印地语、中文等专业优势，逐步展开对金砖五国国别人文状况和金砖国家人文交流的深度研究。为了能让同仁们分享我们的研究成果，同时也为该领域的专家学者提供一个专门的发表园地，研究院决定编辑出版《金砖国家国别与合作研究》系列成果。

《金砖国家国别与合作研究》原则上每年出版一辑，每辑由一至两名主编署名，侧重发表国内外专家学者对金砖国家国别与合作研究的最新成果，特别是以金砖国家国别人文状况和金砖国家人文交流为重点，力求打造国内外金砖国家研究尤其是人文交流研究的重要平台。

《金砖国家国别与合作研究》突出三个特点：1. 国内第一个以金砖国家人文交流为研究重心的系列成果；2. 以中英文双语出版，以便更好地在国内外金砖国家研究领域扩大学术影响；3. 既立足于人文交流，又不局限于人文交流，特别鼓励从人文交流的视角对金砖国家的全方位合作，如政治安全对话与经贸财金合作进行分析和解读，以期产出更多跨学科、跨专业的交叉研究成果。

《金砖国家国别与合作研究》设有三个栏目：1. "理论探讨"主要就人文、人文交流及人文与政治、经济的互动关系进行学理分析，为金砖国家人文交流构建核心概念，搭建分析框架；2. "应用研究"主要就金砖国家国别人文状况和人文交流合作中存在的现实问题进行解读，并针对性地提出应对和解决的方案与建议；3. "学术书评"主要就国内外学者近期发表的学术论文或智库报告进行述评，并就此提出新的观点与看法，激发专家学者的进一步讨论。

我们热忱欢迎国内外专家学者不吝赐稿，共同推动跨学科背景下的金砖国家研究更上一个新台阶。

董洪川
四川外国语大学校长、博士生导师
四川外国语大学金砖国家研究院院长
《金砖国家国别与合作研究》总主编
2021年3月5日

目　录

金砖国家合作研究

新冠肺炎疫情危机下的金砖国家贸易与
　　投资合作 ……………………………… 斯维特拉娜·古萨罗娃 / 003

金砖国家科技外交：成就与前景 ……………… 安娜·库鲁姆奇娜 / 016

金砖国家青年交流的合作与挑战 ……………………… 游　涵 / 026

金砖国家公共卫生合作现状与挑战 …………… 蒲公英　蔡佳菲等 / 035

金砖国家国别研究

俄罗斯农业发展定位及其影响 ………………… 崔　铮　杨越茗 / 051

建立有利于全球稳定、共同安全和创新增长的金砖国家伙伴关系
　　——轮值主席国俄罗斯的任务 ………… 瓦列尼娅·戈尔巴乔娃 / 069

中印人文交流史中的跨文化传播关键点 ……………… 段孟洁 / 075

南非灾难管理能力建设及其挑战
　　——基于应对新冠肺炎疫情的分析 …………………… 孟利君 / 086

学术书评

《巴西与金砖国家：贸易与政策》书评：
　　回顾历史，挑战未来 ……………………………… 刘梦茹　童雪莹 / 103

CONTENTS

Studies on BRICS Cooperation

Intra-BRICS Trade and Investment Cooperation:
　Overcoming the COVID-19 Crisis ·················· Svetlana Gusarova / 121

Science Diplomacy of BRICS: Results and
　Perspectives ·· Anna Kurumchina / 139

Cooperation and Challenges of Youth Exchange in BRICS ······ You Han / 152

Current Status and Challenges of Public Health Cooperation
　among the BRICS ························ Pu Gongying, Cai Jiafei et al. / 165

Studies on BRICS Countries

The Russia's Agricultural Development Orientation
　and Its Influence ···························· Cui Zheng, Yang Yueming / 189

金砖国家国别与合作研究
（第二辑）

BRICS Partnership for Global Stability, Shared Security and Innovative Growth
　　——Priorities of the Russian BRICS Chairship ⋯⋯ Valeriia Gorbacheva / 215

Key Points of Cross-cultural Communication in the History of China-
　　India Cultural and People-to-people Exchanges ⋯⋯⋯ Duan Mengjie / 223

Disaster Management Capacity of South Africa and Its Challenges:
an Analysis of South Africa's Response to the COVID-19
Epidemic ⋯⋯⋯⋯⋯⋯⋯⋯⋯⋯⋯⋯⋯⋯⋯⋯⋯⋯⋯⋯⋯⋯ Meng Lijun / 239

Book Review

Review on Brazil and BRICS: Trade and Policy: Looking Back to
　　the Past and Challenging the Future ⋯⋯ Liu Mengru, Tong Xueying / 263

金砖国家合作研究

美国文学史论

新冠肺炎疫情危机下的金砖国家贸易与投资合作

斯维特拉娜·古萨罗娃[*]

摘　要：未来50年，金砖国家可能成为世界经济的推动力，其拥有巨大的联合潜力和广泛的机会。金砖国家的经济若要获得进一步增长，就要在贸易和投资方面建立起更紧密的伙伴关系。中国作为全球主要的对外投资国和外国直接投资流入国，以及金砖国家中的贸易伙伴，在这一过程中发挥着重要作用。金砖国家的贸易和投资合作是形成经济增长的新范式。本文作者提出确立金砖国家之间贸易和投资合作潜力以及获得金砖国家经济互动的协同效应的方法，并对该方法进行了检验。中国与其他金砖国家的贸易和投资合作对其经济的发展产生了非常大的影响。中国将继续深化与其他金砖国家的经济联系，开放其金融市场，为全球不确定性上升提供缓冲。在新冠肺炎疫情危机的背景下，金砖国家内部贸易和投资合作的发展非常重要。"金砖制造"计划的实施可以考虑参考本研究的成果。

关键词：金砖国家；外商直接投资；贸易投资合作；经济潜力；协同效应

---

[*] 斯维特拉娜·古萨罗娃，经济学博士，俄罗斯普列汉诺夫经济大学副教授，首席研究员。

引　言

　　2020年，世界上几乎所有国家都与新型冠状病毒大流行做斗争，状况艰难。许多州被迫实行封锁，某些行业工作停摆。

　　根据国际货币基金组织的预测，2020年全球经济下滑将为3%。冠状病毒大流行将影响包括金砖国家在内的世界所有国家的经济。信用评级机构惠誉（Fitch）认为，世界上任何国家都无法避免冠状病毒大流行带来的毁灭性影响。[①] 据亚洲开发银行的数据显示，到2020年，因新型冠状病毒大流行引起的世界经济总量将减少5.8万亿—8.8万亿美元。[②] 到2020年，中国的国内生产总值预计将增长1.2%，而印度的经济将增长1.9%。到2020年，其他金砖国家的国内生产总值总量将大幅减少——俄罗斯减少5.5%，巴西——减少5.3%，南非——减少5.8%。[③] 中国国内生产总值增长率的下降不仅受到大流行导致的许多企业活动中断的影响，还受到中美之间"贸易战"的影响。

　　金砖国家相互帮助，共同应对流行病，提供经济、专家和人道主义援助。金砖国家内部贸易和投资合作的发展与深化，使金砖国家可以进口高科技和其他商品。现在，金砖国家从双边对外贸易逐步过渡到其经济关系发展的多边贸易和投资范式，旨在形成和改善互惠、开放、平等的多边关系，以促进经济增长和提高国民经济竞争力。金砖国家内部相互贸易和投资互动的发展，促进了这种合作的扩大及其进一步整合的协同效应。

---

　　① Fitch rezko ukhudshil prognoz dlya rossiyskoy ekonomiki na 2020 god // Interfaks. https: //www.interfax. ru/business/705548.

　　② Aziatskiy bank razvitiya otsenil ushcherb mirovoy ekonomiki ot virusa // RBK. https: //www.rbc. ru/economics/15/05/2020/5ebe145c9a79475ca82eaac8? utm＿source＝RBC&utm＿campaign＝7908d81f1d-EMAIL＿CAMPAIGN＿2020＿05＿15＿03＿02&utm＿medium＝email&utm＿term＝0＿140f2882c5 - 7908d81f1d - 50810719.

　　③ World Economic Outlook 2020 // International Monetary Fund. https: //www. imf. org/en/Publications/WEO/Issues/2020/04/14/weo-april - 2020.

一、金砖国家内部贸易合作

金砖国家正在制定《金砖国家到 2025 年的经济伙伴关系战略》。新战略涵盖了一揽子联合合作计划，包括抗击流行病和克服危机带来的经济影响，支持多边贸易体系，释放数字经济潜力，在新型冠状病毒大流行的背景下实现可持续和包容性发展。

金砖国家在全球商品出口中的份额已从 2001 年的 8.1% 增加到 2018 年的 18.5%，其中中国——13.2%，俄罗斯——2.1%，印度——1.7%，巴西——1.3%，南非——0.5%。在 2001—2018 年间，中国的商品出口增长了 8.5 倍，达到 24870 亿美元；俄罗斯——增长了 3.5 倍，达到 4520 亿美元；印度——增长了 6.8 倍，达到 3220 亿美元；巴西——增长了 3.7 倍，达到 2400 亿美元；南非——增长了 3.4 倍，高达 940 亿美元。① 金砖国家内部商品出口额在 2018 年几乎是 2001 年的 11 倍。

金砖国家商品进口占全球商品进口的比重从 2001 年的 6.8% 上升到 2018 年的 16.1%，其中中国 10.9%（全球第 2）、印度 2.6%（全球第 11）、俄罗斯 1.2%（全球第 20）、巴西 0.9%（全球第 28）、南非 0.5%（全球第 34）。2018 年，中国货物进出口均居世界前列，其中出口居世界第一，进口居第二。

2001—2018 年，金砖国家间贸易额增长了 10 倍。相比之下，金砖国家对外贸易总额同期仅增长 6 倍，全球贸易额仅增长 2.6 倍。金砖国家内部贸易总额占金砖国家对外贸易总额的比重从 2001 年的 6.2% 上升到 2018 年的 10.5%。上述数据证明，金砖国家贸易合作潜力巨大。

中国是世界 100 多个经济体的十大贸易伙伴之一，这些经济体的国内生产总值约占世界的 80%。金砖国家商品出口份额最大的国家是中国（2018 年为 70.3%），其次是俄罗斯（11%——比中国少 6.4 倍），第三是印度（9.3%），第四是巴西（6.8%），第五是南非（2.6%）。在金砖国家中，中国（66.1%）、印度（16.1%）、俄罗斯（8.5%）、巴西

---

① UNCTADSTAT. http://unctadstat.unctad.org/wds/TableViewer/tableView.aspx.

（5.6%）和南非（3.7%）也是商品进口份额最大的国家。

金砖国家在商品出口专业化方面具有独特的比较优势。金砖国家之间可以通过很多方式进行合作。例如，巴西专门经营矿产资源、钢铁、农产品、食品、化学品和飞机设备；俄罗斯——燃料和采矿产品、军事生产和武器、化学品、工业设备、两用技术；印度——高科技产品、化学品、药品、软件、纺织品；中国——高科技产品、电信设备、化工、汽车产品、消费品；南非——各种矿石、珠宝。金砖国家内部商品出口占金砖国家对外商品出口总额的比重从2001年的4.2%上升到2018年的10%。金砖国家内部商品出口的最大份额是中国（56.2%）。

中国是金砖国家主要贸易伙伴之一。由于美国的贸易保护主义破坏了全球贸易体系，中国和印度更加频繁地挖掘彼此间的合作潜力。中印努力促进双边贸易，更加重视彼此关系的发展。2018年，中国对印度的商品出口是金砖国家内部出口中最大的。中印经贸发展具有很强的互补性。中国对印度出口的主要产品为数字加工设备、专业工业设备、电子芯片、实验室工业设备、医疗设备（44.1%）、化学品（20%）等。中国还向印度出口了电机、电动机和发电机（6.9%）、电热设备（0.6%）、电视、无线电接收和录音设备（4.3%）、晶体管（1.5%）、光学设备（1.1%）、采矿设备（0.3%）、家用电工设备（0.5%）和其他产品。由于印度投资环境不断改善，中国希望恢复对印度的奶制品、苹果和梨出口。此外，2018年印度对华商品出口额为125亿美元，是印度对金砖国家商品出口总额中最高的。印度对华出口的主要类别是电子芯片、医疗设备、实验室工业设备、棉花（占中国从印度进口总额的25.2%）、金属矿石（28.1%）、钻石（10.1%）、纺织品（4.5%）、钢铁（2.2%）和其他商品。中国打算增加从印度进口大米、糖、豆粕和油菜籽。

在疫情暴发之际，印度和中国庆祝了建交70周年，并宣布了双方互动交流"新时代"的开始。

俄罗斯和印度是军事技术合作领域的长期合作伙伴。俄罗斯和印度联合开发了布拉莫斯超音速导弹系统。2020年，俄罗斯和印度同意将超音速巡航导弹的射程提高到600千米。该公司还计划在印度供应和组织Igla-S MANPADS的许可生产以及米格29升级版的额外交付。印度将装备俄罗斯

AK-203 突击步枪，从 2020 年开始，印度将在接下来的 10 年内生产这种步枪。该工厂在印度的产能为每年 7.5 万支 AK-203 突击步枪。印度还是世界上最大的羟氯喹生产国，向俄罗斯供应了 1 亿片这种药。

中国已连续 8 年成为俄罗斯第一大贸易伙伴。中俄继续保持高频率互动，2018 年签署多项重要文件，巩固两国关系发展。2018 年，中国对俄罗斯出口 477 亿美元，在金砖国家出口总额中居第二位。中国对俄出口产品主要有数字加工设备、工业专用设备、医疗设备、电机、电动机和发电机、电视和广播设备、矿山设备、电热设备、光学设备等，占比 34.8%。俄罗斯从中国进口的产品包括食品（4.3%）及消费品：鞋类（2.4%）、服装（1.8%）、汽车及其配件（2.6%）、纺织品（0.8%）、女装及童装（1.4%）、电话机及其配件（0.4%）以及其他货品。此外，2018 年俄罗斯对华商品出口总额为 560 亿美元。俄罗斯向中国出口石油（占俄罗斯对华出口总值的 52.3%）、天然气（28.9%）、煤炭（6.1%）、铁矿石（4.9%）和高科技工业设备（7.6%）。[①] 中国是大宗商品的主要进口国。中国对石油和天然气的需求依然强劲。对俄罗斯和中国来说，十分重要的石油和天然气项目之一是"西伯利亚力量"——一份为期 30 年、总额达 4000 亿美元的俄罗斯天然气供应合同。通过俄罗斯的天然气管道长度为 3000 千米，通过中国的天然气管道长度为 5100 千米。中国境内黑河至长岭之间的第一部分天然气管道（中俄东线天然气管道北段）已经建成。另一部分，即长岭至永清的天然气管道已于 2020 年投入使用。这使中国在 2020 年从俄罗斯获得 50 亿立方米的天然气。永清至上海天然气管道的中国部分将于 2023 年建成，这将使俄罗斯对中国的天然气供应增加到每年 380 亿立方米。

中国国家主席习近平指出，俄罗斯和中国的战略合作经过了疫情的考验，必将进一步加强，两国人民的友谊也必将日益加深。[②] 中俄愿与金砖国家一道，加强反流行病学合作，交流防治冠状病毒经验，共同应对卫生

---

① UNCTADSTAT. http://unctadstat.unctad.org/wds/TableViewer/tableView.aspx.
② Xi Jinping uveren, chto sotrudnichestvo Rossii i Kitaya stanet prochneye // RIA Novosti. https://ria.ru/20200416/1570147658.html.

领域的共同威胁和挑战。

2020年1—4月，中俄贸易额增至336亿美元。同期，俄罗斯对华货物出口204亿美元，增长1.1倍，中国对俄出口略有下降，为131亿美元。① 尽管国内对燃料的需求因疫情而下降，但在2020年3月，俄罗斯对中国的石油出口量仍增加了1.3倍，达到702万吨，即每天166万桶。②

2018年，中国对巴西商品出口总额为335亿美元，在金砖国家中排名第三。中国对巴西出口产品主要有数字加工设备、光学工具、空调设备、电热设备、电子芯片、电动机和发电机等，占中国对巴西出口的45.9%。除高科技产品外，巴西还从中国进口了手机零部件（4.6%）、面料（1.7%）、空调、转换器、电视及其零部件、蓄电池（6.5%）等消费品。2018年，巴西对华商品出口642亿美元包括矿产资源、食品（92%）、电子芯片、电动机和发电机、汽车电动设备（3.1%）和其他商品。

中国已连续9年成为南非第一大贸易伙伴。2018年，中国对南非商品出口总额163亿美元。中国对南非的出口产品主要有数字加工设备、专业工业设备、实验室工业设备、医疗设备、电热设备、二极管、晶体管、矿业设备、电机、电动机和发电机、汽车等（38.3%）。中国还向南非出口了鞋类（4.9%）、家具（3%）、旅游用品（2.3%）、电视机、收音机和录音设备（4.3%）、椅子（1.9%）、家用电器设备（0.7%）等消费品。2018年，南非对华商品出口85亿美元。中国从南非进口铁矿石、铂金、钻石、煤炭、铜等矿产资源（77.9%）。

2020年5月，俄罗斯向南非运送了第一批人道主义救援物资。

2001年至2018年，中国对其他金砖国家的商品出口增长了22倍——对巴西增长了13.7倍，对俄罗斯增长了5.8倍，对印度增长了8.4倍，对南非增长了10.5倍。中国对其他金砖国家的商品出口份额为：印度43.9%，俄罗斯27.4%，巴西19.3%，南非9.4%。

相关系数用于衡量两个变量（2001—2018年金砖国家内部贸易总额

---

① Tovarooborot Rossii i Kitaya v yanvare-aprele vyros do $33, 56 mlrd // Informatsionnyy portal BRIKS. https: //infobrics. org/post/30882/.

② Import nefti v Kitay iz Rossii v marte vyros na 31% // Informatsionnyy portal BRIKS. https: //infobrics. org/post/30816/.

与 GDP）之间的线性依赖程度。上述两个变量中，中国与所有金砖国家都存在完全正相关关系：与印度（0.95），与巴西（0.93），与南非（0.90），与俄罗斯（0.84）。

二、金砖国家间外商直接投资合作

2018 年，金砖国家在全球外国直接投资存量中所占的份额仍然较小，但从 2010 年的 3% 上升至 11%，占全球外国直接投资流入的份额为 19%。2007 年，中国投资在金砖国家内部外国直接投资中所占比例为 72%，2018 年下降至 47%，这与其他金砖国家更积极参与集团内投资进程有关。但中国仍是金砖国家外国直接投资的主要出口国。从中国流出的外国直接投资主要投往俄罗斯联邦和南非。中国对这两个国家的直接投资中，服务业占很大比重。

2011—2018 年，从中国流入俄罗斯的外国直接投资存量增长了 4 倍。中国是俄罗斯经济的第四大外国投资者。2001—2018 年，俄罗斯从中国进口的投资增长了近 116 倍。这些投资涉及采矿、能源、石油和天然气、汽车工业、农业、基础设施项目、贸易和服务等领域。俄罗斯和中国的联合项目包括莫斯科地铁站的建设，基础设施的建立——莫斯科和北京之间的高速铁路，俄罗斯（犹太自治区）与中国之间的铁路桥梁（黑龙江省）横跨阿穆尔河，在符拉迪沃斯托克建立自由港，建造浮动核电站，建造新的汽车装配厂等。国有的中国石油天然气集团公司以 11 亿美元收购了 OAO Yamal SPG 20% 的股份。中国参与了俄罗斯东西伯利亚气田与中国东北地区石油管道建设的融资（联合项目价值 1000 多亿美元，天然气管道近 4000 千米）。能源发展仍将是中俄经贸合作的主要目标，也是两国务实合作的重点领域之一。这是两国经济全面战略伙伴关系的体现。中国将成为俄罗斯天然气的最大进口国。在前 10 个绿地项目中，有 5 个是中国投资者在俄罗斯投资的：中国凯盛国际工程公司在工业机械、设备和工具方面投资了 30 亿美元（创造了 3000 个工作岗位）；中国公司华泰汽车集团在汽车 OEM 领域投资了 11 亿美元（创造了 3000 个工作岗位）；中国长城汽车公司开始在图拉地区建造一家汽车工厂，估计价值 5.2 亿美元（创造了

2500个工作岗位）；中国企业新希望集团在食品、烟草、畜禽食品领域投资5亿美元（创造了1267个就业岗位）；中国东风汽车公司在汽车OEM领域投资了5亿美元（创造了2931个工作岗位）。中俄在航天、基础设施等领域的合作稳步推进。2018年双边贸易总额达到1000亿美元。俄罗斯决定在国家财富基金中投资人民币和中国政府债券。

在南非，国有的北京国际汽车公司在南非投资了8.19亿美元的汽车工厂（Coega发展公司），为当地和地区市场生产汽车。中国企业还投资了南非的能源行业和基础设施建设，一半以上的项目是在可再生能源领域（水电）实施的。

中国在印度的主要投资是在汽车工业、冶金、工业工程、能源、电气设备制造等领域。尽管由于中巴经济走廊的建设（"一带一路"倡议的主要基础设施项目之一），两国关系受到影响，但中国仍在增加对印度的外国直接投资（460亿美元）。面对不断上涨的劳动力成本（是印度的1.5—3倍）和经济增长放缓的压力，中国公司正在寻找替代资源和新市场来提高效率。印度是有效投资的潜在国家之一，目前是世界上增长最快的经济体。为了提高竞争力，中国公司正在将生产转移到印度（汽车工业、化学、电子产品开发、信息和通信技术等领域）。中国中车公司在印中合资工厂投资了6300万美元，用于生产铁路运输设备。华为技术公司计划开始在印度生产智能手机。

巴西与中国的双边经济关系最为牢固，但这种关系主要是由贸易推动的（近年来，巴西对中国的初级产品出口激增）。巴西公司在中国的业务有限，主要包括服务（如金融、商务咨询和贸易）、产品销售和分销、采购等。中国投资的领域包括巴西电力行业、采矿业、石油和天然气行业以及基础设施。中国对巴西的投资主要以并购形式进行。例如，中国石化公司投资了巴西的石油和天然气勘探与生产领域。据中国—巴西商业委员会统计，在5年内，44家中国企业向巴西60个投资项目投资685亿美元。巴西在中国的投资比其他地方更加多样化（包括金融服务、食品、金属、电子元件、航空航天）。

中国对金砖国家的外国直接投资是多元化的，主要集中在自然资源、汽车行业和其他工业消费品领域。随着"一带一路"倡议（指"丝绸之路经济带"和"21世纪海上丝绸之路")的推进,中国对外直接投资的快速增长可能会持续下去,尤其是在服务业和基础设施相关行业。在中国,运输、仓储和邮政服务领域的外国直接投资在持续增长。这些举措为金砖国家加强经济合作创设了框架基础。

金砖国家新开发银行(NDB)正在帮助金砖国家克服危机后果,抗击新冠肺炎疫情。中国、印度、巴西和南非各获 10 亿美元信贷额度,作为抗击新冠肺炎疫情的紧急援助。NDB 也为新开发银行成员国设立了应急基金。

三、金砖国家贸易和投资合作的协同效应

国家间合作的协同效应与整合带来的效率提高相关,整合将这种合作的各个要素合并为一个整体。分析各国合作所产生的协同效应,确定加强其积极组成部分的措施是重要且相关的。金砖国家团结在一起的动机之一是有可能从这一过程中获得协同效应,从而为金砖国家的经济发展做出贡献。

为了确定金砖国家内部贸易和投资合作的协同效应,作者提出使用多因素相关和多元回归分析。多重相关性分析(根据公式 1、2、3、4 计算)可以确定三个变量(金砖国家内部贸易交易额、外商直接投资和国内生产总值)之间的依赖关系。

$$R_{y/x_1x_2} = \sqrt{\frac{r_{yx_1}^2 + r_{yx_2}^2 - 2 \cdot r_{yx_1} \cdot r_{yx_2} \cdot r_{x_1x_2}}{1 - r_{x_1x_2}^2}} \quad (1)$$

R_{y/x_1x_2}——金砖国家内部贸易总额、外商直接投资和国内生产总值的多重关联度系数

x_1——金砖国家内部贸易总额,单位为 10 亿美元;

x_2——金砖国家内部外商直接投资,单位为 10 亿美元;

y——金砖国家的国内生产总值,单位为 10 亿美元;

r_{yx_1}——金砖国家内部贸易总额与国内生产总值的相关系数;

r_{yx_2}——金砖国家内部外商直接投资与国内生产总值的相关系数;

$r_{x_1x_2}$—金砖国家内部贸易额与外商直接投资的相关系数。

相关系数的计算公式如下：

$$r_{yx_1} = \frac{\sum (x_1 - \overline{x_1}) \cdot (y - \overline{y})}{\sqrt{\sum (x_1 - \overline{x_1})^2 \cdot \sum (y - \overline{y})^2}} \tag{2}$$

x_1—金砖国家内部贸易总额，单位为10亿美元；

$\overline{x_1}$—2001—2018年金砖国家内部贸易额，单位为10亿美元；

y—金砖国家的国内生产总值，单位为10亿美元；

$\overline{y}$—2001—2018年金砖国家平均国内生产总值，单位为10亿美元。

$$r_{yx_2} = \frac{\sum (x_2 - \overline{x_2}) \cdot (y - \overline{y})}{\sqrt{\sum (x_2 - \overline{x_2})^2 \cdot \sum (y - \overline{y})^2}} \tag{3}$$

x_2—金砖国家内部外商直接投资，单位为10亿美元；

$\overline{x_2}$—金砖国家内部平均外商直接投资，单位为10亿美元。

$$r_{x_1x_2} = \frac{\sum (x_1 - \overline{x_1}) \cdot (x_2 - \overline{x_2})}{\sqrt{\sum (x_1 - \overline{x_1})^2 \cdot \sum (x_2 - \overline{x_2})^2}} \tag{4}$$

在选择分析因素时，进行了分析分组、时间序列比较和线性图的构建，从而可以确定所考虑参数之间关系的存在、方向和形状。基于多重相关系数的分析，证实了金砖国家2001—2018年贸易和投资合作与国内生产总值的密切关系：巴西（多重相关系数为0.97），印度（0.93），中国（0.92），在俄罗斯（0.92）。上述指标的相关性也在南非被证实（0.78）。较高的多重相关系数证实了金砖国家的贸易和投资合作前景，并表明它们具有巨大的经济合作潜力和协同效应。

作者还计算了2001—2018年金砖国家内部贸易投资合作与各自国内生产总值的多元回归方程：

$$\gamma = \beta_0 + \beta_1 x_1 + \beta_2 x_2 \tag{5}$$

γ—金砖国家国内生产总值，单位为10亿美元；

β_0—自由成员，如果阶乘参数（X_1和X_2）等于零，则确定国内生产总值（γ）的值；

β_1—第一个阶乘参数的回归系数（X_1）；

β_2—第二阶乘参数的回归系数（X_2）；

X_1—第一阶乘参数（金砖国家中每个金砖国家的贸易额，单位为10亿美元）；

X_2—第二阶乘参数（金砖国家中每个金砖国家的外商直接投资流入，单位为10亿美元）；

最小二乘法和矩阵法用于求解回归方程。在确定金砖国家贸易与投资合作的协同效应时，获得以下结果。两个因子参数的多元回归方程（金砖国家内部的贸易额；金砖国家内部的外商直接投资流入每个金砖国家）以及由此产生的2001—2018年参数（国内生产总值）可以确定每个金砖国家的回归系数，并且得出以下结论：

a）巴西与其他金砖国家的贸易额每增长1美元，就导致巴西的平均国内生产总值增长17美元；来自其他金砖国家的流入巴西的外国直接投资每增加1美元，导致巴西的平均国内生产总值增长了55.9美元。与其他金砖国家的贸易营业额的增加相比，其他金砖国家对巴西的外国直接投资对巴西国内生产总值的增长影响更大。

b）俄罗斯与其他金砖国家的贸易额每增长1美元，就导致俄罗斯平均国内生产总值增长16.6美元；来自其他金砖国家的俄罗斯外国直接投资流入量每增加1美元，就导致俄罗斯平均国内生产总值增长78.4美元。与其他金砖国家的贸易额相比，其他金砖国家对俄罗斯的外国直接投资对俄罗斯国内生产总值增长的影响更大。

c）印度与其他金砖国家的贸易额每增长1美元，就导致印度的国内生产总值平均增长14.9美元；来自其他金砖国家的流入印度的外国直接投资每增加1美元，就导致印度的平均国内生产总值增长249.1美元。与其他金砖国家的贸易额相比，其他金砖国家对印度的外国直接投资对印度国内生产总值增长的影响更大。

d）中国与其他金砖国家的贸易额每增加1美元，就导致中国国内生产总值平均增长36.5美元；其他金砖国家流入中国的外国直接投资每增加1美元，就导致中国的平均国内生产总值增长488.6美元。与其他金砖国家的贸易额相比，其他金砖国家对中国的外国直接投资对中国国内生产总值增长的影响更大。

e）南非与其他金砖国家的贸易额每增加1美元，就导致南非的平均国内生产总值增长1.6美元；来自其他金砖国家的流入南非的外国直接投资每增加1美元，就导致南非的平均国内生产总值增长降低1.2美元。

多元回归分析的结果证实了金砖国家贸易与投资合作的协同效应。得出的结论是，金砖国家内部的贸易和投资合作与在该领域和世界其他国家的合作相比，前者的国内生产总值有了更大的增长。这一事实表明，金砖国家之间进一步贸易和投资合作具有很大的潜力和协同效应。基于定量方法的使用（多元回归分析），金砖国家之间的贸易和投资合作前景广阔。金砖国家间的外国直接投资流入量的增加导致巴西、俄罗斯、印度和中国的国内生产总值增长更快。从其他金砖国家流入南非的外国直接投资的增长对其经济的发展几乎没有积极影响。

要实现金砖国家贸易投资合作协同效应，必须扩大贸易投资合作类型和形式，扩大贸易投资合作规模；在贸易和投资领域形成联合平台；利用区域联系确保各国的共同发展；金砖国家内部贸易和投资自由化；利用新开发银行的能力实施联合项目；联合投资项目从双边向多边过渡；利用各国在发展经济合作方面相辅相成的可能性；扩大金砖国家战略伙伴关系，发挥协同效应，提升金砖国家在全球经济中的影响力。通过分析，我们可以对金砖国家贸易和投资合作的前景进行总结，这是金砖国家经济合作的重要领域之一，可以从扩大合作中获得协同效应。在制定"金砖国家制造"计划时，上述结论可供参考。

结　　论

本文提出了一种确立金砖国家经济合作潜力的研究方法，并进行了检验。其结论是：a) 金砖国家之间的多边合作存在协同效应；b) 金砖国家内部贸易和投资关系强度超过金砖国家与世界其他国家合作强度，这是衡量金砖国家经济合作潜力的量化指标；c) 由于它们之间的经济具有显著的互补性，相互作用的强度的可能性增大；d) 金砖国家之间开展合作的产业清单不断扩大；e) 金砖国家现有和新建立的共同机构在发展；f) 在现有国际多边经济机构的联合战略行动在加强。

作者开发并检验了确定金砖国家贸易投资合作协同效应的方法。基于所提出的方法（多重相关和多元回归分析），作者发现金砖国家间贸易和投资合作的扩大对其经济增长具有很强的正向影响。金砖国家内部贸易和投资合作增长速度高于与世界其他国家的互动，这一现象并没有被任何经济发展理论充分解释。作者揭示了对这一过程具有决定性影响的复杂因素：金砖国家经济的高度互补性；金砖国家经济互动潜力巨大，合作产生协同效应，对发展金砖国家间贸易和投资合作抱有极大兴趣；金砖国家机制化进程。

当前的新冠肺炎疫情危机证实了金砖国家加强集团内战略合作的重要性，是扩大金砖国家各经济领域关系的催化剂。该研究使世界上许多国家可能面临的风险得以界定：新冠肺炎疫情的持续蔓延可能影响各国取消隔离措施的时间，导致世界经济复苏不平衡；对许多国家的制裁会扩大；世界上许多国家的储油设施出现石油储量溢出效应；国际贸易领域的关系恶化；不同国家政府和中央银行刺激经济政策力度的变化。

金砖国家科技外交：成就与前景

安娜·库鲁姆奇娜[*]

摘　要：当今，科学在人类生活中扮演着极其重要的角色。这体现在以下两个方面：一方面，保护国家内外的利益；另一方面，每个国家的科学、技术和创新都在为解决我们今天面临的全球性问题，比如健康、环境污染、水资源、医药、太阳能、海洋和极地科学等领域的难题做出贡献。在多极世界中，新的强国及其联盟利用科学外交来保护自身地区和国家利益，并宣称自身是新的科学、技术和创新中心，能够参与解决上述全球问题。金砖国家就是这样一个区域合作的例子。2015 年，金砖国家签署了《科技创新框架计划》。5 年间，在此框架下实施了 58 个科学、技术和创新项目，其中大多属于基础科学领域，如物理学、生物学、空间研究等。所有项目都是为了实现国家和全球目标。本文简要分析了该集团各成员国的科学基础设施，表明金砖国家在科技创新领域拥有巨大的潜力。金砖国家在科学外交领域的潜力和机遇初步显现。一切都取决于各成员国政府在利用金砖国家既有资源方面的智慧。通过对科学家之间的合作，以及金砖国家内部及外部科学外交的合理利用，现有困难可以克服。

关键词：金砖国家；科学外交；技术；高科技；合作

---

[*] 安娜·库鲁姆奇娜，俄罗斯乌拉尔联邦大学副教授。

今天，科学在人类生活中扮演着极其重要的角色。这体现在以下两个方面：一方面，保护国家内外的利益；另一方面，每个国家的科学、技术和创新都在为解决我们今天面临的全球性问题，比如健康、环境污染、水资源、医药、太阳能、海洋和极地科学等领域的难题做出贡献。

《维也纳外交关系公约》第 3 条规定，派遣国的职能是在接受国保护派遣国及其国民的利益；促进派遣国与接受国之间的友好关系，发展其经济、文化和科学关系。[①] 该文件描述了传统的国际关系，当代的情况在某种程度上略有不同，因为当今世界的多极格局中出现了一些区域领导者，例如中国、印度、巴西等。全球问题需要所有国家的解决方案及其国家科学，这就是将科学纳入国际决策和外交议程的原因。

根据英国皇家学会的概念，科学外交有三个层面的含义：为外交政策目标提供科学建议（外交里的科学）；促进国际科学合作（外交为了科学）；利用科学合作改善国家间的国际关系（科学为了外交）。[②] 利用一个国家的软实力工具或无形资产是一种新的行动方式或是被视为领导者的证明，如文化、旅游、烹饪、电影或科学、技术和创新（Copeland，2009年），而不是使用强制手段，如军事力量或支付手段，即传统的硬实力工具。因此，各国战略性地将硬实力和软实力工具结合在一起，可以称之为巧实力。[③]

在多极世界中，新的强国及其联盟利用科学外交来保护其地区和国家利益，并宣称自己是新的科学、技术和创新中心，能够参与解决上述全球问题。

金砖国家就是这样一个区域合作的例子，其首次官方峰会于 10 年前（2009 年）在叶卡捷琳堡举行，从那时起，金砖国家之间的合作不仅限于

[①] Vienna Convention on Diplomatic Relations 1961. p. 3. https://legal.un.org/ilc/texts/instruments/english/conventions/9_1_1961.pdf.

[②] New frontiers in science diplomacy. Navigating the changing balance of power. January 2010. The Royal Society, 2010. p. 8. https://royalsociety.org/topics-policy/publications/2010/new-frontiers-science-diplomacy/.

[③] Lorenzo Melchor, Izaskun Lacunza, and Ana Elorza. 2020. What Is Science Diplomacy? S4D4C European Science Diplomacy Online Course, Module 2, Vienna: S4D4C.

政治领域，而且扩展至文化、技术、创新和教育领域。2015年，金砖国家签署了《科技创新框架计划》。它旨在支持第一梯队领域的出色研究，这些领域问题的解决可以得到多国的支持。

该倡议应促进由至少三个金砖国家伙伴组成的联盟研究人员和机构之间的合作。

2016年以来，在金砖国家科技创新框架下启动了多边研究项目协调呼吁，邀请金砖国家的研究人员共同开展多边方法的基础、应用和创新研究项"。[①]

金砖国家的每个成员都指定了明确的组织结构和机构。来自巴西的国家科学和技术发展理事会和巴西创新局参与了这一方案。俄罗斯小型创新企业援助基金会、科学和高等教育部及俄罗斯基础研究基金会都是其代表。印度生物技术部（DBT）和科学技术部也被任命。中国科学技术部和国家自然科学基金委员会亦签署了该项目。科学技术部、国家研究基金会和南非医学研究理事会参加了南非的框架计划。这些机构都是最高级别的政府机构，强调金砖国家集团理解科学外交的重要性。

这5年间，在这一框架下实施了58个科学、技术和创新项目。其中大多属于基础科学领域，如物理学、生物学、空间研究等。所有项目都是为了实现国家和全球目标。例如，用于癌症诊断和治疗项目的硼和钆纳米粒子是对癌症诊断任务的全球搜索的极大补充。"中国研究小组（宁波市中国科学院宁波材料与技术工程研究所所长沈教授）制备了钆基纳米粒子用于MRI研究。俄罗斯团队（俄罗斯莫斯科科学院有机元素化合物研究所所长弗拉基米尔·布雷加泽教授）致力于新型硼化脂及其类似物的合成，以及脂质—硼簇非共价相互作用的模型研究。印度团队（印度加尔各答科学教育研究所教授S. Mandal）研究了硼化合物和MRI造影剂脂质体的形成和封装，通过超分子组装将其包裹到脂质双分子层中。该团队将进行进一步的细胞实验和动物实验，从而验证合成的材料可以作为癌症的早期诊断

---

① About BRICS STI Framework Programme. http://brics-sti.org/index.php?p=about/About+BRICS+STI+FP.

和硼中子捕获疗法的潜在药物。"①

考虑到人类的环境问题，绿色经济是应该尽快实现的全球任务的重要组成部分。金砖国家集团也为实现这一目标做出重要贡献。

大规模环境能量收集元件无线网络项目的设计和开发是关于授权"大规模无线网络与环境能量收集元件和新兴的通信技术，将以更有效、可靠和可持续的方式促进绿色经济。它试图通过利用可再生和（或）射频能源在现有网络资源之间的合作来解决系统性能、规划和资源分配问题，以实现大规模的环境能量收集元件无线网络。特别是，它打算将更吸引人的毫米波（mmWave）技术集成到 LargEWiN 中，用于其潜在的未来部署。这些发展不但有助于满足不断增加的资讯传递需求，也有助于减少流动服务运营商的运营开支，同时保护环境和保护自然资源"。②

对于目前的疫情形势，金砖国家应该赞扬和解决这一对世界各国造成损害的、极其严峻的全球性挑战。所有金砖国家应联合起来研究这种病毒并研制疫苗。该项目于 2020 年 7 月 1 日宣布，截止日期为 2020 年 8 月 18 日。"金砖国家性传播疾病预防和控制中心为应对 2019 冠状病毒疾病流行病，目前计划开展以下专题领域的工作：

（1）诊断 2019 新冠病毒疾病的新技术/工具的研究与开发。

（2）新冠病毒疫苗和药物的研究与开发，包括对现有药物的再利用。

（3）SARS-CoV-2 基因组测序及 2019 新型冠状病毒疾病流行病学和数学模型研究。

（4）面向 AI、ICT 和 HPC③ 的新冠肺炎药物设计、疫苗开发、治疗、临床试验与公共卫生基础设施和系统的研究。

（5）对流行病学进行研究和临床试验，以评估 SARS-CoV-2 和并存

---

① "BGNCDT" - Boron and gadolinium nanoparticles for cancer diagnosis and therapy. http://brics-sti.org/index.php?p=project/9/.

② "LargEWiN" - Design and Development of Large-Scale Ambient Energy Harvesting Wireless Networks. http://brics-sti.org/index.php?p=project/57.

③ Artificial intelligence, Information and communications technology and High-performance computing.

疾病，特别是结核病"。① 众所周知，俄罗斯已经在 2020 年 8 月 11 日申请了第一个疫苗的专利。②

这些项目表明，金砖国家集团在科学外交方面具有巨大的潜力。作者建议将上述项目的成果添加到该平台，以展示这些项目的成果和产出，包含文章链接的出版物数量、这些项目产生的国家和国际专利数量等。

谈到金砖国家的科学外交，有必要提及和分析该组织每个国家的科学基础设施。

俄 罗 斯

根据联邦教育和科学监督服务机构的数据，不包括分支机构，俄罗斯共有 1266 所公立大学和 622 所私立大学，③ 1696 个国家认可的实验室，④ 177 个创业孵化机构和加速机构，⑤ 联邦知识产权服务和 7 个公共资助基金会。俄罗斯主要的创新立法是 2011 年 7 月 18 日关于特定类型法人实体的货物、工程、服务采购的第 223 - FZ 号联邦法律（2015 年 12 月 29 日修订），该法律规范了国家在这一领域的政策。俄罗斯财政支持的主要形式如下：

——补贴——无偿福利补贴严格规定了与项目执行有关的领域；

——补贴——从预算中拨款，以弥补主要参与者创新活动的损失，并发展基础设施；

——实物投资——国家资本对建立科学技术储备的长期投资；

——金融投资；

---

① Pre-announcement BRICS STI Framework Programme Response to COVID-19 pandemic coordinated call for BRICS multilateral projects 2020. http: //brics-sti. org/index. php? p = new/26.

② Минздрав России зарегистрировал первую в мире вакцину от COVID-19. https: //covid19. rosminzdrav. ru/minzdrav-rossii-zaregistriroval-pervuyu-v-mire-vakczinu-ot-covid - 19/.

③ Federal Service for Supervision in the Education and Science. https: //map. obrnadzor. gov. ru/application/university.

④ Eurasian Economic Commission. https: //eaeunion. org.

⑤ All business incubators and accelerators. https: //rb. ru/incubator/·&page = 1.

—融资租赁。

财政支持应有一定的界限，并以下列原则为基础：

—用于获取更多资金来源的多渠道系统；

—政府拨款的优先次序；

—筹资的目的；

—将公共资金与私人投资结合起来。

2017年，俄罗斯共有21037项专利和350多项国际专利。

印　度

印度将创新发展和创新确定为优先事项，并致力于促进包容性发展。关于教育的政策行动和改善创新创业的条件是印度社会创新的关键利益。如今，印度在全球创新指数中排名第52位，在过去三年中提升了9个名次，增幅表现好于此前基于GDP的预期值。印度科技部有责任与印度外交部、印度驻外使团，科学和技术顾问，科学、技术和学术机构的利益攸关方，有关政府机构和印度各行业协会密切协商，谈判缔结和执行印度与其他国家之间的科学和技术协定。主要的政府角色由印度科技部的科学和工业研究局扮演。印度科学外交论坛是科学和工业研究局的主要项目，通过科学外交能力建设、发展网络和战略思维科学外交等手段释放印度的发展潜力。它们与世界各地的印度侨民合作，将他们看作海外的"经济资产"。

印度在科学、技术和创新领域投入了大量资金，全国有865所大学。根据《印度创业生态系统》的报告，"印度拥有全球第二大创业生态系统，创业企业超过2万家，年增长率达10%—12%。仅在2016年就有1400家初创企业诞生，这意味着每天有3—4家初创企业诞生。大多数初创企业集群位于班加罗尔、首都地区和孟买"。[①] 印度还有大量的投资。"自2014年以来，投资者向印度初创企业生态系统投资了336.2亿美元，其中一半

[①] Startup Ecosystem in India: Incubators and Accelerators. https://www.s-ge.com/sites/default/files/publication/free/startup-ecosystem-india-incubators-accelerators - 23 - 01 - 2019.pdf.

以上投资于 2017 年（137 亿美元）和 2018 年第一季度（22.6 亿美元）。"① 其与大学和教育机构合作建立了大量孵化机构，与国外合作伙伴合作开发了许多明星项目。②

巴　西③

巴西由几个发展不均衡的次区域组成。最发达的次区域是圣保罗，它包括几所主要的国立大学和研究中心，如圣保罗大学、坎皮纳斯州立大学、圣保罗州立大学、圣保罗州立技术学院、圣卡洛斯联邦大学、圣保罗联邦大学。有 23 个工程实验室、15 个农业和生物科学实验室、15 个卫生实验室和 7 个社会人文科学机构。该次区域有 16 家创业孵化机构和 10 家孵化加速机构。2019 年，圣保罗获得 2000 万美元的公共资金，由私营公司提供。④ 圣保罗享有约 40% 的专利权。从 2014 年到 2018 年，巴西每年获得约 2000 项国际专利。该地区高新技术产品占总出口的 30%，中高新技术产品占 26%。在科学和创新外交领域，圣保罗有几个项目：圣保罗研究基金会、圣保罗投资与竞争力促进局（Invest SP）、巴西农牧研究院的拉贝克斯中国、欧洲、韩国和美国分公司，创新与科学外交学校。巴西重视对世界各地侨民的支持。他们制定了制度支持，以绘制侨民网络的地图。

中　国⑤

中国的科技创新基础设施如下：全国共有普通高等学校 2688 所，其

---

① Startup Ecosystem in India: Incubators and Accelerators. https://www.s-ge.com/sites/default/files/publication/free/startup-ecosystem-india-incubators-accelerators - 23 - 01 - 2019. pdf.
② Chaturvedi, S. and Mulakala A. India's Approach to Development Cooperation. Routledge, 2016. p. 190.
③ 该部分数据来源于奥古斯托·科斯塔 2020 年 8 月 4 日在"科学外交与创新外交：圣保罗大学强化班"的演讲。
④ Secretariat for Economic Development. http://www.desenvolvimentoeconomico.sp.gov.br/.
⑤ 该部分数据来源于何舟 2020 年 8 月 6 日在"科学外交与创新外交：圣保罗大学强化班"的演讲。

中独立学院 257 所；拥有 20 个国家级实验室，2000 多家创业孵化机构和孵化加速机构，以及国家专利局、国家自主创新示范区和高新技术产业开发区。截至 2018 年 8 月，国家科技成果转化指导基金累计投资 247 亿元，完成科技成果转化项目 161 个。截至 2017 年底，科技期刊 5052 种，医药卫生期刊 1196 种。2019 年国家专利申请数量为 58990 件。高新技术产品出口占出口总额的 30% 左右。中国制定并实施了"一带一路"技术创新合作计划，以加强国际科技人才交流与合作。

南　　非

南非实际上与苏联是在同一时期去工业化的。南伊利诺伊斯大学的学者还写了一篇专门讨论这个话题的文章。① 尽管如此，南非仍然尽最大努力重建和革新这一制度。为此，南非签署了《南部非洲发展共同体科学、技术和创新议定书》，并制定了 2015—2020 年科学、技术和创新战略计划。开发计划署调整了南非的全球发展目标。② 南非的创新基础设施包括 26 所公立大学，其中 8 所是技术型大学，6 所是汇集传统学科与技术类分支的综合性大学。该国有 4 个大学合作项目，例如开普高等教育联盟与南方教育和研究联盟。南非还有 20 家科技创新加速机构和孵化机构。③ 根据南非认证体系，全国大约有 120 家血库，还有许多其他血库。关于此的更详细的资料记载于南非国家认证系统的官方网站。④ 根据世界银行收集的发展指标，南非 2018 年的高技术出口（占制成品出口的百分比）为 5.3197%，这些指标是根据官方承认的来源汇编的。⑤

---

① Grabowski, R. Deindustrialization of Africa. https://scholarworks.wmich.edu/cgi/viewcontent.cgi?article=1041&context=ijad.
② Sustainable Development Goals. https://www.za.undp.org/content/south_africa/en/home/sustainable-development-goals.html.
③ Here are 20 accelerators, incubators for African startups to apply for in 2020 // VentureBurn, 2 Jan, 2020. https://ventureburn.com/2020/01/accelerators-incubators-african-startups-2/.
④ The South African National Accreditation System. https://www.sanas.co.za/Pages/index.aspx.
⑤ Trading Economy. https://tradingeconomics.com/south-africa/high-technology-exports-percent-of-manufactured-exports-wb-data.html.

因此，正如所显示的那样，所有金砖国家在科技创新领域都具有巨大的潜力，其中一些国家可以与世界强国竞争。应该强调的是，金砖国家的大多数成员国都属于南方，只有俄罗斯来自北方，这种独特性使得这个群体独一无二。联合的科学、技术、创新机会和潜力可用于发展这种区域领导之间的合作。本文尝试对金砖国家的 STI 领域进行 SWOT 分析，见表 2-1。

表 2-1　金砖四国科技与创新的 SWOT（态势分析法）分析

优势	弱势
金砖国家成员具有巨大的科技和创新潜力 全球 43% 的人力资源，包括高级知识分子 整个联盟拥有储量最大的矿产和自然资源 丰富的农业经验和机会 核潜能 金砖国家一些成员的大型工业和生产基础设施 发展金砖国家独立金融体系	一些金砖国家的投资潜力低 与西方国家相比，金砖国家的生活水平较低 金砖国家的购买力较低 部分国家受环境污染困扰
机遇	挑战
金砖国家可以利用彼此的国内市场应对来自其他国家的制裁 金砖国家的潜力可以用来克服上述劣势 金砖国家科技创新基础设施互惠使用	来自美国和欧盟的制裁，以及应对与一些金砖国家的全球竞争 一些金砖国家成员难以进入全球性的科技和创新市场 金砖国家之间的武装冲突 依赖美元的经济体系

资料来源：笔者自制。

当然，这离理想状态还很远，但它可以不断完善并且发人深省，即如果我们将金砖国家视为一个科技创新机构，它会带来巨大的发展机会。

结　　论

　　金砖国家在科学外交领域的潜力和机遇初步显现，一切都取决于各成员国政府在利用金砖国家既有资源方面的智慧。通过对科学家之间的合作，以及金砖国家内部及外部科学外交的合理利用，现有的困难可以克服。

金砖国家青年交流的合作与挑战[*]

游 涵[**]

摘　要：随着金砖国家越来越多合作机制的形成，加强人文交流已发展成金砖合作的"第三支柱"，而青年交流也在金砖合作的框架下逐渐机制化，日益成为社会议程的主要组成部分。当前，金砖国家青年交流特点鲜明：承载着多重目标；平台日趋丰富；政府积极引导。但是，金砖各国青年政策的关注点不同、青年的代表性不够，以及活动效果缺乏巩固，给金砖国家青年交流的进一步深化带来了阻碍。因此，只有继续重视金砖国家青年交流，加强与民间社会力量的合作，拓展交流形式，才能凝聚各国的青年智慧，推动金砖未来的发展。

关键词：金砖国家；青年交流；青年政策

---

[*] 本文系国家社会科学基金项目"中俄全球治理战略比较研究"（项目批准号：19CGJ021）的阶段性成果。

[**] 游涵，四川外国语大学国际关系学院副教授。

一、金砖国家青年交流的发展历程

根据联合国的定义，青年是指介于 15 岁与 25 岁之间的那些人，在此范畴内实则包括青少年（年龄介于 13—19 岁之间）与低龄成年人（年龄介于 20—25 岁之间），而这个年龄段的人群是社会中最脆弱的群体。在全球新增艾滋病感染者、赤贫人口、没有读写能力等问题方面，青年人口都占据非常大的比例。因此，金砖国家自 2009 年举办首届领导人峰会以来就一直关注青年这一议题，近年来青年议题更是成为社会议程的主要组成部分。

（一）初始阶段

2010 年，金砖国家领导人第二次会晤发布的《巴西利亚宣言》就在消除贫困领域表示，必须加强技术和财政能力建设以促进社会发展和社会保护，弱势群体（如穷人、妇女、青年、移民及残疾人）则是重点的发展和保护对象。2011 年，金砖国家领导人第三次会晤中再次承诺"在社会保护、体面工作、性别平等、青年、公共卫生包括艾滋病防治等领域加强对话与合作"。可以看出，这一时期金砖国家主要将青年看作社会中的弱势群体，合作的重点是在保护青年方面。

2012 年，金砖国家领导人第四次会晤发表的《德里宣言》中正式倡议将"金砖国家青年政策对话"作为新的合作项目，旨在将青年声音纳入金砖国家议程，并在各个国家的年轻人中推广金砖国家机制，这一举措有利于促进金砖青年之间的相互交流，夯实金砖合作的青年基础。

（二）过渡阶段

2014 年，巴西金砖峰会主题为"包容性增长的可持续解决方案"，而青年是实现包容性增长、稳定社会的关键，因此为青年创造就业机会、促进金砖国家之间的技术和职业教育交流成为金砖青年交流的重点。

作为 2014 年轮值主席国，巴西在联合国开发计划署包容性增长国际政策中心的支持下，在金砖峰会前发布了《金砖国家青年和就业》与《金砖青年的社会计划和工作促进》①的研究报告。两项报告对金砖国家的人口结构、青年就业率及失业率、非正式待遇等进行了综合分析，比较了金砖各国以青年为导向的促进就业政策和方案，这些研究为金砖国家青年合作指明了方向。最终，2014年金砖国家领导人之间的会晤中提出建立金砖国家青年对话机制的想法。

（三）机制化阶段

2015年7月4日，在俄罗斯喀山举行了金砖国家青年事务部长/机构负责人会议，会后金砖国家青年事务部长/机构负责人签署了《青年事务理解与合作备忘录》。该备忘录规定了青年合作的主要领域，包括相互交流各国在国际青年交流、商业、研究、创新活动等青年政策的经验，此外还设想了有关青年事务的年度技术会议。

2015年7月4—7日，在金砖国家领导人第六次会晤的前夕于喀山举办了第一届金砖国家青年峰会，峰会的主要目标是进一步发展金砖国家的青年对话，增进青年间的互动，促进人文交流。来自金砖五个国家的200多名青年代表在俄罗斯喀山召开了为期三天的会议，与会代表在致力于政治、经济、人道主义、信息和科学技术合作的小组框架内签署了《青年行动计划》。该计划一致通过了联合国改革、在金砖国家内部制定国际实习计划、建立金砖国家联合通讯社等内容。他们认为金砖国家应创造有利于青年的经济和社会环境，为青年提供平等的机会，将青年问题纳入学术、议会、外交等其他金砖国家论坛的活动中，呼吁扩大金砖国家所有会议中的青年代表比例，确保青年参与金砖国家政策的决策过程和战略制定。《青年行动计划》具有建设性的性质，旨在使金砖国家领导人了解青年群体的关切，因此它作为正式文件被提交至乌法峰会上。

自2015年开始，金砖国家青年峰会成为金砖活动一年一度的固定议程，而2016—2019年青年交流的不断深化使其成为人文交流中的重要

---

① MacLennan Michael, ed., Youth and employment among the BRICS, International Policy Centre for Inclusive Growth UNDP, Brasilia, April 2014, No. 28.; PL de Arruda, AK Slingsby: Social programmes and job promotion for the BRICS youth, International Policy Centre for Inclusive Growth UNDP, Brasilia, Oct. 2014., No. 130.

议题。2020年俄罗斯担任轮值主席国期间，举办了第六届青年峰会和金砖国家青年事务部长/机构负责人会议，该活动于2020年11月29日至12月2日在乌里扬诺夫斯克举行，讨论了青年在扩大金砖国家活动方面的作用。

二、金砖国家青年交流的特点

随着金砖国家青年交流的不断发展与机制化，其交流的目标、方式、议题也逐渐丰富。金砖国家青年交流有着独特的"金砖"特点：首先，金砖国家的人群构成普遍不同于西方发达国家，其青年人口占比较高。全球超过60%的青年人住在亚太地区，总数约为7.5亿。在2010年，仅印度就有2.34亿青年，占其人口总数的19%，并且这一比例还在上升，而中国有2.25亿青年，占人口总数的17%。[①] 其次，金砖国家是新兴市场国家和发展中国家的代表，是国际体系的重要参与者与贡献者，对于改革和完善现行全球治理体系的诉求较为一致，因此金砖国家的特殊构成使得青年有着不同的利益诉求。

（一）承载多重目标

首先，保护青年是金砖国家青年交流的初始目标。金砖国家成立伊始，青年议题的讨论是基于联合国标准15—25岁这一年龄段的人群，因此青年被当作完全的弱势群体进行讨论，加强对青年的保护是金砖国家促进社会发展与社会保护的众多领域之一，这也符合联合国对青年议题的基本设置。

其次，金砖国家机制的建立是为了构建跨区域的经济合作及共同行动机制，因此促进青年就业与发展，使青年成为推动金砖国家创新和经济增长的重要力量是金砖国家青年交流的又一个目标。各金砖国家对年龄、社会地位、价值观的判断标准不同，它们各自的青年年龄范围与联合国的标

---

① Regional Overview: Youth in Asia and the Pacific. Unitied Nations Youth. https: //www. un. org/esa/socdev/documents/youth/fact-sheets/youth-regional-escap. pdf.

准有所出入，例如巴西的青年政策针对的是 15—29 岁，俄罗斯是 14—30 岁，印度是 10—35 岁，中国是 15—30 岁，南非是 15—35 岁。青年作为承上启下的重要群体，只有当年轻人口健康、受过教育、有工作时，国家才能实现人口红利，推动创新和经济增长。

最后，青年议题是金砖国家参与全球治理的重要路径。2014 年正值联合国可持续发展议程制定过程中，国际社会正对摆脱全球金融危机、促进全球经济增长和社会发展进行评估，金砖国家作为推动世界经济稳步增长的重要动力，应积极增加青年议题的讨论及制定有效的青年政策：一方面，有助于为国际社会实现可持续发展的目标做出贡献；另一方面，参与全球议程的设置有助于提高金砖国家参与全球治理的话语权。

（二）平台日趋丰富

金砖国家利用国家、教育机构、企业、学生的多方共同参与，在青年交流发展中构建了多领域、多层次、多主体的互动平台。目前金砖国家青年交流的主要机制有：

1. 金砖国家青年峰会。2015 年在俄罗斯喀山举办了第一届峰会，此后每年作为金砖国家的重要组成部分。峰会的重点是团结金砖国家的年轻人，扩大金砖国家在经济、政治、信息、科技和人道主义领域的合作。

2. 金砖国家青年外交官论坛。首届论坛于 2015 年 10 月 29 日在俄罗斯莫斯科举行，旨在为金砖国家青年外交官之间建立直接联系，促进他们对金砖国家合作重要性的认识和了解。

3. 金砖国家青年科学家论坛。该论坛囊括一系列科技问题及科技对社会影响的专题论坛，并涵盖了青年创新创业大赛等子项目，旨在共同促进科学进步，提供创新性增长。

4. 金砖国家青年能源署。该机构是 2015 年根据喀山举行的第一届金砖国家峰会的行动计划而建立的，其目的是增进青年对能源发展的了解和研究，为金砖国家能源转型提供建设性意见。该机构定期发布《金砖国家青年能源展望》，召开金砖国家青年能源峰会，创建金砖国家 YEA 网络。

此外，金砖国家之间的青年交流平台还包括金砖国家国际青年论坛、金砖国家青年领袖国际论坛、上海暑期学校金砖国家项目等一系列活动。2020年俄罗斯举行了金砖国家国际学校和金砖国家青年领袖竞赛等活动，作为金砖国家领导人峰会的配套项目。

（三）政府积极引导

随着金砖国家政治安全、经济金融和人文交流三大合作支柱的形成，人文交流合作的范围逐渐扩大，而青年作为人文交流的一部分也得以逐步实现机制化。目前，金砖国家青年交流的具体形式和主题都是基于历届峰会的"行动计划"倡议而执行的，其主要手段有：一是在金砖国家峰会期间举办各领域的青年对话论坛和会议；二是利用高等教育领域的合作，增加学生之间的互访和交流。可见，金砖国家青年交流充分体现了各国关于金砖国家青年交流的顶层设计和战略谋划。

三、挑战与应对

近年来，金砖国家青年交流取得不小的成果，各国青年通过交流和合作加深了对彼此的了解，真正奠定了金砖合作的民众基础。金砖合作的未来在青年一代身上，一系列深入的交流合作对金砖青年一代的影响非常深远，加深和强化了青年对金砖机制的了解与支持，鼓励青年对相关领域进行思考、提出建议，对推动金砖的务实合作和长远发展起到重要作用。

但与此同时，金砖国家青年交流也面临不少挑战，需要各国及时对交流的困境做出调整，以便进一步推动其交流合作。主要的挑战有以下几方面：

（一）各国青年政策的关注点不同

金砖国家尽管是新兴市场国家和发展中国家的代表，但隶属于不同区域，其国家的政治与经济发展模式、人口比例、社会保障制度有所不同，因此各国青年政策的关注点也有非常大的差异性。例如，印度在其《2014

年国家青年政策》①　里为印度青年规划了一个整体愿景，即"赋予青年权力以充分发挥他们的潜力，并通过他们使印度在国际社会中找到应有的地位"，因此印度青年政策的重点是加强青年的技能，以及赋权提高青年的治理参与；中国则将青年教育、青年保护、青年创新列为国家青年政策的重点；② 俄罗斯着重关注本国青年的社会化问题，强调青年在国家公共机构中的服务，塑造青年在国家发展和社会转型中的重要作用；③ 巴西由于犯罪和暴力活动加剧，青年政策侧重于通过教育、职业发展、数字包容来促进青年的社会融入，培养和平文化；④ 而南非由于高失业率，劳动就业问题一直是其关注的重点，⑤ 早在2013年，时任南非总统雅各布·祖马就指出促进青年就业与发展是南非参与金砖合作的重点。

各个国家青年政策的不同必然会增加金砖国家青年交流议题设置的难度，提出的某些倡议可能难以得到其他金砖国家的积极响应。例如，在第五届金砖国家峰会上，南非为解决青年的失业问题，曾提议设立金砖国家青年基金来鼓励和支持青年创业的计划，但这一倡议至今并未实现。

（二）青年的代表性不够

当前，金砖国家青年交流主要是在金砖峰会的整体框架下进行，所有的青年代表由金砖国家各自的政府机构进行筛选，最终能参加金砖国家青年峰会或者对话论坛的将是一些优秀的大学生、青年企业家、青年学者，即参与金砖国家青年交流的仍是各个国家的精英代表。例如，2018年赴南

---

① National Youth Policy - 2014. Ministry of Youth Affairs and Sports Government of India, Dec 2014. http://yas.nic.in/sites/default/files/National-Youth-Policy-Document.pdf.

② 《中长期青年发展规划（2016—2025年）》，中共中央国务院，2017年4月13日，http://www.gov.cn/zhengce/2017-04/13/content_5185555.htm#1。

③ Основы государственной молодежной политики Российской Федерации на период 2025 года. Правительство Российской Федерации. Москва: 29 ноя 2014. №2403 - p. http://static.government.ru/media/files/ceFXleNUqOU.pdf.

④ Guia das políticas públicas de juventude / Secretaria Nacional de Juventude. . Brasília : SNJ, 2010，p. 24. https://www.youthpolicy.org/national/Brazil_2010_National_Youth_Policy.pdf.

⑤ National Youth Policy 2015 - 2020. The presidency republic of South Africa. https://www.gov.za/sites/default/files/gcis_document/201610/nationalyouthpolicy.pdf.

非参加金砖国家青年峰会的中国代表团只有 8 人，① 有人批评金砖国家青年活动为"穿着商务休闲装"，"仪式化严重且缺乏实质性内容"。他们指出"金砖国家青年代表讲的语言与年轻人不同……他们的讨论只是反映了政府的优先事项，并非青年的优先事项"。② 这意味着，如果青年政策只局限于官员层面和学术层面，受益的只是少部分青年群体，那仍然很难获得各国青年对金砖国家的支持。

（三）活动效果缺乏巩固

随着一年一度金砖国家峰会的召开，金砖国家青年的活动也应期举行。但是大部分活动的延续性比较短，最主要的交流模式是各领域的青年论坛，此外可能还会有一些短期的文化体验活动，但这些活动往往举办的时候轰轰烈烈，一旦金砖峰会结束，青年之间的交流就几乎悄无声息了，"民心相通"未达到理想的效果。因此，必须建立长效机制，才能有效巩固交流的成果。

尽管当前金砖国家青年交流还面临各种挑战，但青年无疑是人文交流中的主力军，它既是金砖教育合作最直接的受益者，又是金砖国家文化、科技、卫生、体育、旅游的重要参与者。2018 年 6 月 9 日，在重庆举行了2018 年金砖国家智库国际研讨会暨第二十一届万寿论坛，该论坛由金砖国家智库合作中方理事会主办，四川外国语大学承办，论坛的主题是"金砖国家人文交流：政府引导与民间互动"。其中许多促进人文交流的举措都与青年相关，例如中国社科院欧洲所研究员、上海大学特聘教授江时学倡议"金砖国家高校应设立金砖国家奖学金，专门资助研究金砖国家的青年学子"；北京吉利学院校长霍伟东建议应"开展金砖国家大学生艺术展、科技竞赛、体育比赛、'双创'大赛等活动"；复旦大学金砖国家研究中心项目主管侯筱辰提出应"开设金砖国家课程，帮助青年学生更多了解金砖

---

① "中国青年代表一行 8 人赴南非参加 2018 金砖国家青年峰会"，新华网，2018 年 7 月 24 日，http://www.xinhuanet.com/gongyi/2018-07/24/c_129919660.htm。

② Brics Youth: Everything about us without us? https://mg.co.za/article/2018-06-21-00-brics-youth-everything-about-us-without-us/.

国家与全球治理"等。① 总之，青年是一个以年龄为区分的群体，因此它与各种人文交流的领域交叉重叠。总而言之，金砖国家青年交流的推进需要从以下几个方面进行改善：

第一，继续重视金砖国家青年交流，这是实现金砖国家"民心相通"的重要手段。青年的发展与金砖国家发展基本同步，是推动国家发展的重要力量，迟早会成为社会发展的中流砥柱。只有不断深化各领域的青年合作，使更多的青年能参与其中并从中受益，才能得到广大青年对金砖国家这一机制的认可和支持。

第二，加强与民间社会力量的合作。金砖国家青年交流除了政府引领外，还必须深化民间合作。当前，金砖国家中的许多青年组织发挥着凝聚和联系青年的作用，② 金砖国家应设置相应的机构，展开与各国青年组织的联系与合作，为深入了解、帮助和引导青年搭建更多平台。

第三，拓展交流形式。如今，互联网在青年生活中扮演的角色越来越重要，传统的线下论坛和峰会模式不仅增加了活动的成本，而且不利于在青年中传播金砖活动。因此，有必要在金砖国家青年常用的软件中开设公共账号，加大新媒体对金砖国家信息的传播，积极建构金砖国家的共同理念，这样才能加深青年对金砖国家的身份认同。

---

① 吴沛斌："金砖国家人文交流促进五国民心相通——2018 金砖国家智库国际研讨会暨第二十一届万寿论坛会议综述"，2018 年 7 月 17 日，http://world.people.com.cn/n1/2018/0717/c187656-30152590.html。

② 龚爱国、徐艳玲：《"金砖四国"青年组织联系凝聚青年的路径》，《中国青年研究》2014 年第 3 期，第 115—119 页。

金砖国家公共卫生合作现状与挑战

蒲公英[*] 蔡佳菲等[**]

摘　要：金砖国家总人口占全世界人口的42%，金砖国家公共卫生合作是对金砖国家人民生命健康的保证，也是顺应全球化的理性选择。近年来，金砖国家公共卫生合作特色鲜明，领域不断拓宽，在对抗传染性与非传染性疾病方面取得一定成绩。在当前全球对抗新冠肺炎疫情的关键时期，金砖国家作为新兴市场国家和发展中国家的代表，在公共卫生领域积极开展合作，通过高层网络会议、疫苗研发合作、新开发银行提供贷款等方式不断探索公共卫生领域合作的新途径，主动承担全球卫生治理责任。未来，由于公共卫生事件的突发性和金砖国家自身存在的一系列问题，金砖国家公共卫生合作将面临诸多挑战。

关键词：金砖国家；公共卫生；新冠肺炎疫情

---

[*] 蒲公英，博士，四川外国语大学俄语学院副教授，硕士生导师。
[**] 蔡佳菲、武雅文、黄月、罗丹、许函睿，四川外国语大学俄语学院学生。

一、金砖国家公共卫生合作现状

公共卫生是金砖国家重要的合作领域。近年来，金砖国家无论是在公共卫生领域的合作广度上，还是合作深度上，都呈现了积极向好、蓬勃发展的态势，也逐渐形成属于自身的特点。

（一）金砖国家公共卫生合作领域不断拓宽加深

从2011年至今，金砖国家共举行了9次卫生部长会议。为在医疗卫生合作框架内紧密贴合"提高公共卫生水平、健全医疗卫生体系"的共同需求，金砖国家逐年增加公共卫生领域新议题，如疾病防控、药品研发及可及性、疫苗研发、技术转让等，其涉及领域不断拓宽（见表4-1）。

金砖国家在公共卫生领域合作加深。以结核病为例，金砖五国占全球结核病负担和死亡率的40%，在全球耐多药、抗药性结核病病例中至少占50%。过去十年，结核病始终是金砖国家卫生合作的重点防控防治对象，金砖五国在结核病控制方面已投入至少200亿美元。[1]

为应对结核病的严峻挑战，金砖国家逐步深化在该领域的合作，努力取得阶段性进展。在2012年的《德里公报》中，金砖国家提出"决定在能力和基础设施建设发展方面加强协作，以减少结核病的患病率和发病率；通过新药、疫苗和诊断技术的创新以及结核病研究人员的联合，在药品疫苗临床试验方面开展合作；促进获得可负担的药品，提供高质量保健服务"。2014年，在巴西举行的第四届金砖国家卫生部长会议中，金砖国家商定在结核病的研究和创新方面进行合作并努力实现技术共享，药品制造能力和结核病筹资为重点合作内容。2016年12月，金砖国家卫生部长提出"同意建立金砖国家结核病研究网络，成立结核病、艾滋病毒和疟疾研究与发展联盟，并考虑筹集国际资金"。2017年金砖国家在《厦门宣言》中表示将建立结核病研究网络。截至2020年8月，金砖国家共举行

---

[1] Global tuberculous report 2017, p160, 162, 170, 186, 188. https://www.who.int/tb/publications/global_report/gtbr2017_main_text.pdf·ua=1.

了6次结核病研究网络技术会议。[1]

表4-1 金砖国家历届卫生部长会议相关信息

时间	地点	发表文件	合作方向
2011	北京	《北京宣言》	公共卫生、卫生服务、药品可及性、技术转让、医疗产品出口、保健技术
2012	新德里	《德里宣言》	非传染病、传统医学、药品研发、技术转让、远程医学
2013	开普敦	《开普敦公报》	卫生监测系统、全民健康覆盖、传染病和非传染性疾病、医疗技术、药品开发、孕产妇和儿童健康、生物技术应用合作
2014	巴西利亚	《联合公报》	埃博拉防控、结核病防控、药品可及性、热带病防治、抗生素耐药性、慢性非传染性疾病
2015	莫斯科	《莫斯科宣言》	艾滋病、热带病、非传染性疾病监测、烟草控制、全民医保
2016	新德里	《德里宣言》	医疗产品研发、传染病挑战、结核病研究网络、健康监测、抗微生物耐药性、药品可及性、幼妇健康、精神疾病
2017	天津	《天津公报》	传统医学、医疗产品研发、降低孕产妇及新生儿死亡率、疾病监测、卫生服务可及性
2018	德班	《德班宣言》	全民健康覆盖、医疗技术、加强卫生系统、药品可及性、疫苗研发合作、抗微生物耐药性、非传染性疾病、烟草控制
2019	库里蒂巴	《库里蒂巴宣言》	初级卫生保健、降低孕产妇及新生儿死亡率、疫苗接种、医疗产品监管、技术转让、金砖国家结核病研究网络、非传染病、稀有疾病、远程医疗、数字医疗

资料来源：http://brics.utoronto.ca/docs/index.html#health

（二）金砖国家公共卫生合作特色分工持续发展

在开展卫生合作初期，金砖五国便在公共卫生领域开展特色分工。在

---

[1] BRICS TB Research network. http://bricstb.samrc.ac.za/.

金砖国家国别与合作研究
（第二辑）

2013年世卫组织第66届世界卫生大会期间，金砖五国强调要致力于5个领域的专题合作：印度将加强卫生监测体系建设合作，南非主要负责减少非传染性疾病的危险因素、非传染病预防、健康促进和全民健康覆盖，巴西发挥自身优势重点关注传染病战略性卫生技术，俄罗斯加强对医疗技术的研究，中国着重药品研发。① 五国的明确分工、通力合作在提高了合作成效的同时，也增进了经验的交流与共享。

此外，金砖国家轮值主席国凭借其主场优势，在议程设置上结合国家发展需求，充分发挥本国资源特长。2016年9月在印度班加罗尔举办了主题为"金砖国家传统医药合作"的健康研讨会，该研讨会框架下的阿罗亚博览会为金砖国家传统药物、原材料制造商与进口商提供了大量交流机会，有利于其他四国亲身体验印度传统医药产品和制造设施。2017年中国将"推广传统中医药"纳入金砖国家卫生合作议程，同年7月在中国天津举行的金砖国家部长级会议和中医药高级别会议上，金砖国家就加强中医药合作发表联合声明，表示要"加强传统医学在国家卫生保健系统中的整合，以此作为促进和鼓励传统医学实践、教育培训、疗法和药物的宝贵手段，促进传统医学从业者有系统地提高保健服务质量和外展服务"。② 巴西作为全球母乳库的领导者，拥有全球550家母乳库中的230家，③ 被认为是全球效益最高的母乳库系统，巴西已经帮助拉丁美洲、非洲和欧洲的32个国家建立了母乳库，巴西的母乳库体系正逐渐走向全球发展模式。④ 在2019年金砖巴西利亚峰会上，巴西提出建立金砖国家母乳库网络的倡议，金砖国家在此次峰会宣言中承诺，"在金砖国际技术合作框架内，动员各方努力，建立金砖国家母乳库网络，以扩大在新生儿和哺乳婴儿护理方

---

① BRICS Nations to Establish Extensive Human Milk Bank Network. https://www.who.int/bulletin/volumes/92/6/14-141051/zh/.
② Tianjin Communique of BRICS Health Ministers Meeting. http://en.nhc.gov.cn/2017-07/17/c_71977.htm.
③ The Surprisingly Simple Way To Save Babies' Lives. https://storytracker.solutionsjournalism.org/stories/the-surprisingly-simple-way-to-save-babies-lives.
④ BRICS Nations to Establish Extensive Human Milk Bank Network. https://eurasiantimes.com/brics-nations-to-establish-human-milk-bank-network/.

面，以食物和营养安全为重点的知识技术共享，并将健康权作为其核心价值"。[1] 由此可见，金砖五国在确立了固定的卫生合作议程基础上，结合本国发展特色，自主创新合作议题，拓展合作广度与深度，有效丰富了金砖公共卫生合作。

二、新冠肺炎疫情下的金砖国家公共卫生合作

基于人口分布密集、医疗卫生条件系统欠发达等特点，金砖国家共同面临传染性疾病暴发的高风险。当前新冠肺炎疫情在全球暴发，对金砖国家突发公共卫生事件应对机制带来了严峻挑战。

在金砖五国中，中国新冠肺炎疫情防控已取得良好成效，但俄罗斯、巴西、南非及印度的新冠肺炎疫情仍有待遏制。截至9月14日，印度新冠肺炎确诊人数达到500万余人，巴西超过400万人，俄罗斯超过100万人，南非超过65万人，中国确诊人数8万余人[2]。作为最早出现新冠疫情的国家，中国发挥自身制度优势，调集各方力量支援疫情重灾区，并采取封城、隔离等有效举措，已取得疫情防控阶段性胜利，当前已积极投身对外援助，为"全球战疫"贡献自身力量；俄罗斯疫情防控工作起步较早，1月底就成立了疫情防控指挥部、新冠肺炎病毒通讯中心等机构，对防控中国输入病例采取了有效措施，但由于疫情暴发中期大量欧洲病例涌入，加上执法不严和民众配合度较低等因素，导致确诊人数激增，当前疫情形势仍令人心忧；南非于3月中旬成立国家指挥委员会并实施旅游禁令，在疫情早期为强制执行封锁令动用军队以协助警察维持社会治安，但从5月起，分阶段放松防疫封锁，使得疫情大幅反弹；巴西是南美洲疫情受灾大国，抗疫工作举步维艰，一方面总统博索纳罗对疫情防控持消极态度，另一方面逾510万巴西人民生活在贫民窟中，其不利的生活条件也为疫情防控带来巨大压力；同样将贫民窟疫情防控工作视为难点的印度情况也不容

---

[1] Declaration of thr First BRICS Meeting on Human Milk Bank. http: //brics2019. itamaraty. gov. br/images/documentos/Declaration_of_thr_First_BRICS_Meeting_on_Human_Milk_Bank. pdf.

[2] Worldometer. https: //www. worldometers. info/.

乐观，印度政府2020年3月开始"封城"，到同年5月为兼顾经济发展调整政策，逐步解封，各地方防疫政策也在封锁和解封之间不断摇摆。

"疫情大考"是对金砖国家公共卫生应对机制的严峻考验。在2020年4月召开的金砖国家抗击新冠肺炎视频会议上，金砖五国外长表示应把公共卫生领域合作摆在更突出的位置。① 为携手共克新冠肺炎疫情，金砖国家公共卫生合作主要体现在以下几个方面：

（一）金砖国家高层会议：合作抗疫新声音

2020年4月28日，为动员合力防控疫情，金砖国家举办了新冠肺炎疫情特别外长会议，会议围绕新冠肺炎的影响和金砖国家的应对措施展开。在此次会议上，五国外长就坚持多边主义、携手抗击疫情、深化金砖合作等问题深入交换意见，表示金砖国家必须坚持多边主义，加强团结协作，密切疫情信息分享和经验交流，开展药物和疫苗研发合作，以更加有效地应对疫情，维护世界公共卫生安全，努力减缓疫情的负面影响。多数金砖成员谴责将疫情政治化、污名化的行为，反对削弱世卫组织的作用，认为抹黑世卫组织甚至切断其资金供应将严重损害国际社会合作应对疫情、特别是帮助非洲国家抗击疫情的努力。各方应坚定支持世卫组织等联合国机构在全球抗疫合作中发挥领导作用。②

为进一步讨论五国针对疫情的公共卫生合作，2020年5月7日，俄罗斯在担任金砖轮值主席国期间，举行了金砖国家高级卫生官员视频会议。会议总结了五国在疫情防控方面已取得的主要成绩，各国进一步表示将继续相互支持新冠肺炎的预防和治疗工作，以及为提供药品、诊断工具、免疫生物药品和医疗设备创造有利环境。此外，各国赞成俄方建议，即金砖五国需要建立一个生物威胁风险综合预警系统，并编写一份最佳防范措施概览，以供金砖国家和其他国家专家后续使用，新开发银行将对这些项目提供资金支持。金砖国家各国代表对今后在传染病防治领域采取一致行动

---

① 王毅出席金砖国家应对新冠肺炎疫情特别外长会，http://www.chinanews.com/gn/2020-04-28/9170943.shtml。

② 王毅出席金砖国家应对新冠肺炎疫情特别外长会，http://www.gov.cn/guowuyuan/2020-04/29/content_5507226.htm。

的必要性达成共识，俄罗斯联邦卫生部副部长奥列格·格雷德涅夫指出："我们必须加强合作，开发低成本、可持续的传染病检测方法，关注疫苗问题，开展全球治疗研究。"[①]

（二）新开发银行：合作抗疫新保障

金砖国家新开发银行成立于2015年，主要资助金砖国家及其他发展中国家的基础设施与可持续发展建设。2019年第九届金砖国家卫生部长会议宣言指出，金砖国家"同意探讨新开发银行支持卫生项目融资，以保证人民健康福祉的可行性"。2020年新冠疫情肺炎的暴发成为落实这一共识的切实动力。

2020年4月22日金砖国家新开发银行理事会关于应对新冠肺炎疫情发表声明称，"欢迎新开发银行建立一个紧急援助基金，以满足成员国的紧急需求。"自新冠肺炎疫情暴发以来，金砖国家新开发银行以发放贷款、发行债券等形式积极支持各国应对疫情。

自2020年3月起，金砖国家新开发银行分别向中国、印度、南非、巴西发放约10亿美元紧急援助贷款（见表4-2），以支持各国抗击新冠肺炎疫情。新开发银行的迅速反应在一定程度上降低了金砖国家的社会经济损失，缓解了疫情对金砖各国所造成的负面影响。

表4-2 新冠疫情爆发以来新开发银行向金砖各国贷款发放情况表
（数据统计截至2020年8月）

时间	对象国	金额
2020.3	中国	70亿元人民币（约10亿美元）
2020.5	印度	10亿美元
2020.6	南非	10亿美元
2020.7	巴西	10亿美元

数据来源：https://www.ndb.int/

---

① Минздрав России провел встречу старших должностных лиц стран БРИКС по вопросам здравоохранения. https://brics-russia2020.ru/news/20200508/395175/Minzdrav-Rossii-provel-vstrechu-v-formate-videokonferentsii-starshikh-dolzhnostnykh-lits-stran-BRIKS-po.html.

除了发放紧急援助贷款之外，金砖国家新开发银行还以发行债券的方式助力金砖国家抗疫。2020年4月2日，新开发银行在中国银行间债券市场发行规模为50亿元人民币的抗击新冠肺炎疫情债券，帮助中国政府抗击疫情。筹集到的资金用于向中国提供抗击疫情方面的紧急援助贷款项目，为疫情下的紧急公共卫生支出提供资金支持，重点支持疫情影响严重的湖北、广东和河南。[1]

2020年9月4日，王毅在金砖外长会议中指出："新开发银行是金砖经济合作的旗舰项目，为五国经济社会发展发挥了积极作用，成为国际金融架构的有益补充。我们要争取在今年领导人会晤前取得实质性进展，拓展银行的国际影响力，提升金砖国家全球金融治理话语权"。[2] 当前，金砖国家新开发银行在公共卫生合作领域承担起了共抗疫情的重要职责，同时也扩大了自身的业务覆盖范围。未来，金砖国家新开发银行或将抗疫特别贷款提升至100亿美元。[3] 金砖国家新开发银行将持续为金砖五国及其他发展中国家建设、提升公共卫生防控和应急反应能力提供支持，为金砖国家公共卫生合作持续助力。

（三）医疗卫生技术合作：合作抗疫新方向

为应对突发疫情，金砖国家提出医疗卫生技术合作的关键任务，即在金砖国家框架内开展技术研究与开发项目，推动疫苗的研发与生产，为人类健康安全贡献金砖力量。

在新冠肺炎疫情的大背景下，金砖国家的科学技术部门共同举办了科技创新框架计划合作研究项目评选活动，该活动有助于在金砖国家间开展大规模技术交流与研究合作，为寻找应对全球挑战办法添砖加瓦。活动项目征集围绕以下五个主题："COVID-19诊断新技术、新设备的研究与开

---

[1] 新开发银行发行债券支持中国抗击新冠肺炎疫情，http://www.xinhuanet.com/politics/2020-04/03/c_1125811913.htm。

[2] 王毅国务委员兼外长在金砖国家外长视频会晤时的发言（全文），http://new.fmprc.gov.cn/web/wjbzhd/t1812434.shtml。

[3] Meeting of BRICS Ministers of Foreign Affairs/International Relations. http://www.brics.utoronto.ca/docs/190926-foreign.html。

发""研究和开发可利用的药物""SARS-CoV-2 基因测序及 COVID-19 的流行病学和数学模型研究""以人工智能和通信技术为导向的 COVID-19 药物和疫苗研发""评估 SARS-CoV-2 与合并症，进行流行病学研究和临床试验"。①

此外，新冠肺炎疫情的暴发更加坚定了金砖国家共同建立疫苗研发中心的决心。早在 2015 年金砖国家乌法峰会宣言中，金砖国家就提出建立联合开发和使用疫苗机制的任务，2018 年金砖约翰内斯堡峰会进一步细化了此项任务，并首次倡议成立金砖国家疫苗研发中心。② 新冠肺炎疫情暴发后，在 2020 年 4 月召开的金砖国家应对新冠肺炎疫情特别外长会上，中俄外长均表示金砖国家要加快落实这一倡议，开展药物和疫苗研发合作。③ 中国外交部部长王毅在 9 月金砖国家外长会议上表示，"金砖国家在疫苗研发、生产等领域各有优势，关键要形成合力，共同为实现疫苗在发展中国家的可及性和可负担性做出贡献，推进金砖国家疫苗研发中心建设，推动疫苗研发和信息共享。可考虑率先建成虚拟研发中心，探讨联合研发、联合境外Ⅲ期临床试验、授权生产、疫苗标准相互认证等，并以此次新冠肺炎疫苗合作为契机，推进金砖国家在药品监管、研发机构之间的对接和交流"。④

（四）媒体与青年交流：合作抗疫新渠道

在当前新冠肺炎疫情的大背景下，金砖国家以更加灵活的方式开展人文交流活动，聚焦线上信息交流，分享五国抗疫经验与疫情动态，为金砖国家人民携手攻克疫情增添信心。

新闻媒体是人文交流与信息推广的主要媒介，金砖国家与"金砖联合

---

① BRICS STI Framework Programme Response to COVID-19 pandemic coordinated call for BRICS multilateral projects 2020. http://brics-sti.org/files/BRICS_STI_Framework_Programme_Call_2020.pdf.
② 张清敏.新冠疫情考验全球公共卫生治理，东北亚论坛，2020（4）：57。
③ 王毅出席金砖国家应对新冠肺炎疫情特别外长会，https://www.fmprc.gov.cn/web/ziliao_674904/zt_674979/dnzt_674981/qtzt/kjgzbdfyyq_699171/t1774273.shtml。
④ 王毅国务委员兼外长在金砖国家外长视频会晤时的发言（全文），http://www.chinanews.com/m/gn/2020/09-05/9283146.shtml。

电视频道"(金砖 TV)合作推出"金砖国家国际媒体网络抗击新冠病毒专题信息交流频道"。金砖 TV 于 2017 年厦门金砖国家峰会期间被提出创立，现使用金砖五国官方语言开展报道，为金砖国家人民提供资讯获取便利。"金砖国家国际媒体网络抗击新冠病毒专题信息交流频道"报道疫情下金砖五国关于自我隔离、防止传染措施以及新冠肺炎病毒诊断方法的最新消息，分享金砖五国普通人民群众的抗疫故事。①

作为金砖人文交流的主力军，金砖国家青年开展线上以"COVID‐19 全球情景：金砖与别国"为主题的网络研讨会议。会议由金砖国家研究委员会和金砖国家俄罗斯专家委员会共同举办。会上，来自金砖五国的青年学者围绕"COVID‐19 大流行对本国的社会、经济和政治影响是什么？""金砖国家在不断变化的世界中扮演什么角色？""青年人能做些什么？"三个问题进行探讨。②

中国外交部部长王毅在 2020 年 9 月 4 日的金砖外长会议上表示，"金砖合作最深厚的力量在于人民。在疫情的特殊形势下，我们要继续集思广益，以灵活方式开展人文交流。"金砖国家的媒体合作与青年交流跨越国境壁垒，有效促进了防疫信息在金砖国家人民间的传播，加深了金砖国家不同群体对于共同抗疫的理解。

三、金砖国家公共卫生合作面临的问题与挑战

当前，特别是在新冠肺炎疫情的背景下，金砖国家在公共卫生领域仍有很大的合作提升空间，金砖国家公共卫生合作也面临着以下问题与挑战：

(一) 金砖国家公共卫生合作基础差异大

虽然金砖国家都是新兴市场国家，存在诸多共性特征，但反映到公共

---

① Международная сеть TVBRICS запустила информационный обмен материалами о борьбе с COVID-19. https://news.rambler.ru/other/44093704-mezhdunarodnaya-set-tvbrics-zapustila-informatsionnyy-obmen-materialami-o-borbe-s-covid-19.

② International youth webinar "The Scenario of COVID-19 across the Globe: BRICS and beyond". http://www.nkibrics.ru/posts/show/5ee8d9466272695143170000.

卫生方面，各成员国在医药产业水平、疾病负担等方面存在着较大的客观差异。

一个国家在国际医药市场的竞争力一定程度上能够反映其医药产业发展水平。据2013—2017年金砖国家的医药贸易竞争力指数显示，在这五年中，只有印度的竞争力指数始终为正数，维持在0.75左右，其他四国每年的医药贸易竞争力指数均为负数。这表明，金砖国家中，只有印度在医药国际贸易中具有相对的国际竞争优势。而在其他四国中，每个国家医药产业都拥有自己的比较优势产品（如中国的原料药等），① 医药产品竞争力和优先发展方向各不相同，难以形成合力。

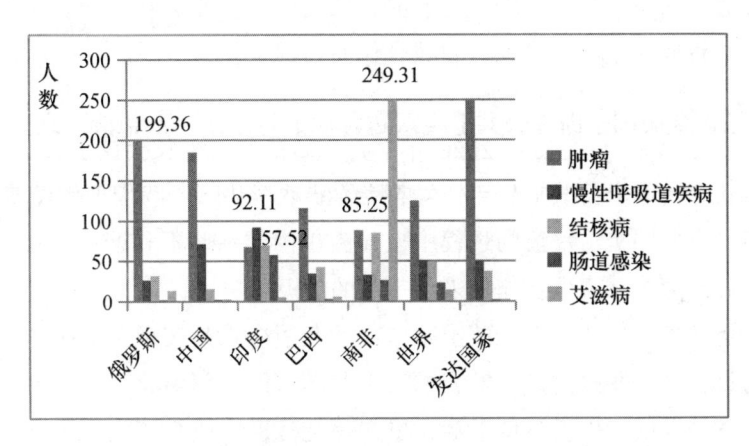

图4-1：2017年金砖国家、发达国家、世界每10万人中因各种疾病死亡人数对比图

数据来源：GBD Viz Hub.

金砖国家在高发疾病负担方面存在一定共性，但各国间差异更不容忽视，甚至呈现出一定的地域特征。影响中国、俄罗斯、巴西的主要是肿瘤、慢性呼吸道疾病、心血管疾病等非传染病；而影响南非、印度的主要是艾滋病、结核病等传染性疾病；在印度与中国，慢性呼吸道感染是致死的首要原因之一；在巴西，2017年每10万人中有超过1929人因与精神有

---

① 刘晓慧，金砖国家医药贸易竞争力分析，时代经贸，2018（25）：37.

/ 045 /

关的疾病而死亡，数据是其他金砖国家的1.18—1.22倍；在俄罗斯，除了肿瘤之外，心血管疾病也正危害着许多普通人的身心健康，是最突显的主要疾病之一，2017年俄罗斯心血管疾病死亡人数是其他金砖国家的2.2—4.9倍，是世界平均水平的2.9倍；印度慢性呼吸道疾病的死亡人数是俄罗斯之一指标的3.52倍；艾滋病传播在南非的形势最为严峻，因患艾滋病而死亡的人数远超其他金砖国家近百倍①（见图4-1）。

金砖国家医药水平参差不齐、高发疾病负担差异明显，这些都导致金砖国家在公共卫生合作的优先方向上较难达成共识。当前，由于新冠肺炎疫情的突发性和严重性，共同抗击新冠肺炎病毒成为金砖国家公共卫生的首要任务。未来，如何兼顾客观差异，实现公共卫生合作的全面发展和共同进步，将成为金砖国家在该领域合作面临的难题。

（二）金砖国家内部公共卫生双边合作中尚存在"不和谐"之音

深化金砖国家公共卫生合作是符合金砖国家利益的大势所趋，但在此次金砖国家共同抗击疫情的过程中也显露出内部一些不和谐的声音，客观上为金砖国家公共卫生合作带来了一定的消极影响。

新冠肺炎疫情背景下金砖国家内部的双边合作是实现共同抗击疫情的重要力量，而一些政治人物发表的对某些国家的"污名化"言论，不仅对双边关系的发展产生了不良影响，也在一定程度上成为了疫情下开展合作的阻力。例如，巴西个别国会议员在社交媒体上发表不当言论，称"中国刻意隐瞒疫情，对全球抗击疫情产生负面效应"，这一言论在巴西各界引起轩然大波。对此，中国驻巴西大使馆发表声明，表示"该议员发表的涉华言论造成十分恶劣的影响，严重侮辱中国的国家尊严，严重伤害了14亿中国人民的感情，同时也损害了巴西在中国人民心中的良好形象，对两国开展务实合作带来干扰"。②2020年4月27日，印度医学研究理事会在对从中国进口的新冠肺炎病毒抗体快速检测试剂盒进行实地测试后，对测试结果表示不满，要求各邦停止使用这些试剂并予以退货。针对此次事

---

① GBD Viz Hub. https://vizhub.healthdata.org/gbd-compare/.
② 中国驻巴西使馆声明，http://br.china-embassy.org/chn/gdxw/t1758511.htm。

件，中国驻印度使馆发言人嵇蓉参赞表示，"中方支持印度抗疫的心意是真诚的，中国出口的医疗产品坚持质量优先。对于目前出现的问题，我们希望印方本着实事求是的态度，充分考虑中方的善意和诚意，及时与相关公司加强沟通，予以合理妥善解决"。[①]

正如中国驻印度大使孙卫东所说，"病毒没有国界，疫情不分种族。我们都是疫情的受害者，都在同一条船上。危机面前，任何埋怨、指责与推诿，都无助于集中精力应对好本国疫情，可能造成国际社会的分裂，带来对个别群体或种族的歧视，最终损害所有国家的利益。我们主张摒弃意识形态偏见，反对病毒标签化、抗疫政治化以及对特定国家污名化的言论和做法"。当前，金砖国家同世界其他国家一道面临着这场疫情防控的大考，如何正确处理双边合作交流中所遇到的问题，维护良好的双边关系，使其成为推动金砖国家公共卫生合作的动力，是金砖国家仍将面临的挑战之一。

（三）金砖国家公共卫生合作的落实水平有待提升

当前金砖国家卫生合作机制化程度较低，在合作倡议的落实上普遍缺乏执行力。除2013年提出建设五个主题领域的合作外，金砖国家并未对共同的卫生合作发展目标进行分工，对每个成员的权、责、利尚缺乏清晰的界定。[②]

俄罗斯高等经济学校国际组织与合作研究所所长拉里欧诺娃及部分学者将金砖国家参与全球治理的过程量化为五个步骤，即：会议讨论、确定行动方向、通过决议、落实决议、全球治理取得进展，并在运用定量和定性的方法分析2008年至2014年金砖国家关于卫生领域的文件后发现：金砖国家关于"通过决议"的讨论占比持续增加，但在"全球治理取得进展"方面的讨论逐渐缩水，而关于真正付诸行动的"决议落实"层面的探

---

① 中国驻印度使馆发言人嵇蓉参赞就印宣布停止使用中国有关公司生产的检测试剂答记者问，https://www.fmprc.gov.cn/ce/cein/chn/sgxw/t1773984.htm。
② 金砖国家人文交流机制建设：作用、挑战及对策，http://theory.people.com.cn/n1/2018/0823/c40531-30246463.html。

讨更是逐年减少。①

在经历了 2014 年埃博拉病毒和 2016 年寨卡病毒等大流行病之后，金砖国家于 2017 年 7 月召开的卫生部长会暨传统医药高级别会议中提出"共同加强传统医学教育培训；发挥传统医学临床优势；共同规范传统医药产品生产；科学探索和创新传统医学；务实传统医学从业人员交流"。然而，金砖国家在传统医学教育培训和从业人员交流方面，目前仍未建立有效合作机制。

由此可见，尽管金砖国家面临着共同的公共卫生挑战，但合作成果多体现在声明和各类文件的签署上，而实际落实则明显滞后。

四、结　　语

加强公共卫生合作不仅有利于保障人民生活福祉，深化国家间政治互信，也是解决全人类突发性公共卫生事件的有效方案。面对 2020 年新冠肺炎疫情，进行公共卫生领域的多边合作已经成为世界各国人民的期望与共识。金砖国家经过近十年的努力，在公共卫生合作领域达成了诸多共识，取得了一定成效，特别是在共同抗击新冠肺炎疫情中做出了及时的共同反应和团结努力，这些努力彰显了全球公共卫生治理中的"金砖态度"，传递出了积极有力的"金砖声音"，提出了属于自己的"金砖方案"，为世界共同应对公共卫生威胁提供了典范。由于金砖国家的自身原因和公共卫生危机的突发性，金砖国家共同抗击新冠肺炎疫情的合作效果还有较大的提升空间。除此之外，如何将合作声明具体化、实效化，如何在重大突发事件中摒弃偏见、同舟共济，也是金砖国家需要思考的重要命题。

---

① М. В. Ларионова, М. Р. Рахмангулов, А. В. Шелепов, А. Г. Сахаров Формирование повестки дня БРИКС в сфере здравоохранения//Вестник международных организаций，2014，№4.

金砖国家国别研究

俄罗斯农业发展定位及其影响[*]

崔 铮[**] 杨越茗[***]

摘 要：本文围绕俄罗斯农业战略变化和影响，对冷战后俄各阶段农业政策、主要调整方向及其对中俄农业合作产生的影响进行梳理。俄罗斯农业战略具有长期性，随着国家的发展和国家利益的调整，农业发展目标在不同时期呈现出阶段性变化的特征。俄罗斯农业之所以能在经济下滑时期逆势增长，根本原因在于国家长期以来从战略高度给予补贴与扶持。如今俄罗斯农业生产力大幅提升，农业战略作出新的调整，国家出台了新的发展规划以应对经济结构失衡带来的不利影响。新的战略将深化农业产业结构改革，保障该领域向创新型可持续方向发展。其中积极开展农业合作是改革过程中的重要内容，俄罗斯农业合作以国家利益为核心，以吸引外国直接投资为目的，在开拓贸易市场的同时可以改善外交孤立的被动局面。中俄伙伴关系的提质升级也将深化双方在农业领域的合作。

---

[*] 本文系辽宁大学校立"十三五"教育部人文社科重点研究基地重大项目"普京复任总统后俄罗斯内政外交的重大调整及后果研判"（LNUJD201702）、2017年度辽宁省社会科学规划基金项目"特朗普时期俄罗斯在中美竞合关系中的角色研究"（L17BGJ004）阶段性研究成果。

[**] 崔铮，副教授，硕士生导师，辽宁大学转型国家经济政治研究中心副主任。

[***] 杨越茗，辽宁大学国际关系学院研究生。

关键词：出口型农业；经济结构；多边合作；技术创新

2014年乌克兰危机爆发后，俄美关系跌入冷战结束以来的最低谷。美国及其盟友利用经济优势，在金融、信贷、外贸等领域对俄罗斯实施了一系列制裁措施。同时，俄罗斯也出台了一系列反危机政策，其中农业作为"进口替代"政策的重要实施领域取得了显著成果。农业是当前俄罗斯经济转型发展的关键，随着一系列农业发展战略陆续出台，积极加强产业合作、推动相关基础设施建设、扩大产品出口、提高产品加工能力、完善相关合作机制成为俄罗斯农业合作机制中的新内容。

一、俄罗斯农业发展历程回顾

第一阶段：进口配额时期。苏联解体后，俄罗斯在向市场经济过渡阶段采取了强有力的去集体化与市场化手段，大批集体农场转变为私有农场和农业公司，2000年大约只有1/4的生产者盈利，农业在国内生产总值中的占比从1990年的15.4%下降到1997年的6.5%，同时，由于农业的生产周期较长，高额的农业贷款给国家银行业带来巨大负担。[①] 在此背景下，进口肉类开始大量涌入俄罗斯市场。除了民众对肉类产品的消费需求外，俄罗斯开放市场面临着发达国家农业企业带来的严峻挑战，特别是在市场贸易层面，俄罗斯的应对能力尤其有限。俄罗斯从国际货币基金组织获得了用于"高价"购买粮食的定向贷款以及人道主义援助等，这使俄罗斯家禽业遭受沉重打击，美国鸡肉以倾销价格交货，因此俄罗斯国内产品几乎不占据竞争优势。1999年12月30日普京在文章《千年之交的俄罗斯》中提出，推行农业现代化是俄罗斯的一项基础性工程，俄罗斯正在将国家扶持调控措施同农村、土地所有制方面的市场改革有机结合。普京上任后陆续出台一系列农业政策，确立了富有俄罗斯特色的农业发展方向，在国家规划的指导下，建立起农业组织协同发展新机制。普京强调，农业

---

① "1990-e：сложное время для АПК," РБК, http://madeinrussia.rbc.ru/article/1990-ye-gody/.

的发展是俄罗斯回归世界舞台的必备条件，是实施强国富民战略的必然要求。2003年，俄罗斯联邦政府正式提出禽肉的年进口量要减少25%，牛肉与猪肉的进口量要减少20%，禽肉实施进口配额（进口量不得超过配额额度），猪肉与牛肉实施关税配额，配额外进口牛肉征收60%关税，配额外猪肉进口关税为80%。[①] 通过对比俄罗斯国内肉类生产年增长率与国民需求年增长率，发现其国内肉类生产速度略高于居民消费速度，这也直接反映了配额制度在这一时期带来的积极影响。

表5-1 肉类产品的需求与产量及其增长率[②] （单位：千吨）

	2003年	2004年	2005年	2006年	2007年	2008年	2009年
国内生产	4936	—	4972	5259	5790	6268	6688
同比增长率	105.6%	—	—	105.8%	110.1%	108.3%	106.7%
国内个人消费	7464	—	7871	8287	8774	9353	9545
同比增长率	103.6%	—	—	105.3%	105.9%	106.6%	102.1%

数据来源：根据俄罗斯联邦统计局《农业、畜牧业与林业报告》整理

第二阶段：农业长期战略形成时期。俄罗斯联邦于2010年通过粮食安全战略，这意味着国家将根据经济状况维持居民合理的消费水平，而物质和经济的可及性是确保粮食独立的主要条件。衡量一个国家的粮食安全水平通常以该国的粮食自给率为评估指标。虽然进口配额刺激了国内生产商的生产能力，但仍然有近30%的食品需要进口，这严重威胁到俄罗斯的粮食安全。因此，如果没有国家政策的进一步支持，俄罗斯农业将无法在市场关系条件下取得更大发展。

从经济层面上看，俄罗斯对某些食品进口的高度依赖极大地降低了自身的经济安全性。在外债增加的背景下，大量购买外国食品和食品原料进

---

① "Импорт мяса в Россию значительно сократится" РБК https://www.rbc.ru/economics/28/01/2003/5703bfe49a7947afa08c df41.

② 《Сельское хозяйство, охота и лесоводство в России - 2004г》《Сельское хозяйство, охота и лесоводство в России - 2011г》，доклад《Ресурсы и использование мясо и мясопродуктов》, https://gks.ru/bgd/regl/b04_38/Main.Htm.

一步增大了对俄罗斯有限外汇资源的压力。此外，为偿付粮食进口增加而产生的高额费用，俄罗斯被迫出售的越来越多不可再生资源，严重削弱了俄罗斯在全球经济中的作用。俄罗斯粮食安全的主要目标是：及时预测、查明和预防粮食安全的内部和外部威胁；国内食品和原料生产可持续发展，确保国家粮食独立自主。对此，俄罗斯规定了各类国产食品的市场占有率：谷物产品至少占 95%；糖至少 80%；植物油至少 80%；肉类和肉类产品不低于 85%；牛奶和乳制品不低于 90%；鱼产品至少 80%；土豆至少 95%；盐至少 85%。① 该原则被认为是对前一阶段农业保护政策的升级，已将减少进口上升到保护粮食安全的高度。

第三阶段：农业发展受阻时期。俄罗斯的入世谈判长达 18 年，直到 2012 年俄罗斯才正式成为世贸组织成员国。俄罗斯国内对于入世影响看法不一，大多数专家学者认为，短期内俄罗斯入世的积极影响可能不太明显，降低关税甚至会对国内脆弱的生产制造业造成冲击。近十年来，俄罗斯农业在国家保护政策的支持下逐渐恢复生产，但是与大量廉价的进口农产品相比仍然缺乏市场竞争力，俄罗斯国内对于入世以后开放的农业市场持消极态度。在谈判入世协议的过程中，打开农业市场是俄罗斯入世的重要条件之一。俄罗斯长期以来都是欧美国家农产品的主要进口国，国内农业生产力水平远不能保障国家粮食安全，打开国内市场势必会对刚发展起来的农业生产造成冲击。在签署的入世协议中，俄罗斯在农业领域的主要限制性条款包括：取消牛肉配额，在 2020 年 1 月 1 日前取消猪肉配额，根据组织框架内的农业协定的金额减少"黄箱补贴"②。

俄罗斯加入世贸组织在参与世界资源再分配、融入世界秩序等方面具有重要影响，取得这种战略优势也许需要花费比入世谈判更长的时间。降低关税、控制"黄箱"补贴势必会对俄罗斯刚发展起来的农业生产造成重大冲击。同时，俄罗斯在入世谈判时也争取到了 5—7 年的过渡期，在最

---

① Указ Президента Российской Федерации от 30. 01. 2010 г. № 120, http: //www. kremlin. ru/acts/bank/ 30563.

② 世贸组织《农业协定》中约束了成员国对国内农业的相关保护政策，按照可能对贸易产生的扭曲程度分为黄箱、蓝箱和绿箱政策，黄箱政策指对贸易扭曲程度较高的保护政策，其中包括政府对农产品的价格干预，种子、肥料等农业投入的补贴等。

终形成的协议中确定肉类产品的进口配额制度可以保留，但是配额内的进口猪肉免税，配额外进口猪肉的关税下降了 10 个百分点，[1] 2013 年俄罗斯对于国内生产者的补贴不得超过 90 亿美元，到 2018 年前该补贴应逐步缩减至 44 亿美元。[2]

第四阶段：进口替代阶段。为应对西方国家的制裁，俄罗斯宣布推行进口替代政策。在严峻复杂的经济形势下出台进口替代政策，目的在于推动俄罗斯经济多样化，逐渐摆脱对国外技术与产品的依赖。通过加强国家对外贸领域的管理，制定有效实施进口替代政策的标准机制，为俄罗斯经济增长、科技发展、克服技术差距、改善投资环境提供了难得的机遇。

2014 年 8 月，俄罗斯针对美欧制裁正式实施反制裁措施，对从欧盟国家以及美国、澳大利亚、加拿大进口的某些食品实施限制。被禁食品涉及牛肉、猪肉、家禽、鱼、海鲜、奶酪、牛奶、水果、蔬菜等。此举推动了俄罗斯国内农业生产发展，某些国产农产品替代了进口产品，俄罗斯国产农业食品开始在本国市场上占据主导地位，农业几乎成为了俄罗斯经济下滑时期唯一实现增长的产业。

根据俄罗斯农业部 2017 年 8 月发布的报告，俄罗斯农业预算从 2014 年的 1900 亿卢布增加到 2017 年的 2420 亿卢布，增幅为 27%。同时，俄罗斯还出台了一系列补贴与贷款政策，其中农业部制定了统一的地区补贴标准，允许各地区按照具体情况独立确定重点支持的产业。这些措施保障了俄罗斯进口替代政策顺利实施，其中肉类产业取得的成果最为显著。猪肉进口份额下降了 2/3（从 2013 年的 26% 降至 2016 年的 8%），禽肉下降了 3/5（从 2013 年的 12% 降至 2016 年的 5%）。蔬菜进口量下降了 1/2（从 2013 年的 86.6 万吨降至 2016 年的 46.3 万吨），与此同时，俄罗斯国内蔬菜产量逐年增加，在过去的三年中，温室蔬菜产量增加了 30%。

由于新的温室综合体的建设及新耕地开垦，2017 年，面对恶劣的天气

---

[1] "Таможенный союз обновил пошлины с учетом вступления России в ВТО," РИА, https://ria.ru/20120823/729063890.html.

[2] "Процесс присоединения России к Всемирной торговой организации (ВТО)," РИА, https://ria.ru/20130614/943153184.html.

情况（霜冻、雨水、冰雹、洪水），水果和蔬菜产量仍保持上年水平。①

表 5-2　近五年蔬菜与乳制品的生产与消费②　　（单位：千吨）

蔬菜

	2014	2015	2016	2017	2018	占比% 2017	占比% 2018
国内生产	14352.1	14967.8	15064.4	15426.7	15655.0	61.2	61.5
进口	2952.5	2643.6	2356.7	2669.9	2484.6	10.6	9.7
共计	24161.1	24632.0	24608.4	25195.2	25471.0	100	100
损耗	483.2	509.3	510.4	511.5	472.2	2.0	1.9
出口	76.4	197.5	269.1	248.0	282.2	1.0	1.1
个人消费	14833.4	14918.3	14946.9	15219.4	15651.0	60.4	61.5

乳制品

	2014	2015	2016	2017	2018	占比% 2017	占比% 2018
国内生产	29995.1	29887.5	29787.3	30185.0	30611.1	77.5	79.0
进口	9157.9	7951.3	7578.6	6996.9	6493.0	10.6	9.7
共计	41134.8	39959.2	39313.6	38927.9	38743.0	100	100
损耗	35.2	33.7	30.3	29.4	31.3	0.1	0.1
出口	628.9	606.0	644.8	607.6	576.3	1.0	1.1
个人消费	34953.1	34148.2	33832.9	33736.9	33552.0	86.6	86.6

数据来源：根据俄罗斯联邦统计局《2019年俄罗斯联邦居民主食消费报告》整理

---

① "Минсельхоз России подвёл итоги реализации программы импортозамещения за 3 года," Министерство сельского хозяйства Российской Федерации, http://mcx.ru/press-service/news/minselkhoz-rossii-podvyel-itogi-realizatsii-programmy-importozameshcheniya-za-3-goda/.

② "《Потребление основных продуктов питания населением Российской Федерации》," Федеральная служба государственной статистики, https://www.gks.ru/compendium/document/13278.

二、美欧制裁背景下俄罗斯的农业发展战略

在宏观经济再次受到挑战的背景下，深受地缘政治因素影响的俄罗斯农业在基本完成粮食自给后进入了新的发展时期。尽管此前受到多重压力，但在进口替代过程中，俄罗斯农业发展的总体趋势向好，所有产品都保持着较高的利润水平。2018年10月，普京出席了在斯塔夫罗波尔边疆区召开的农业会议，并在会议上对农业部门的成果进行了评估，确定了未来国家重点产业的发展战略方针。普京将农工综合体的成就称为一项突破，指出这五年来，农业生产增长超过20%，国内生产商几乎完全可以保障本国食品供应，同时还积极参与国外市场开拓，扩大与中国、印度、东南亚、非洲和波斯湾沿岸国家的贸易往来。2017年，俄罗斯食品和农业原材料出口同比增长21%，总额超过200亿美元，比武器销售额多50亿美元，成为了俄罗斯第二大出口商品。

早在2016年11月30日，俄罗斯就批准了"农产品出口"优先项目，这意味着俄罗斯农业逐渐向"出口型"转变。2019年7月，在俄罗斯农产品出口会议上，俄总理梅德韦杰夫首先肯定了近5年来俄罗斯在农业领域取得的显著成就。农工综合体迅速发展，谷物、饲料、牛奶及肉类的生产和加工量日益增加，已经初步解决了粮食安全问题。2018年，俄罗斯农产品出口额接近260亿美元，远超联邦项目"农产品出口"中设定的230亿美元的目标。[①] 俄罗斯是谷物出口领先国家之一，出口地域不断扩大，亚太、非洲和中东地区均成为俄罗斯的主要合作区域。

预计至2024年俄罗斯农产品出口额将达到450亿美元。首先，俄罗斯政府将对农产品深加工的投资项目提供支持，出口产品将从原材料优势转变为深加工产品优势。目前，谷物产品已开始朝这个方向转变，海鲜产品也将加快转变速度。目前90%的海产品在出口前只经过冷冻处理，下一

---

① "Паспорт федерального проекта《Экспорт продукции АПК》" Министерство сельского хозяйства Российской Федерации, http: //mcx. ru/upload/iblock/c2a/c2a05c48403 632531fc69dc891 db4a97. pdf.

步计划将高附加值鱼产品的份额提高到40%。其次，要加快物流基础设施建设，完善出口商批发配送中心网络。2018年共有8个批发配送中心投入运行，另有14家将在四年内陆续建成。在2024年的基础设施扩建和现代化综合计划中将考虑农民对农产品运输的需求，通过优惠关税向农业生产者补偿铁路运输农产品的部分成本。第三，统一俄罗斯国产产品检疫标准，消除其他国家对俄罗斯食品质量的顾虑。[1]

（一）农业战略转变的条件

第一，地缘政治环境依旧复杂。首先，西方国家对俄罗斯的敌视态度依然是影响俄罗斯国家安全无法回避的因素。2019年6月，欧盟宣布延长对俄罗斯部分经济部门的制裁，其中包括：限制五家由俄罗斯国家控股的金融机构及其在欧盟境外的控股子公司进入欧盟的一级和二级资本市场，限制俄罗斯三大能源公司和三大军工企业在欧盟融资；禁止与俄罗斯进行武器进出口贸易；禁止向俄罗斯出口具有潜在军事用途和涉及国防的军民两用商品；限制俄罗斯获得某些可用于石油开发和生产的具有战略意义的技术和服务。俄罗斯也出台了相应的《反制裁法》以及法令，确认俄罗斯总统与政府有权对其他国家的"不友好行为"进行反制裁。

俄欧双边关系虽然存在着巨大的矛盾，但双方均逐渐意识到长期以来形成的经济贸易关系带来的益处，同时美国"单边主义"的做法也使欧洲国家感到失望，这给俄欧展开合作创造了机会。由于地理位置优越等诸多原因，俄罗斯已成为欧盟国家不可或缺的经济伙伴，双边跨境合作从未间断。对于欧盟而言，因为与俄罗斯拥有最长的陆地边界，终止跨境合作将违反睦邻政策，双方关系将从友好变为敌对。因此，2014年欧洲委员会决定继续实施跨境合作计划，数十个小型联合项目继续执行。这有助于减少双方政治矛盾，对双方官员定期会面，地方当局和执法机构保持联系起到了有力的推动作用。

其次，独联体国家作为俄罗斯重要的战略空间，一直以来都是俄罗斯

---

[1] "О стимулировании экспорта сельскохозяйственной продукции," Правительство России, http://government.ru/news/37430/.

外交工作的重中之重，这是俄罗斯维持自己"大国身份"的底线。俄罗斯在"欧亚伙伴关系"的基础上，在该地区建立了多层次多领域的合作机制，从而向其合作伙伴传达本国的主要理念——后苏联空间一体化进程的目标不仅限于建立关税同盟和共同经济空间，而是要建立一个广泛的欧亚合作区。实现这一目标的最重要条件是对后苏联空间进行经济整合，同时这也是俄罗斯在独联体的战略目标。对于俄罗斯而言，整合后苏联空间的需求主要与其地缘政治目标及经济发展前景有关。俄罗斯希望本国商品在欧亚地区拥有市场竞争力，并努力与周边国家建立友好合作带。俄罗斯与独联体国家之间的合作可以通过建立洲际工业协会、国际金融中心、工业公司等形式发展。

俄美关系十分尖锐并且存在继续恶化的风险，两国关系恶化的趋势具有长期性，这是由美国政治精英阶层的意识形态决定的，其特点是新保守主义力量不断增强，美国外交政策中出现理想主义与现实主义交织的现象。在不断变化的世界格局中美国的战略体现了其对权力边界的现实认识，决定了俄美关系的不稳定性。俄美关系一直处于最低水平，国际安全中俄美关系的"失衡"可能导致两国爆发直接军事冲突，双边关系中最敏感、最根本的战略稳定与安全问题极大地限制了俄罗斯的发展。

复杂且紧张的地缘政治环境给俄罗斯经济发展提出迫切要求，为俄罗斯农业转型、加强农业合作提供了契机。粮食作物具有重要的战略地位，俄罗斯可凭借粮食出口国身份进入世界市场，这对于提振国家发展信心具有重大的政治意义，有利于提高俄罗斯国民经济的投资吸引力。2019年9月，俄罗斯联邦农业部副部长率代表团参加金砖国家农业部长第九次会议，会议期间，各方强调要优先落实"2030年可持续发展议程"的目标。会议还强调，成员国间应分享交流经验并加强专业人员的国际合作。俄罗斯代表在会议报告中谈到了俄罗斯农业部门的数字化转型，以及有关农村地区发展的国家规划。在此后的金砖国家部长级会议上签署了一份联合宣言，内容涵盖金砖国家在通信领域使用新技术、农业创新公司的发展、贸易和区域化及农业可持续发展等多个主题。①

第二，国家宏观经济发展不稳定。2018 年，世界银行在发布的《俄罗斯经济报告》中预测 2018—2020 年俄罗斯经济增长前景温和，预计为 1.5%—1.8%。② 2019 年初，俄罗斯经济发展部、中央银行及国家统计局相继公布 2018 年经济增长数据。据俄罗斯联邦国家统计局估计，2018 年俄罗斯联邦 GDP 增长率为 2.3%，高于经济发展部和中央银行的估值。经济发展部估计的 GDP 增长率为 1.8%（后又提高到 2%），中央银行预测增幅在 1.5% 至 2% 之间。③ 但是年增长率浮动是由油价上涨等短期原因导致，并未体现劳动和资本等基本要素的作用。

将经济增长率提高到全球平均水平以上是俄罗斯国民经济进一步发展的关键任务，这将提升俄罗斯国民的生活水平，保证国家粮食安全并提高俄罗斯农产品等在国内外市场的竞争力。俄罗斯正竭力开发出口产品以确保这一目标顺利实现。谷物、面粉、油脂、糖、淀粉、糖果行业的深加工出口的发展进一步受到国家重视。家禽、猪肉和牛肉的出口也呈现出积极态势。俄罗斯产品的主要出口对象国位于亚速海—黑海、里海沿岸地区和亚太地区。联合国贸易和发展会议编写的报告特别指出："在全球需求低迷的形势下，世界贸易极有可能无法实现广泛增长。"全球经济中存在的这种状况为各国发展带来了一定风险。"在全球需求低迷的情况下，除非个别国家和某些特殊情况，否则世界贸易不太可能出现广泛的增长。俄罗斯农产品出口是国家长期发展规划中的优先发展项目，因此需要国家制定合理的贸易保护主义政策，并为该政策确立必要的体制和提供基础设施支持，推动俄罗斯农产品走向国际市场。

---

① "На встрече министров сельского хозяйства стран БРИКС обсудили трансформацию российского АПК," Министерство сельского хозяйства Российской Федерации, http://mcx.ru/press-service/news/na-vstreche-ministrov-selskogo-khozyay stva-stran-briks- obsudili-transformatsiyu-rossiyskogo-apk/.

② "世界银行调高 2018 年俄罗斯经济增长预期，"中华人民共和国商务部 http://www.mofcom.gov.cn/article/i/jyjl/e/20181 2/20181202817419.shtml.

③ "Самый быстрый ВВП," коммерсантъ, https://www.kommersant.ru/doc/3873845.

（二）制裁背景下俄罗斯农业政策的角色

第一，国际层面：有利于实行经济外交和吸引外资。俄罗斯在西方受挫后，战略目标上更加重视"东方"，亚太地区在经济、地缘政治、国家关系等诸多方面都与俄罗斯的重大战略利益紧密相关，理应成为俄罗斯全面发展最重要的地区之一。其中农业领域的合作是落实"东向"战略的重要支点。首先，在全球化背景下，世界农产品市场中发展中国家的作用日益增强：经济增长、减贫、消费和进口增加促使西方伙伴在世界贸易中逐渐将目光投向东方，这显然对俄罗斯农业发展利好。与能源行业或其他产业相比，全球农业市场对投资政策变化的敏感度较小，对政治形势的波动依赖性有限。世界某些地区的人口增长和气候变化成为俄罗斯农产品出口的有利因素。根据联合国粮食及农业组织的数据显示，世界上最大的农产品进口国是欧盟、美国、中国、日本、加拿大和墨西哥，最大的出口国是欧盟、美国、巴西、中国、加拿大和阿根廷[1]。俄罗斯农产品出口最有前景的市场就是消费持续增长的亚太地区国家，其中包括中国、日本、韩国等。

俄日在远东地区的农业和能源合作就是一个最典型的例子。日本借着俄罗斯转向东方的机会，积极与俄罗斯接触，希望与俄罗斯就领土争端进行谈判，即使该目的暂时无法达成，也能通过经济合作与俄罗斯展开对话与合作。2016年5月，日本正式宣布出台对俄关系的"新方法"，包括延长人均寿命；发展现代化城市；提供整洁便利的生活环境；中小企业的互动；扩展合作；能源合作；提高俄罗斯工业的多元化水平；提高生产率；发展远东工业；建立出口基地；在先进技术领域进行合作；加强俄日民间交流共八项内容。2019年9月4日，在第五届东方经济论坛召开期间，俄农业部副部长与越南、日本农业、林业和渔业部副部长举行了工作会议，重点讨论了俄日联合项目的实施情况，旨在提高俄罗斯远东地区的农业和渔业生产力以及建立适应远东气候条件的温室和养猪场等。

---

[1] "The state of agricultural commodity markets," 联合国粮农组织，http://www.fao.org/3/I9542EN/i9542en.pdf.

除了亚太地区，俄罗斯也积极与中东、非洲等地区发展贸易关系。俄罗斯农业部副部长谢尔盖·莱文在2019年10月举办的"农业领域的可持续伙伴关系：制度、方法、保障"俄非经济论坛小组会议上表示，俄罗斯认为非洲是在农业领域建立建设性合作的可靠伙伴。自2016年以来，俄罗斯对非洲国家的出口增长了73%，2018年底达到46亿美元，俄非双边贸易具有长足的发展潜力。在未来几年中，俄计划将非洲大陆的农产品供应增加一倍，预计增长将超过50亿美元。① 目前，俄罗斯农产品出口大部分流向北非，俄罗斯计划扩大与其他非洲地区的合作，以满足非洲不断增长的粮食需求。莱文副部长强调，俄罗斯小麦、大麦、葵花籽油、禽肉、糖果和鱼产品出口至非洲大陆国家的潜力巨大。与会者还讨论了建立物流基础设施以发展与非洲国家的伙伴关系、农产品和食品贸易领域的互惠伙伴关系问题及俄罗斯在该地区农业领域基础设施的投资前景。2019年11月，俄罗斯农业部长出访约旦，对促进双方在农业领域的合作起到推动作用。长期以来，约旦需要进口俄罗斯大麦、豆类和蔬菜。两国就俄罗斯肉类和肉制品、牛奶和奶制品的供应检疫标准达成一致，准备增加粮食供应，特别是谷物、牲畜和鱼产品的出口。②

第二，国家层面：有利于解决国家经济结构性矛盾。农业是俄罗斯国民经济最重要的领域之一。农业生产不仅为民众提供食品，作为加工业的原料来源还能满足社会的其他各种需求。居民生活水平、营养结构、人均收入、商品和服务的消费以及社会生活条件等许多方面都取决于农业的发展。当前，俄罗斯在国民经济和社会发展上追求"突破式发展"，急须改善经济结构。农业是所有国家国民经济的支柱产业之一。不论土壤和气候条件如何，即使是最发达的国家也在大力发展农业经济，世界上任何一个强国都需要强大的农业做支撑，所以俄罗斯必须发展本国独立的农业产

---

① "Россия удвоит поставки продовольствия в Африку," Министерство сельского хозяйства Российской Федерации, http://mcx.ru/press-service/news/rossiya-udvoit-postavki-prodovolstviya-v-afriku-/.

② "Россия и Иордания укрепляют торгово-экономическое сотрудничество," Министерство сельского хозяйства Российской Федерации, http://mcx.ru/press-service/news/rossiya-i-iordaniya-ukreplyayut-torgovo-ekonomicheskoe-sotrudnic hestvo/.

业。况且俄罗斯具备发展农业的先天优势，即土地广阔平坦且肥沃。

同时，发展农业有利于农村地区稳定，保障国家安全。俄罗斯城乡地区差距巨大，农村地区地理位置偏僻，许多村镇缺少自来水、电力、通信等基础生活设施，农村劳动力大量向城市转移。据 2019 年初公布的地区生活质量排名，等级最高的莫斯科与最低的图瓦地区人均总产值相差 25 倍。推动农业领域发展可以有效吸引劳动力回迁，其外溢作用还可带动相关基础设施的建设。

然而，"进口替代"作为国家实施的经济策略具有矛盾性：一方面，它是出于保护经济而实施的经济政策之一；另一方面，它也是一种侧重经济增长目标融入全球经济的方式。目前进口替代的策略对俄而言非常重要。进口替代可理解为旨在增加国内对国产产品需求的国家政策，通过采取积极措施减少对国外同类产品的消费依赖，从而创造具有全球竞争力的国内生产商和产品。值得注意的是，进口替代政策具有两面性，从实施制裁和报复措施的发展趋势来看，该政策有可能成为刺激国内产业发展的激励措施。但是，进口替代的目的不仅是在国内市场上用国内商品替代进口商品，而且还在于提高商品及服务质量，从而提高与外国商品在世界市场上的竞争力，就这一层面而言，对待进口替代政策还需持有更加谨慎的态度。

表 5-3 俄罗斯家庭月均支出① （单位：卢布）

	2011 年	2012 年	2013 年	2014 年	2015 年	2016 年
家庭月均消费	11715.1	13066.3	14153.8	15094.3	15295.4	16632.5
月均食品消费	4078.1	4375.1	4694.9	5111.0	5707.8	6220.7
农村家庭月均消费	8156.8	9305.4	9739.5	10611.9	11271.3	12070.4
农村家庭月均食品消费	3579.3	3842.8	4073.8	4457.0	5100.5	5486.2

数据来源：根据俄罗斯联邦统计局《俄罗斯居民社会地位和生活水平报告》整理

---

① "Социальное положение и уровень жизни населения России - 2015г"、доклад "Состав расходов на конечное потребление домашних хозяйств различных социально-экономических катеторий"，Федеральная служба государственной статистики, https: //gks.ru/bgd/regl/b15 _ 44/ Main.htm.

(三) 未来农业发展前景

第一，积极方面：有机农业是俄罗斯出口的新特点。有机农业是俄罗斯农业的特色之一，满足了俄罗斯对本国农产品"洁净提质"的要求，而其他农业大国以发达工业、科技能力推动农业发展，发展建立大型集约化农场的模式，这也是俄罗斯与其他农业大国的最大不同之处。在发展有机农业的过程中，俄罗斯不仅提高了进口标准，还在外交中利用这一因素对部分国家实施制裁。俄罗斯农业部享有有机产品商标的所有权，专利证书则由俄罗斯联邦知识产权局负责颁发。"有机产品法"自2020年起开始生效，目前，俄罗斯农业部正与其他主管部门一同制定包括维护有机生产者登记注册在内的法规以及多项国家标准。实行统一商标将有助于提高俄罗斯国内市场的产品质量，促进俄罗斯农工综合体的发展。借助俄罗斯政府和农业部实行的其他措施创建有机和环保农产品品牌，将有利于实现俄总统提出的增加农产品出口进而提高俄罗斯食品质量的目标。

2018年5月16日至18日，联合国粮食及农业组织第三十一次区域会议在沃罗涅日举行。会议前夕，俄罗斯联邦有机农业联盟发布了一项俄罗斯有机农业市场调研成果，该调研起止时间为2017年3月至2018年4月，由俄联邦有机农业联盟、俄罗斯农业部以及农业科研机构共同合作完成。会议以"电子农业、农业生态学和有机农业"为主题。会上沃罗涅日代理州长亚历山大·古谢夫对在当地发展有机农业表示支持，并指出未来将会面临一系列挑战，但近期会将发展有机农业纳入地区农业发展优先事项。

有机农业是一种农业生产方式，指的是在农业生产过程中不使用杀虫剂、除草剂、化学肥料、生长调节剂和转基因种子。俄罗斯国内总共有70家有机农业认证企业，其中53家符合国际认证标准。目前，已有16家获得有机认证的俄罗斯农业生产商将产品出口到欧盟国家，主要包括谷物、油籽和精油。2018年1月，俄联邦国家杜马通过了有机农业法案，前总理梅德韦杰夫援引专家的估计称，未来俄罗斯可以在全球有机农业市场上占据10%—25%的份额。① 这将使俄罗斯农产品具有不可替代性，稳定俄罗斯农产品出口市场，同时刺激农业相关科学技术发展。有机农业的发展是俄罗斯农业的一大亮点，其政治意义在于扭转了俄罗斯在俄欧贸易中处于劣势的局面，增加了俄罗斯的主动权。

第二，消极方面：国内农业综合生产链尚未形成。农业发展的主要趋势之一是技术现代化，国家极力支持大棚蔬菜种植、养猪和种子生产等。同时农业生产者补贴缺乏保障，高额农业补贴吸引了大量投资者进入农业市场。然而，也出现了一些亟待解决的问题，例如补贴分配不合理、大部分补贴被用于畜牧生产和饲料生产等。

俄罗斯植物化学制造商联盟执行董事奥贡卡说："我们确实在许多产业上都落后于世界其他国家，除谷物作物外，几乎所有农作物对种子的进口依存度都很高。"俄罗斯国内市场上几乎有一半的种子都来自国外，对进口的依赖程度超过50%，甜菜品种种子进口甚至高达90%。在发达国家，农业已成为高科技产业之一，而俄罗斯农业科学筹集的资金却很少。虽然俄罗斯农业部制定了相应的战略和计划，但到目前为止并没有取得实质性成果。俄罗斯针对农产品原料、农业科学技术不发达等情况，与拜耳公司达成了合作意向，拜耳公司将向俄罗斯研究人员提供种子材料和传授加速农业发展的生产技术。"俄国内种子市场价值为500亿卢布，其中进口部分为241.4亿卢布"。根据俄罗斯农业部科技教育司的数据：蔬菜种子的进口依存度为47%，饲料作物达90%，水果、浆果和坚果类作物的育种和苗圃达70%。② 拜耳技术转让项目负责人表示，俄罗斯科学家将获得玉米、大豆、油菜和小麦等重要作物的外来种子材料，并掌握加快番茄、黄瓜和卷心菜三种蔬菜作物生产率的相关技术。俄罗斯农业科技研究所的科研人员可以进行本地化改良，对外来种子进行研究实验，获得本地化杂交种子以及将其作为商品出售。作为技术转让的一部分，拜耳还将提供专家支持，包括教育活动和俄罗斯代表赴拜耳欧洲研究中心培训。拜耳

---

① "ГД в первом чтении приняла законопроект об органическом сельском хозяйстве" РИА, https: //ria. ru/20180403/1517 829156. html?

② "Что посеешь?" Коммерсантъ, https: //www. kommersant. ru/doc/3888725? query = bayer.

还将参与创建植物生物技术科学教育中心，重点研究玉米、油菜、大豆和小麦四种作物。

21世纪前20年，俄罗斯农业政策随着国家发展而不断调整，虽然俄罗斯发展农业有一定地理优势，但仍存在发展起点低、劳动力不足、气候条件不佳、机械技术依赖进口等问题，要真正实现农产品自给，俄罗斯政府需要加大资金技术投入，因为强大的农业生产力有赖于长期的投资与关注，而俄罗斯农业部门的平均投资回收期约为4—5年，难以吸引外部资金。独立的农业生产产业链涉及人力、科技、工业现代化等多种因素，而当前俄罗斯的农业发展仅停留在提高农业生产力层面，未来农业领域可持续发展前景尚不明朗。

三、东向战略对中俄农业合作的影响及前景

当前，俄罗斯对外贸易方向发生了明显转变，俄罗斯正逐步加强与东方国家的经贸合作。如今充满活力的亚太地区已成为世界经济中心之一，与东方国家开展经贸合作对俄罗斯越来越有吸引力。中国是俄罗斯在亚太地区最大的贸易伙伴，同时中俄关系也是俄罗斯最重要的双边关系之一，中俄经贸合作30年的发展历程呈现出与政治关系相似的阶段特征。20世纪90年代以来，随着中俄政治关系的不断改善，经贸合作也逐渐扩大，现阶段俄罗斯和中国都在进行经济结构调整和转型，寻求新形式的互动与合作。随着两国政治关系进入"新时代"，中俄经贸合作进一步深化，农业作为中俄经贸合作的重要领域也迎来新的合作契机。2018年，俄罗斯农业部部长德米特里·帕特鲁舍夫与中国农业农村部部长韩长赋就远东、俄罗斯贝加尔湖地区和中国东北的农工联合体的共同发展达成了共识。俄罗斯和中国计划在农业关键领域开展合作，重点规划了两国在谷物、畜牧和渔业综合体建设方面的合作，计划促进大豆、水稻的种植，发展蔬菜种植、奶牛和肉牛育种及猪和家禽养殖。有望建立统一的苗圃和水产养殖场，提高高附加值产品的产量。中俄双方将共同发展农业基础设施，并在实施创新农业技术和科学发展方面进行合作。中俄总理第二十三次定期会晤联合公报中明确指出，要加强监管机构合作交流，加快食品农产品准入

进程，以进一步扩大两国农产品贸易规模，推动实施农工综合体领域投资和基础设施合作项目；并且继续就制定双方感兴趣的农产品清单和具有出口潜力的主要农产品和食品生产企业清单开展建设性合作。①

由于双边经贸合作水平受到两国产业结构与经济模式的制约，经贸合作相对于两国政治互信而言明显滞后，以 2018 年为例，双边贸易额超过 1000 亿美元，达到历史最高水平，但在中国 4 万亿外贸总额中却占比不大。现阶段中俄农业合作重心仍然是贸易，但因两国经济体量差距过大，贸易总体水平并不高。中俄农业贸易结构具有一定的互补性，在农业领域，俄罗斯可与中国在种子培育、农机生产及劳动力方面展开合作。在此基础上，扩大中俄农业合作更重要的是国家层面的创新合作模式，中俄两国农业合作历史不长，农产品贸易更是新兴的贸易方向，如今通过建立合作区，降低了农产品生产成本并提高了通关效率。建立农产品自由贸易区可以消除中俄农业合作发展的长期障碍，并强化两国的互动协作，大大提高合作效率和水平。同时，进一步加强海关合作与协调，亟待建立系统有效的具体规则，简化农产品检疫流程和手续。

四、结　　论

俄罗斯农业在经济制裁的背景下逆势上扬。国家长期出台的保护政策为俄罗斯农业发展创造了有利条件，俄罗斯农业已呈现出良好的发展趋势。在基本满足国家粮食安全的需要后，俄罗斯新的农业战略正向"出口型"转变，其目的体现在两个方面：一是改善国家经济结构，减少经济对燃料出口的依赖；二是在实施东向战略的基础上，利用农产品贸易优势与亚太地区国家积极开展外交活动。在地缘政治局势复杂、国家经济结构矛盾突出的形势下，重视农业发展是俄罗斯应对国内外各种风险和挑战的重要策略之一。

但是，俄罗斯农业发展也存在不足与劣势，影响农业发展的关键因素

---

① "中俄总理第二十三次定期会晤联合公报"新华网，2018 年 11 月 7 日，http: //www. gov. cn/guowuyuan/2018 - 11/07/content_5338172. htm.

包括宏观经济前景不明朗、劳动力不足、农业机械与种子进口率高、农业人才培养和科技研究等，这些可能要经过十年甚至二十年才会有所改善。此外，许多农作物不适应俄罗斯的地理条件，过分坚持国家主义、实施全面的进口替代将产生高昂的成本，只有广泛参与国际合作才符合国家经济利益。中俄农业合作具有巨大的发展潜力，是双边经贸合作的重要组成部分，双方应重点加强两国的顶层设计，扎实推动与深化合作，使农业合作的硕果造福于两国人民。

建立有利于全球稳定、共同安全和创新增长的金砖国家伙伴关系

——轮值主席国俄罗斯的任务

瓦列尼娅·戈尔巴乔娃[*]

摘 要：2019年11月，俄罗斯宣布2020年金砖峰会的主题为"金砖国家加强战略伙伴关系有利于全球稳定、共同安全和创新增长"，这三个关键议题的设置表明了俄罗斯与金砖国家合作的优先方向。随着新冠肺炎疫情的暴发，俄罗斯不得不对关键议题的内容进行调整：在全球稳定方面，俄罗斯将"加强多边平台上的对外政策协调"调整为"对新冠肺炎病毒的应对采取共同行动"，这既有利于应对疫情，也将加强金砖国家作为"稳定岛"的作用；在安全领域，俄罗斯为金砖国家制定的共同反恐战略现已退位于"后疫情时代"的国家计划；在创新增长方面，俄罗斯将结合目前世界的经济状况调整未来五年的金砖国家经济合作战略。尽管新冠肺炎疫情极大地影响了俄罗斯作为主席国的许多既定方案，但金砖国家仍然是应对全球稳定的唯一机制。

关键词：金砖峰会；全球稳定；俄罗斯；优先方向

---

[*] 瓦列尼娅·戈尔巴乔娃，俄罗斯金砖国家研究国家委员会政府关系总监，俄罗斯科学院经济研究所亚洲战略研究中心研究员。

在2019年11月举行的巴西、俄罗斯、印度、中国、南非金砖国家领导人会晤活动上，俄罗斯总统弗拉基米尔·普京肯定了保持金砖国家议程连续性的重要性，并提出，在2020年担任主席国期间，俄罗斯将继续推动金砖国家在多个主要领域的合作，为金砖国家所有成员国造福。

轮值主席国俄罗斯的口号是："建立有利于全球稳定、共同安全和创新增长的金砖国家伙伴关系"，它指明了三个主要的优先发展方向，这些优先发展方向已成为俄罗斯发起的同金砖国家合作伙伴议事的重中之重。但是，新冠病毒的肆虐改变了国际事务的方向标，并使得俄罗斯调整了主席国任期内的计划，因此重新确定了重点。

全球稳定问题一直是俄罗斯与金砖国家伙伴议事的重点问题之一。俄罗斯坚定不移地支持扩大金砖国家在一些国际重要场合中的外交政策协作，尤其是在成员国之间已经积累了正面协作经验的联合国。然而疫情迫使许多国家调整内政计划，从而加剧了一系列国际冲突。在中美贸易战不断升级的背景之下，包括俄罗斯在内的金砖国家面临着选边站的问题，这似乎是符合逻辑的。但是金砖国家中没有任何一个成员国，尤其是俄罗斯对加入针对美国或者中国的对抗感兴趣。这也意味着，尽管在"新冠肺炎疫情危机"之下金砖国家组织陷入分裂，但应该进一步加强其在确保全球稳定及世界秩序可持续方面的作用。对于俄罗斯而言重要的是利用这个机会，邀请伙伴国家拟定统一协调的行动方案，以应对疫情挑战，增强金砖国家在当下动荡不安的世界中作为"稳定岛"的力量。

安全——又一个永恒的首要问题，俄罗斯同金砖国家成员国的协作关系是建立在安全这个基础之上的。金砖国家成员国在包括维和、反恐、打击跨国犯罪、共同解决全球及区域关键问题在内的国际安全议程上的一切事务一贯保持统一立场。俄罗斯支持金砖国家在推动联合国这一确保和平与安全的关键组织发起的倡议上发挥更加积极的作用。金砖国家在联合国协作的首要任务之一就是制定统一的预防恐怖主义、阻止恐怖主义意识形态传播（包括网络传播）的国际标准。[①] 在任主席国期间，俄罗斯计划从

[①] 俄罗斯总统弗拉基米尔·普京于2019年11月14日在巴西利亚举行的金砖国家峰会上的讲话。http://kremlin.ru/events/president/news/62045

巴西手中接过接力棒，加强金砖国家成员国在打击洗钱、恐怖主义融资和回收犯罪所得资产方面的合作。俄方提议制定金砖国家反恐战略，① 这将大大推动打击国际恐怖主义全面公约的制定和联合国大会采纳工作的完成。但是由于防止新冠肺炎病毒传播所采取的限制性措施，这些任务，哪怕是暂时的，仍退居到了次要地位，让位于抗击疫情及其影响的国家计划。

疫情中断了许多计划。2020年本是全世界欢庆第二次世界大战结束及联合国成立75周年的一年，作为主席国，俄罗斯向金砖国家成员国提议考虑针对这些重大事件准备联合声明的可能性。对于金砖国家来说，坚定支持以国际法和联合国宪章为基础的世界秩序本是十分重要的，但是新冠肺炎病毒导致全球秩序的结构性转变，到目前为止，我们只能推测"后疫情时代"世界秩序的走向。

第三个重点是创新发展，这能为金砖国家开辟新的机遇，即引导国际经济议程、形成世界经济发展与合作的新模式，并将其推广到其他发展中国家。这种新模式的实质在于不限制主权的平等合作、公平竞争和倡议对接，以实现包容性经济的发展，但是世界经济的现状使得金砖国家在进一步发展经贸、金融以及投资方面的合作上做出重大调整。

尽管如此，俄罗斯在2020年的主要任务始终是更新至2025年金砖国家经济合作伙伴战略。该战略的第一个"版本"于2015年由金砖国家批准通过。

这份文件对金砖国家成员国在多领域开展经济合作产生了积极影响。②如今在疫情及其对世界经济造成的不良后果背景之下，俄罗斯需对未来五年经济伙伴战略提案做出调整。

俄罗斯从巴西手中接过的另一个任务是继续丰富金砖国家的合作内容。首先就是巩固金砖国家现有的组织机构和金融机制，即金砖国家新开发银行、外汇储备库及在外汇储备库框架下运行的宏观经济信息交流体

---

① 帕特鲁舍夫提出制定金砖国家反恐战略/俄新社. 2019. 10. 18. https: //ria. ru/20191018/1559938410. html

② 金砖国家经济合作伙伴战略/2015年俄罗斯任金砖国家主席国时期官方网站。2015年7月9日。http: //brics2015. ru/documents/。

系。2020年在莫斯科计划开设新开发银行欧亚地区分支机构。俄罗斯和金砖国家成员国打算继续进行设立金砖国家本币债券基金的工作。俄方也准备发起一批新倡议,以扩大金砖国家成员国税务机关、海关及反垄断机构间的合作。这类具体的工作旨在实现金砖国家战略发展目标。

俄罗斯任主席国期间的任务清单上还包括发展"金砖+"模式,金砖国家正在与其他国家及一体化联盟建立合作并不断向前发展。同时正在进行扩大新开发银行股东成员国的协商工作,这将有助于缓解金砖国家组织本身成员国扩员问题的紧迫性。

2020年俄罗斯任金砖国家主席国期间的优先发展方向如下:

(一)巩固全球政治多边原则,在国际舞台上维护金砖国家成员国的共同利益:

——在遵守国际法公认原则和规范的基础及考虑到所有国家的利益前提上推动合作议程;

——巩固联合国在国际关系中的中心地位;

——增强集体力量以应对全球及区域挑战与威胁;

——加强金砖国家在打击恐怖主义、极端主义、腐败、跨国犯罪、毒品及武器贩运方面的合作;

——进一步增强在和平利用和研究外层空间方面的协作;

——继续开展关于确保国际信息安全及打击信息犯罪的对话交流;

——加强金砖国家在关键多边场合的协调机制;

——在"金砖+"及"拓展"模式下扩展金砖国家伙伴国协作;

——加强国际发展领域合作的对话交流;

(二)发展经贸金融领域的合作:

——更新金砖国家经济合作伙伴战略;

——加强金砖国家间的贸易往来;

——推动新开发银行提升潜力;

——完善金砖国家外汇储备库;

——发展及统一金砖国家结算系统;

——开展金砖国家女性工商联盟实践活动；

——促进金砖国家偏远地区经济发展；

——加强金砖国家成员国税务机关、海关及反垄断机构间的合作；

——深化能源领域合作；

——推动在数字经济及创新领域的互动协作；

——加强卫生保健领域的联系，包括在防治传染病及非传染病问题上采用联合措施；

——加强金砖五国关于农业和粮食安全问题的对话交流；

——在预防紧急情况、消除其影响方面加强联系；

（三）人文交流合作：

——加强议会间的联系；

——扩大文化领域协作；

——加强金砖国家教育机构协作；

——进一步发展金砖国家网络大学；

——推动青年交流；

——扩大公共外交模式框架下的合作；

——加强金砖国家新闻界代表的联系。

俄罗斯的主要任务之一仍然是推动金砖国家能源议程发展。俄方正在继续推行建立金砖国家能源研究合作平台的倡议，以便在石油、天然气和能源效率等领域进行联合研究。

俄罗斯认为人文交流是金砖国家另一个重要合作方向。特别需要关注的是金砖国家青年这一赛道的发展。

在扩大及深化高等教育领域合作方面，俄罗斯专注于发展金砖国家网络大学、扩大金砖国家学术科研中心（在俄罗斯任主席国期间学术领域的作用显著增加）、研究机构及高校之间的联系。一批俄罗斯高校已经开始实施金砖国家大学生交流项目。第一个国际大学生交流项目在远东联邦大学开展，该大学在2020年2月接纳了150名来自金砖国家的大学生前来学习。

民间合作领域也在积极发展。2015年俄罗斯发起创建金砖国家民间组织合作发展平台的倡议。在俄罗斯的倡议之下，金砖国家议会和妇女工作继续向前发展。

在科学和创新领域，俄罗斯打算继续致力于实施"金砖国家清洁河流项目"。重点方向包括发展数字经济和人工智能、创造舒适智慧城市环境、实现可持续发展目标、导入创新等。

新冠肺炎病毒大流行也凸显了现如今金砖国家发展的其他重点任务。日前金砖国家已经提出创建疫苗中心的倡议。当下在由新冠肺炎病毒传播引起的疫情期间确保金砖国家国民的生命安全、总结金砖国家防疫措施应用情况和国家卫生保健体系协作问题成为卫生保健领域的中心话题之一。俄方提议概括总结金砖国家成员国采用的先进防疫措施，不仅能为金砖国家继续使用，也能为其他国家专业人员所用。[①]

尽管疫情在很大程度上打断了俄罗斯的计划（例如，在任主席国一年期间计划举办约 200 场不同级别的活动），但金砖国家的议程并未变得不重要。相反，在错综复杂的变局之中，在国际关系范式可能发生转变的背景之下，金砖国家仍然是能确保全球稳定的热门组织，而这是其他国家或者一体化联盟所无法提供的。

[①] 俄罗斯卫生部召开金砖国家卫生高官会议，2020 年金砖国家轮值主席国俄罗斯联邦官方网站。https://brics-russia2020.ru/news/20200508/395195/Minzdrav-Rossii-provel-vstrechu-v-formate-videokonferentsii-starshikh-dolzhnostnykh-lits-stran-BRIKS-po.html。

中印人文交流史中的跨文化传播关键点[*]

段孟洁[**]

摘　要："中印交流，质在人心"，中国与印度间的人文交流传统已有两千多年，与两国的文明发展史息息相关，其深度及广度远超我们想象，是两国间友好交流的传承与见证，也是未来两国深层次民心相通的基础与铺垫。2018年末，中印高级别人文交流机制首次会议取得圆满成功，由此拉开了中印人文交流的新帷幕，成为中印人文交流的又一关键性节点。2020年是中印建交70周年，本文旨在梳理中印人文交流史中的文化关键点，为中印文明间的跨文化传播铺路架桥。

关键词：中印人文交流；中印关系；跨文化传播

---

[*] 基金来源：本文是四川外国语大学年度科研青年项目"印地语报刊镜像下的中国形象"（SISU202034），重庆市高校国际化人文特色建设非通用语国别区域研究项目"一带一路背景下金砖国家人文交流研究"（CIISFTGB1903）以及重庆国际战略研究院研究项目（CIISFTGB2005）阶段性研究成果。

[**] 段孟洁，博士生，四川外国语大学重庆非通用语学院印地语专业教师，主要从事印度语言与文化、中印人文交流和跨文化传播研究。

一、引　　言

中国和印度两国比邻千年，既是历史悠久的东方文明大国，又是亚洲广袤大地上的两颗耀眼的明珠。尼赫鲁在《印度的发现》一书中写到：中国和印度"这两个国家有着彼此间几千年来和平相处的值得自豪的记录……它们彼此的关系，不仅对这两个国家本身是极其重要的，而且对世界也是有重大意义的"。[①] 人文交流是中印关系中极为重要的一部分，贯穿中印关系史的始终。早在中印实现高层互访之前，中印间的民间交流互动便已开始，佛教从印度传入中国后，人文交流程度达到顶峰，中印跨文化传播中的文化关键点不断显现，为之后的中印人文交流打下了深厚的基础。在中印人文交流过程中，什么是中印文化交流关键点？我们又应该在中印跨文化传播过程中如何利用好这些文化关键点？以上均是本文试图梳理探究的问题。

二、中印人文交流的定义

（一）人文交流的内涵

"观乎天文，以察时变，观乎人文，以化成天下"，所谓"人文"，在《易经》中原指人类社会的各种现象，而今《辞海》对于"人文"的定义是"人类社会的各种文化现象"。由此，"人文"的内涵得到具化，从广义的人类社会的各种现象，具化成了狭义的人类社会的各种文化现象。中国对外关系的三大主要组成部分是战略互信、经贸合作和人文交流，这三个方面同时也是新时代中国特色大国外交的三大支柱。其中，人文交流的覆盖面最广，主体最多，习近平曾提出，人文交流是中外关系的地基。而当今全球化背景下中外人文交流中的"人文"，指的是"人类文化中先进的、科学的、优秀的、健康的部分，包括先进的价值观及其规范，是一种重视

---

① ［印］尼赫鲁：《印度的发现》，世界知识出版社1956年版，第1页。

人的文化。"①

教育部中外人文交流中心主任杜柯伟在四川外国语大学举办讲座时，对人文交流的内涵做出了明确的界定，"人文交流指在各相关领域各类主体通过各种形式开展的人与人的交流。"② 其中的各相关领域包括教育、科技、文化、卫生、体育、旅游、媒体、新闻出版、影视艺术、青年、妇女、语言文字、档案、智库等，还可以拓展到生态保护、扶贫减灾、遗产保护、人力资源开发、军事文化交流等领域；各类主体包括政府、学校、企业、社会团体、个人等。由此内涵可知，人文交流涉及范围广，层次具有多样性，形式具有灵活性，是人与人的交流，文化与文化的互通。2017年7月，在中共中央办公厅、国务院办公厅印发的《关于加强和改进人文交流工作的若干意见》文件中，说明了当前加强和改进中外人文交流工作的宗旨是"促进中外民心相通和文明互鉴"，③ 同时要创新高级别人文交流机制。

（二）中印人文交流的内涵

历史上，中印文化交流是世界各大文明友好交流的典范。④ 目前，中印两国的高级别人文交流机制的建立已经步入正轨。2018年12月21日，中印两国外长在印度首都新德里共同主持召开中印高级别人文交流机制首次会议，确定了八个重点合作方向。2019年8月12日，中印高级别人文交流机制第二次会议在北京举行，两国外长共同签署《2020年中印外交部交流合作行动计划》并见证签署文化、体育、传统医药、博物馆等人文领域双边合作文件。⑤ 中印人文交流机制已经初步建立。2020年是中印建交

---

① 2019年9月18日，教育部中外人文交流中心主任杜柯伟在四川外国语大学举办主题为"秉承人文交流理念，深入推进高等学校中外人文交流工作"讲座，杜柯伟主任在讲座上的讲话记录。
② 同上。
③ 新华社："文件《关于加强和改进人文交流工作的若干意见》"，中华人民共和国国务院新闻办公室官网，2017年12月22日，http://www.scio.gov.cn/tt/zdgz/Document/1614051/1614051.htm。
④ 尹锡南：《中印人文交流研究：历史、现状与认知》，时事出版社2015年版，第12页。
⑤ 外交部："中印高级别人文交流机制第二次会议在北京举行 王毅同印度外长苏杰生共同主持"，外交部官网，2019年8月12日，https://www.mfa.gov.cn/web/wjbzhd/t1688111.shtml。

70周年，也是中印关系将迎来大发展的一年，中印人文交流在其中起着关键性的作用。中印两国的高级别人文交流机制如何建立，如何为中印关系打好"地基"，我们应当从历史的视角进行溯源，从中印人文交流的传统出发，发掘中印人文交流的更多可能性。

三、中印人文交流史中的文化关键点

在中印人文交流史上，有许多人文互通经典案例，有的广为人知，有的不为人所知，中印人文交流中的文化关键点值得加以总结借鉴。

（一）支那及丝衣

"中国"两字，在英文中是 China，在法文中是 Chine，其来源都是梵文चीन（Cina），曾被音译为"支那"，这一叫法一直延续到现代印地语中，也在世界范围内被广泛使用。至于"支那"这个名字是如何传入印度的，这可能与中印间最初的交往息息相关。चीन（Cina）的读音近似"秦"，来源于中国的"秦"字，这一说法最早是由法国汉学家保罗·伯希和（Paul Pelliot，1878—1945 年）提出的。目前可考的最早对其有所记载的印度文献是孔雀王朝初期考底利耶（Kautilya）的《政事论》，文中出现了"丝及丝衣产于支那国"[①] 这样的词句。此书作于公元前 4 世纪，这正好与秦统一蜀地的时间一致。另外在印度两大史诗之一《摩诃婆罗多》中，चीन（Cina）一词也有体现，[②]《摩诃婆罗多》被印度人民尊为"历史"，在印度有着极其广泛的影响力，चीन（Cina）一词能被写入大史诗，可见当时印度人民已对中国有了初步的认识。这一认识的来源很有可能与当时活跃在中国北部和西北部的游牧部落匈奴、月氏、大宛等有关，这些游牧部族很早就将中国人称为"秦人"，随着部落迁移这一叫法被传到了古印度。从

[①] 薛克翘著：《中印文化交流史话》，商务印书馆1998年版，第6页。
[②] "Cina（支那）"一词，出现于《毗湿摩篇》第10章，持国向全胜询问战争双方的情况的时候，全胜向持国介绍了难敌的支持者的情况，在其中的第64节提到了"支那"。这个国家的国王属于刹帝利种姓，在这场战争中，他支持难敌，最后全军覆灭。这个叫"支那"的国家，就是中国。

《政事论》中"丝及丝衣产于支那国"这样的词句可以进行推断，在秦大一统之前，中印两国已经开始了直接或间接的民间贸易往来，中国的丝和丝衣已经在部分印度地区得到了肯定和推广，并被作为一个国家形象，写入印度大史诗《摩诃婆罗多》中，चीन (Cina) 一词也得到了大范围的传播，促成了中印间最初的了解和交往。

通过以上考证可知，中印人文交流开始的时间节点可以大致确定在公元前3世纪秦朝统一中国之前，至今中印人文交流史已超过两千年。

（二）月兔及星宿

提起中印文化的交流，普遍的认知是在佛教传入中国以后。不可否认，佛教东传极大地带动了中印人义交流，但早在佛教传入以前，中印文化交流就已经开始了，并且这一时期的文化交流是双向的交流，在此有两个经典案例可以作为例证。

中国有个古老的民间传说——月兔，为什么在古人的想象里月亮里会有一只兔子？为什么不是别的动物呢？根据季羡林先生考证，玉兔的由来与印度息息相关，这个故事在中印两国都有广泛流传，在《大唐西域记》卷七中也有记载，讲述了月兔产生的缘由：帝释天化身为一位老人来到烈士池旁考验狐狸、兔子和猴子三种动物，请它们为自己找寻食物。狐狸衔来了一尾鲤鱼，猴子爬树摘来了果子，唯有兔子两手空空。老人发了通牢骚，兔子随即让狐狸和猴子去拾柴生火，说道："仁者！我身卑劣，所求难遂。敢以微躬，充此一餐"。[①] 说罢纵身入火，帝释天恢复原形，哀叹良久，为了使兔子不灭，将它送上了月亮，以传后世，至此，就有了月兔。

这个故事开头便写道："烈士池西，有三兽窣堵波，是如来修菩萨行时烧身之处"[②]。"窣堵波"一词，音译自梵语स्तूप (stupā)，是印度一种塔的形式，在印度教和佛教建筑中都有大量的应用，另外由"如来修菩萨行时烧身之处""时天帝释欲验修菩萨行者"[③] 等语句，可见这个故事属于佛

---

① 玄奘、辩机原著，季羡林等校注：《大唐西域记校注》下，中华书局2004年版，第579页。
② 同上。
③ 同上。

本生故事जतक (Jātaka)。据目前的考古发掘考证，佛本生故事的大致形成时间不晚于公元前3世纪。而中国最早关于月兔的记载是战国时期屈原的《天问》，其中有这样的语句："厥利维何，而顾菟在腹？"① 意思是：月中黑点那是何物，是否兔子腹中藏身？表达了对月兔存在的怀疑。成诗的具体时间不可考，但根据屈原的生卒年份（约公元前340—公元前278年）可以推断，成诗时间晚于佛本生故事。关于这个故事的来源，季羡林先生也作出过一个判断，"根据这个故事在印度起源之古、传布之广、典籍中记载之多，说它起源于印度也是比较合理的"。②

月兔这一"巧合"是中印文化交流的一个见证，也是早期印度文化对中国文化产生影响的一个例证，说明了中印两国文化的吸引性和互通性，其背后隐藏着的人文交流传播途径也值得我们去发掘。

如前文所言，这一时期的中印文化交流是双向的，"月兔"来源于印度，同样，中国文化也对印度产生了一定影响，特别是在天文学方面。

中国自古有二十八星宿之说，印度的古代天文学也是这样划分的，这跟月兔的故事一样，显然不是什么巧合。关于中印二十八宿，据竺可桢先生的考证，"印度之二十八宿与中国同出一源似无疑问"。③ 中印二十八宿有许多相似之处，足以证明其同源论，那么孰先孰后呢？关于"二十八宿从何起源"这一问题，中外学者已经争论了近二百年，有"中国、印度和巴比伦三种观点，而以中国起源说最为有力"。④ 日本天文学者新城新藏认为二十八宿起源于中国，时间大约在周朝时，这与目前的考古发现是一致的。在考古发现中，"长沙马王堆帛书《五星占》（公元前168年）、湖北睡地虎竹简《日书》（公元前2世纪中叶）、安徽双古堆圆盘漆器（公元前165年）和湖北曾侯乙漆箱盖（公元前433年）均出现了完整的二十八宿名"⑤。

由此可见，中印文化之交往是双向的，无论是月兔的起源，还是二十

---

① 屈原著，董楚平译注：《楚辞译注》，上海古籍出版社2006年版，第80页。
② 季羡林著：《中印文化交流史》，新华出版社1991年版，第11页。
③ 竺可桢著：《竺可桢文集》，科学出版社1979年版，第235页。
④ 赵永恒，李勇："二十八宿的形成与演变"，《中国科技史杂志》2009年01期，第110页。
⑤ 同上。

八宿,都是中印文化交流的一个早期结果,是文化与文化间的碰撞与互通。

(三) 佛教东传

两汉之际佛教初传至中国,在隋唐时期,中印人文交流达到了历史上的巅峰。以佛教东传为载体,中印间的人文交流模式得到了极大的丰富,这一巅峰体现在许多方面:

1. 音乐互通

相传,张骞通西域时,在西域得到了两支曲子,其中一支叫做"摩诃兜勒",李延年因之更进二十八解,乘舆以为武乐,对后世军乐产生了很大影响。[①] 曲名带有明显的梵语特点,"摩诃"在梵语中意为"伟大、广大",可以证明其来源于古印度,中印间的音乐交流古已有之。

随着佛教东传,印度的佛教音乐也传到了中国,并且产生了极大影响,出现了中国特色的佛教音乐。印度佛教徒在传授佛经的过程中,除了要背诵经文外,还要特别讲究音韵,讲究富于抑扬顿挫的念诵和歌咏,讲究"散韵相间",遇到散文体的经文就念诵,遇到韵文体的诗歌就歌唱,既不枯燥又便于记忆。佛教传到中国以后,人们把念诵经文称为"转读",把歌唱偈颂称为"梵呗"。佛教音乐的奠基人,即"梵呗"的创作者,一般被认为就是三国时著名的文学家和诗人曹植。[②] 曹植是魏武帝曹操的儿子,魏文帝曹丕的弟弟。因为曾被封为陈王,死后谥号为"思",所以又被后人称为陈思王。关于他创作佛教乐曲的故事,记载于南朝梁僧祐的《出三藏记》卷十二《陈思王感鱼山梵声制呗记》中,可惜目前只传下来一个题目,原文没有流传下来。曹植所创作的梵呗被后人称为鱼山梵呗。从某种程度上说,曹植也是在中国传播印度音乐的使者,这不仅是中国佛教史上的一段佳话,更推动了中印间的人文交流。

2. 人才互通

三国时期,佛教信徒逐渐增多,佛教文化在与中国传统文化的撞击中

[①] 王福利:"《摩诃兜勒》曲名含义及其相关问题",《历史研究》2010 年 03 期,第 103 页。
[②] 薛克翘著:《中印文化交流史话》,商务印书馆 1998 年版,第 25 页。

逐步在中国形成了自己的影响力。一般认为，魏晋南北朝时期是印度佛教徒来华传教的第一个高潮。据《高僧传》记载，这一时期来华的印度僧人有三四十人之多。

同期，中国也开始有人西行求法，但这些人西行求法不是政府层面公派，完全出于宗教信仰。三国时期有朱士行西行于阗（新疆和田）求法，派弟子将梵文正本《大品般若经》送回内地，虽未能至天竺，但他作为西行求法第一人，具有"先驱者的意义"。① 据《高僧传》记载，西行求法的代表人物还有：西晋有精通36种语言文字的竺法护，前秦有中印混血的佛学家和翻译家鸠摩罗什，魏晋南北朝时期有写出了《佛国记》的法显，唐朝有西天取经的玄奘。这些高僧不仅西行求得佛法，更极大地推动了中印文化的交流互通，中印人文交流达到了一个空前的高潮。中印高僧的往来互通，在某种程度上也是人才的交流互通，每位高僧都是佛经翻译家，从语言层面达到了交流互通的目的。

3. 文学互通

鲁迅先生曾在《痴华鬘》的题记中写道："尝闻天竺寓言之富，如大林深泉。他国艺文，往往蒙其影响"。② 其中所指的"他国"就包括了印度。印度的神话故事和寓言对中国文学产生了很深的影响，从前文提到的"月兔"的故事，到后来的六朝志怪故事和唐朝传奇变文，皆可证实。这个影响主要表现在两个方面：一是故事母题，许多我们熟悉的中国故事，据考证都是由印度传入的，比如说"黔驴技穷"，柳宗元的文章《黔之驴》与印度古代故事集《五卷书》第四卷第七个故事就极为相似；比如说"曹冲称象"，《三国志·魏书》中的记载与《杂宝藏经》中的称象故事有异曲同工之妙。③ 二是文体，"框架结构"或"连环穿插式结构"在唐传奇结构上开始体现，故事的组织从篇篇独立到互相联系，与印度两大史诗之

---

① 薛克翘著：《中印文化交流史话》，商务印书馆1998年版，第30页。
② 鲁迅著：《鲁迅全集》第七卷，人民文学出版社2005年版，第103页。
③ 季羡林著，王树英选编：《季羡林论中印文化交流》，新世界出版社2006年版，第279—286页。

一《摩诃婆罗多》、巴利文《佛本生经》和故事集《五卷书》等文体相通，[①] 以唐初王度的《古镜记》为例，都是由一个主干故事开头，借不同人物之口串联起许许多多的小故事。由此可见，古代中印之间的文学互通是十分丰富且深入的，这从一个侧面反映出当时中印人文交流的盛况。

（四）制糖技术

中印间高层推动的人文交流也自古有之，代表案例便是制糖技术。由于印度得天独厚的气候因素，自古便生产甘蔗，熟悉制糖方法，因而当时制糖技术较为落后的中国在唐代初期，便从官方层面派使者去印度学习制糖方法，[②] 学习后经过改进，唐朝制出的精炼白糖无论从颜色还是从口味上都超过了印度，后又传回了印度。因而在现代印地语中，白糖、白砂糖叫做चीनी （cīnī），这个词在印地语中还有一个意思，意为"中国的"。制糖技术的交流互换，是高层推动人文互通的一个典型例证，在中印人文交流史上，在科技交流方面都有其重大的影响和意义。

四、中印间跨文化传播的可能性

通过上文的梳理，可见中印人文交流的历史传统悠久且深厚，两千多年的中印人文交流史为中印高级别人文交流机制的建立打下了坚实的基础，也给中印间跨文化传播提供了如下几个方面的启示：

（一）淡化文明冲突论，挖掘文化相通点

"国家都倾向于追随文明相似的国家，抵制与它们没有文明共性的国家"。[③] 在"文明冲突论"甚嚣尘上的今天，我们应当将目光从西方转向东

---

① 段孟洁："《五卷书》框架结构在东西方民间文学中的发展"，《文学教育（下）》，2019年第六期，第22页。

② 见《新唐书》卷二二一《西域列传·摩揭它国》上的记载：贞观二十一年……太宗遣使取熬糖法，即诏扬州上诸蔗，拃沈如其剂，色味愈西域远甚。

③ [美] 塞缪尔·亨廷顿，周琪等译：《文明的冲突与世界秩序的重建》，新华出版社2010年出版，第135页。

方。中华文明与印度文明同属东方文明，在地缘上相近，在文化上相亲，两种文明都具有极大的包容性，且自古以来，中印间的交流互通从未间断，特别是在佛教东传的带动下，中印人文交流得到了极大的发展。像上文所提到的"月兔"等文化点，就是中印之间的文化互通点，挖掘这类文化互通点有利于增进中印两国民众的互相了解，降低中印人民相互间的隔阂感，促进中印人民民心相通。

（二）吸取佛经翻译经验，加强中国经典外译

两汉隋唐时期对佛经的大量译介，一方面极大地促进了佛教在中国的传播，另一方面也将印度的文化介绍进了中国，这一点在中国的故事文学领域得到了突出体现。古时的经典互译主要以佛经翻译为主，高僧们将从天竺取回的真经翻译成汉语并举办讲经法会，这一"只引进，不输出"的情况导致了中印人文交流发展的不平衡，印度民众缺乏了解中国的文字窗口，因而我们应当加强中国经典的外译。由于印度语言状况复杂，英语与印地语并行，因此在外译过程中也应当注意双语并行，一方面在印度大力推介已经被翻译成英文的中国经典，另一方面加大中国经典的印地语文本翻译力度，增进印度基层民众对中国的了解。

（三）双轨并行，高层助力民间人文互通

制糖技术之所以能得到发展，得益于中印两国的高层推进，但自古以来，中印间的人文交流多以民间自发交流为主，并未建立高层人文交流机制。近年来，随着中印两国首次高级别人文交流会议的召开，中印两国的人文交流逐渐走上"由上自下"的道路，高层人文交流活动频频，但民间交流未见广泛开展。人文交流作为人与人的沟通，应当以古为鉴，大力发展民间人文互通，促使中印两国民众进行自发的民间活动组织，高级别人文交流机制应当为民间人文交流活动铺路，在举办高层次会议和活动的同时，更应该多向民间活动倾斜，双轨并行，将人与人的交流落到实处。

五、结　　语

2018 年在习近平主席和莫迪总理的倡导下建立起来的中印高级别人文交流机制，对中印关系的积极向好发展具有极大意义。2020 年是中印建交 70 周年，中印两国领导人确定 2020 年为"中印人文交流年"，并同意举办 70 项活动庆祝中印建交 70 周年。然而在新冠肺炎疫情这一"黑天鹅"事件的影响下，庆祝活动的进行受到了极大阻碍，中印间也因为边境历史遗留问题再起摩擦，这也是 1962 年以来中印人文交流活动面临的最大阻碍之一。

人文交流，在于人心相通。中印关系虽"长期受领土争端、西藏问题、跨境河流问题、中巴关系问题、海洋战略竞争问题等主要结构性因素的制约",[①] 但搁置争议、谋求发展才是两国当前的合作之道，因此应当积极寻找中印间的文化共性，以文化关键点为抓手，促进中印民心相通。

[①] 张家栋："中印关系中的问题与超越"，《中国周边外交学刊》2016 年第 1 期，第 164 页。

南非灾难管理能力建设及其挑战
——基于应对新冠肺炎疫情的分析

孟利君[*]

摘 要：南非重视灾难管理并建立了完善的灾难管理体系。这一体系在南非应对新冠肺炎疫情中发挥了重要作用，也暴露出其所面临的诸多挑战。这些挑战主要包括应急资源保障压力、民生保障压力与经济运行压力等。

关键词：南非；灾难管理；新冠肺炎疫情；挑战

南非重视对灾难事件的管理，先于1997年制定了《紧急状态法》，以应对各类突发事件，后于2002年制定《灾难管理法》，进一步完善了其灾难管理体系。这一体系以《灾难管理法》为核心，以依该法制定的《灾难管理框架》为行动指南，涉及灾难管理的机构设置、人员任命、运行机制、责权划分、部门协调、央地联动等各个方面，同时也涵盖了灾难预防、准备、响应、恢复等各阶段的具体管理措施。

《灾难管理法》是南非应对各类灾难事件的专门法律。该法于2002年制定，2003年颁布，自2004年4月起施行，共8章65小节，对灾难定义、灾难预防、灾害减损、应急准备、应对措施、灾后恢复、政府三级（国家、

---
[*] 孟利君，四川外国语大学国际关系学院讲师。

省、市）灾难管理中心的设立、自愿者管理及其他事项做出统一规定。根据该法的定义，灾难指"突发或进行中的、本地或大范围的、自然或人为引发的导致或威胁导致：死亡、伤害、疾病的事件，财产、基础设施或环境损害的事件，干扰社区生活的事件以及受影响群体无力自行应对的其他事件"。[①]"灾难管理"指"着眼于预防、降低灾难风险，做好灾难应对准备，减轻灾难严重程度，快速有效处置灾难，开展灾后恢复与重建的一系列综合、跨部门、跨领域的应对灾难的计划及实施过程"。[②] 上诉定义表明，南非的灾难管理全面覆盖了通常所说的"突发事件""紧急事件""公共事件"等各类非常事件。同时，其灾难管理体系也是统一调动各级政府、各政府部门及各类社会力量共同参与的涉及灾难预防、处置、恢复各阶段的综合性体系。

一、南非灾难管理体系概述

（一）灾难管理的机构与职责

南非灾难管理的协调机构为政府灾难管理联席委员会，由总统依法设立。委员会成员包括涉及灾难管理及立法工作的中央政府各部部长，灾难涉及省份省长选任的省行政会议成员代表及南非地方政府联合会选任的市政委员会成员代表。委员会主席由灾难主要涉及的内阁部门部长担任。委员会的职责包括根据宪法第三章就灾难管理事务协调政府内部合作，向内阁汇报灾难管理的政府内部协调情况，就灾难管理相关事宜向内阁提供建议及推荐措施，同时就制定一个涵盖各级政府、政府各部门、各职能机构、非政府组织、私营部门、私人及社区的统一的综合性灾难管理框架向内阁提供建议。

南非同时建立了灾难管理的咨询机制，其组织机构为国家灾难管理咨询论坛，由灾难主要涉及的部门部长组织成立，国家灾难管理中心主任担任主席。论坛成员包括国家灾难管理中心主任，由政府灾难管理联席委员会成员部门部长指定的各部代表，由各省参加政府灾难管理联席委员会的

---

① Disaster Management Act 2002, section 1, Chapter 1.
② 同上。

省行政会议成员指定的代表，由地方政府联合会选任的市级代表，论坛主管部门部长指定的相关行业、领域（如商务、矿业、农业、医疗卫生、教育、劳工、保险、宗教与社会福利、科技等）的代表，灾难管理专家及因特定事务而纳入的其他人员。论坛的作用主要是方便参与灾难管理的各执行人员相互咨询并协调其各自行动，其职能包括就灾难管理框架向政府灾难管理联席委员会推荐措施，并向政府组成部门、法定职员、非政府组织、社区、私营部门等就灾难管理相关事宜提供建议。

南非合作治理与传统事务部负责《灾难管理法》的执行，其下设的国家灾难管理中心具体负责联合各级政府部门、法定职员、灾难管理相关执行人及社区力量，推动建设统筹、协调的灾难管理体系，以防灾减灾。中心主任由合作与传统事务部部长任命，负责中心全面事务。中心职员除主任外，还包括合作与传统事务部内调任人员，其他政府部门根据需要调任的人员及主任选用的人员。中心主任可在其职权范围内将部分职责分派给中心职员或省、市级灾难管理中心。国家灾难中心的职责众多，其日常工作包括：确定灾难管理事项，监督各政府机构及官员是否遵守《灾难管理法》及《灾难管理框架》，监管灾后恢复及重建进程，交流并保存灾难及灾难管理信息，为政府机构、职员、社区及其他主体提供灾难管理咨询，提出建议并采取行动获得灾难管理资金，就国家灾难管理相关立法工作及国家、省、市级灾难相关法律的衔接提供意见，协助落实灾难相关立法工作，对是否宣布国家进入灾难状态提供意见，推动灾难管理志愿者的招募、培训及使用，推动民众灾难管理能力的形成、培养及教育，推动开展灾难管理研究并与省级及市级灾难管理中心联络并协调其行动。国家灾难中心还应建立顺畅的联络机制，建档记录灾难管理所需信息，包括各应急处置主体（如各级政府机构、非政府组织、私营部门、专家、志愿组织、国际机构、国外非政府组织等）的联系方式、分工、应急服务能力等。国家灾难管理中心的另一项工作是建立并维护灾难管理信息系统，收集、整理并保存灾难预警、预防、应急处置能力与资源、灾难管理研究与培训设施等与灾难相关的各种信息。此外，国家灾难管理中心的职责还包括制定灾难管理预案及策略，监督、衡量并评估各政府机构提出的灾难管理预案及灾难预防、处置及减灾提议，发布公报或采取其他行动为各类灾难管理执行人员提供建议及指导，研判已发生或即将发生的灾难的类别、危害程度及影响以决定采取何等级别的响应。最后，国家灾难管理中心每年还需向主管部门部长提交年度报告，汇报当年灾难发生情况、减灾救灾情况及应急预案和策略的执行及评估情况等。

（二）灾难管理体系的运行

南非灾难管理工作的运行在国家、省、市三个层面同时展开并相互联系，本文主要介绍国家层面的运行情况。南非根据《灾难管理法》制定了《灾难管理框架》，对灾难管理流程做了清晰的描述。南非国家层面的灾难管理流程共分为决策、执行、建议、国际合作4个板块，如图8-1所示：

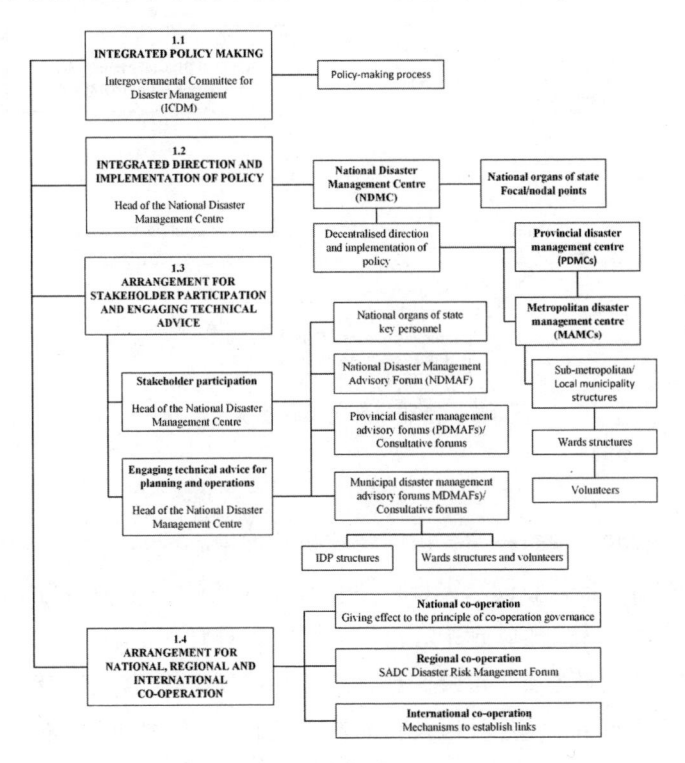

图8-1：南非灾难管理体系运行流程

来源：《灾难管理框架》①

---

① *Disaster Management Framework*, section 1.1.1, chapter 1.

第一个模块为中央政府的决策模块，流程如图 8 - 2 所示。首先，国家灾难管理中心收集有关灾难风险管理的政策建议并提交给国家灾难管理咨询论坛；其次，论坛成员商讨后将建议提交至内阁序列相关委员会；再次，经各委员会商定的建议被提交至国家灾难管理联席委员会；之后，国家灾难管理联席委员会审议建议并提交至内阁；最后，内阁做出决定后交由国家灾难管理中心完善并执行。

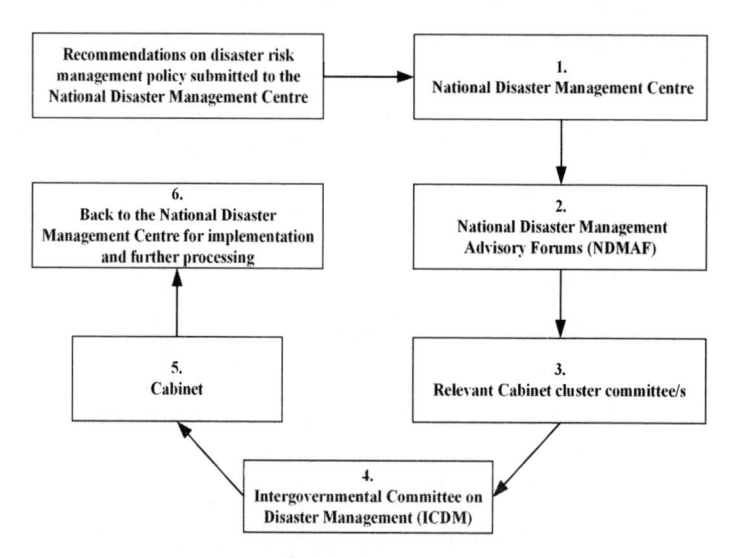

图 8-2：南非政府灾难管理决策流程

来源：《灾难管理框架》①

第二个模块为执行模块，由国家灾难管理中心统筹负责。经中央政府涉灾各部门合作商议，国家灾难管理委员会审定并经内阁批准的灾难管理政策最终交由国家灾难管理中心落实。国家灾难管理中心结合具体情况制订细化意见并指导各省、市级灾难管理中心按规定执行。各下级管理中心则进一步落实政策至基层社区及其他参与灾难管理的机构及个体。

第三个模块为建议模块。这一模块的运行主要是为政府决策提供意见，因而通常与决策过程相联系并成为其中的一个环节。政府决策的意见

---

① *Disaster Management Framework*, section 1.1.2, chapter 1.

来源主要为职能部门意见（包括省、市级灾难管理中心意见）和专业意见两类。意见的沟通与协调平台为国家灾难管理咨询论坛，由国家灾难管理中心组织，各部门及专业人士参与，意见由管理中心汇总并提交上级。

第四个模块为区域及国际合作模块。这一模块主要涉及灾难信息分享、政策协调及国际援助等，由外事部门主导推进。

（三）灾难管理的措施

南非灾难管理的具体措施可分为灾前准备、应急响应及灾后恢复与重建三个阶段。

南非《灾难管理框架》要求涉及灾难管理的政府各部门都应制定灾难管理预案，将其作为本部门工作计划的一部分，并提交国家灾难管理中心。各部门预案应明确灾难管理涉及本部门业务的哪些方面，本部门在国家灾难管理整体工作中的角色与责任，在应急处置、灾后恢复与重建中的角色与责任，履行责任的能力，灾难管理的具体策略，灾难发生时的处置措施、程序以及实现这些措施的财政保障。此外，各部门应定期评估并更新其灾难管理预案，且将其与其他部门与机构的预案协调衔接。

此外，南非还非常重视灾难预警和灾难教育与研究。预警主要涉及灾难风险信息收集、监测及传播。南非国家灾难管理中心根据不同灾难类型（地质、生物、气候、技术、环境）制定了相应的风险信息收集规范及指南，要求各级政府及各类政府机构将灾难风险评估与生产开发规划相结合，每年提交风险评估报告。灾难风险监测主要包括灾害隐患跟踪、灾难事件跟踪及危害监测。国家及省级政府部门及相关研究机构根据各自业务范围负责灾难风险信息的监测、更新并报告国家灾难管理中心。此外，各级灾难管理中心建立了明晰机制，以获取并研判灾难风险信息并发出风险预警。

灾难教育与研究主要涉及灾难相关知识教育、技能培训、公众意识培养及灾难管理研究。南非国家灾难管理中心负责制定全国性灾难教育、培训、研究的框架，结合中小学课程、相关职业人士执业资格与政府职员能力培养等推行教育与培训项目，以提高公众、专业人士及政府人员应对灾难事件的能力。

灾难的应急响应涉及国家进入灾难状态后可采取的一系列应对措施。当国家级的灾难发生时，灾难主要涉及部门的部长可依法宣布国家进入灾难状态。此后，该部长有权在咨询其他涉灾部门部长后发布或授权其他部门发布法规或指令以应对灾难。这些法规及指令主要涉及：中央政府可用资源的开放，如商店、设备、车辆、设施等；中央政府部门应急服务人员的派遣；国家灾难管理预案中部分或所有条款的适用；受灾地区人员的疏散及避难；受灾地区的内外交通联系；受灾地区人员及物资的内外输送；受灾地区房屋的征用；临时应急住所的供应、管制及使用；受灾地区酒精饮料销售、分发或运输的暂停或限制；受灾地区内外临时通讯线路的安装与维修；灾难信息的发布；应急采购程序；灾难响应及灾后恢复与重建的促进措施；防止灾难升级或缓解灾难影响的其他措施；获取国际援助的步骤等。上述各法规与指令都包含被违背时的惩罚措施。国家灾难状态经宣布后可持续3个月，主管部门部长可视情况宣布提前结束或延长灾难状态，每次延长不超过1个月。

南非《灾难管理框架》仅对灾后恢复与重建做了一些原则性规定，如灾难管理的首要责任部门应促进灾后重建团队的成立、确定重建任务、保障重建顺利开展、监督重建进程并使重建工作有利于受灾地区后续发展等。

二、南非对新冠肺炎疫情的管理

（一）南非的疫情管理措施

南非对新冠肺炎疫情的应对可分为"严格管控"与"放松管控"两个时期，以是否采取严格的隔离措施为分水岭。

南非新冠肺炎疫情部级顾问委员会主席将南非政府对新冠肺炎疫情的响应分为8个阶段，[1] 如图8-3所示。第一个阶段为准备阶段，包括建立

---

[1] Salim S. Abdool Karim, The South African Response to the Pandemic, The new england journal of medicine, 382（24）, June 11, 2020.

病毒检测能力等。南非卫生部一直关注疫情发展，在世界卫生组织1月31日宣布新冠肺炎病毒构成"国际公共卫生紧急事件"当日即启动紧急行动中心，在全国9个省均成立快速反应小组，确保各地有能力隔离、管理或控制病毒疑似病例，并根据已建立的灾难风险信息收集、监测机制动员大量工作人员监测并报告疫情风险，及时预警。2020年3月5日，南非出现第一例确诊病例。

在发现首例病例十日后，南非确诊病例达到51例，南非疫情防控进入第二阶段。3月15日，南非总统拉马福萨即根据该法宣布南非进入国家灾难紧急状态，同时成立新冠肺炎疫情管理委员会，启动政府应急处理机制，并根据该法制定新冠肺炎病毒防控条令，授权卫生、财政、交通、教育等政府部门根据需要颁布相关指令。此外卫生部还成立了一个高级别咨询委员会，由51名专家构成，包括临床医生、病毒学家、流行病学家、数学建模专家、公共卫生从业人员和其他专家，负责为卫生部长提供策略建议和政策指导。

在这一阶段以及后续第三阶段，南非出台了一系列应对疫情的综合性措施，具体包括防控、救治、民生保障三方面内容。防控措施主要有关闭海陆口岸、取消社交活动、停止商店营业、关闭学校和部分护理场所、暂停惩教及拘留中心探视、开展疫情防护宣传运动、建立隔离场所等，并调动国防军协助警方维持社会秩序。救治措施包括指定11家公立医院定点免费收治新冠肺炎患者；鼓励私营实验室提供检测服务，设立"得来速"检查站、流动检查车等扩大检测规模；改建扩建医院，执行"应急采购程序"，培训医生，与中国等交流救治经验以提高救治能力。在民生保障方面，南非政府要求基本商品和服务不得随意涨价，供应商不得囤积商品，商品销售须公平分配；为无家可归者提供符合卫生标准的收容所，为无法在家隔离的居民提供隔离场所；通过"雇员临时救济计划"向陷入困境企业的雇员支付工资，为超过400万名收入低于6500兰特的私营企业雇员提供每月500兰特的税收补贴。此外，拉马福萨还于4月21日宣布推行约263亿美元的经济扶持和社会救助计划，用于抗疫、帮助贫民及受困企业、复工复产。

第四阶段主要为大规模测试，积极发现感染患者的阶段。南非政府雇佣了超过28000①名社区工作者深入疫情高风险社区入户进行病例筛查。第五个阶段着眼于控制热点地区疫情的本地传播。第六个阶段注重患者的治疗，包括建立临时医院为轻症患者提供医疗服务。第七个阶段主要针对病亡患者的安葬，病亡患者亲属及治愈患者的心理救助事宜。最后一个阶段主要涉及群体免疫情况的监测及后续疫情的防范。

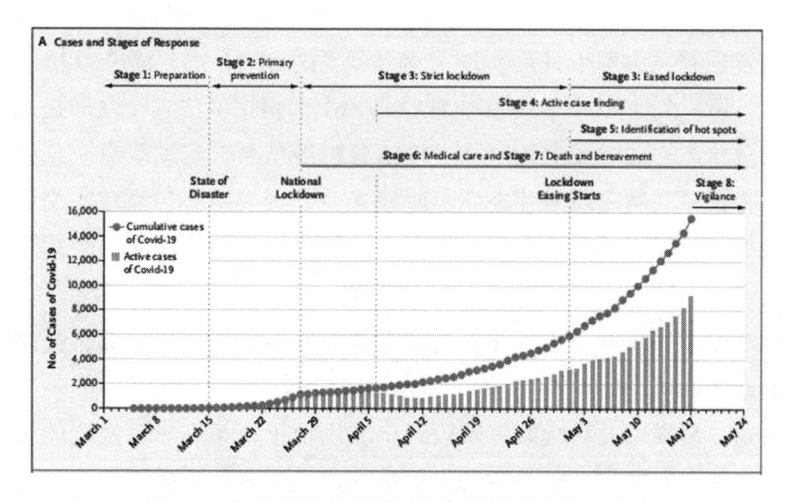

图8-3：南非疫情响应的不同阶段及疫情发展情况

来源：Salim S. Abdool Karim②

（二）南非的疫情管理效果

纵观新冠肺炎疫情在南非出现并蔓延的整个过程，体现了政府应对灾难事件的能力和领导力。果断的领导力在新冠肺炎疫情响应中不可或缺，而果断领导力的共知特征即为清醒认识危险及行动迟缓的后果并在此基础上采取快速的行动。③ 研究表明，对新冠肺炎疫情采取严格措施的速度会

---

① Salim S. Abdool Karim, The South African Response to the Pandemic, The new england journal of medicine, 382 (24), June 11, 2020.
② Salim S. Abdool Karim, The South African Response to the Pandemic, The new england journal of medicine, 382 (24), June 11, 2020.
③ Ahmed Mohammed Obaid Al Saidi, Fowsiya Abikar Nur, Ahmed Salim Al-Mandhari, et al. Decisive leadership is a necessity in the COVID-19 response. *The Lancet*, Vol 396, 295 - 298.

产生明显不同的结果。① 南非政府从疫情初期即果断宣布国家进入灾难时期，及时颁布防控条令，建立应急管理机构，授权交通部、贸工部、卫生部、教育部等政府部门迅速发布分项应对条例，并动用国防军协助警察维持社会秩序，保障各项措施执行到位。从决策、计划到落实，体现出政府面对紧急事件时准确的判断力和周密高效的执行力。这些措施的效果十分明显的，如研究表明，单是禁酒令这一措施即对控制疫情起到积极作用，② 迅速的隔离措施和广泛的筛查是应对病毒的关键也是南非早期成功的特征。③ "政府在利用现有的政策包有效控制新冠肺炎病毒传播上的领导成效显著。"④ 同时，政府对贫民、流浪人员有针对性的救助措施也赢得了民众的普遍支持。⑤

然而，南非2020年3月26日开始的严格"封城"措施从5月1日起逐步解封，并于6月1日起进一步放开各项防控措施，疫情随之反弹。截至8月底，南非累计确诊病例超过62万，每百万人口确诊数超过11000人。南非为何在早期防控措施取得明显成效的情况下逐步放松防控力度从而导致更为严重的后续疫情？其原因与南非灾难管理体系面临的挑战紧密相关。"南非的新冠肺炎疫情响应就像一艘边航行边修建的大船。"⑥

---

① Hale T, Angrist N, Kira B, et al. Variation in government responses to COVID-19 (version 6.0). Blavatnik School of Government working paper. May 25, 2020. https://www.bsg.ox.ac.uk/sites/default/files/2020-05/BSG-WP-2020-032-v6.0.pdf (accessed June 25, 2020)

② Reuter, H., Jenkins, L. S., De Jong, M., Reid, S., & Vonk, M. (2020). Prohibiting alcohol sales during the coronavirus disease 2019 pandemic has positive effects on health services in south africa. African Journal of Primary Health Care & Family Medicine, 12 (1).

③ Bibi-Aisha Wadvalla. (2020). Covid-19: Decisive action is the hallmark of south Africa's early success against coronavirus. Bmj, 369.

④ Ataguba, J., Ayo-Yusuf, O., Greeff, M., Hofman, K., Lutge, E., Madhi, S., ... Wright, C. (2020). COVID-19 statement: The unanticipated costs of COVID-19 to south africa's quadruple disease burden. South African Journal of Science, 116 (7), 1-2.

⑤ Marcus, T. S., Heese, J., Scheibe, A., Shelly, S., Lalla, S. X., & Hugo, J. F. (2020). Harm reduction in an emergency response to homelessness during south Africa's COVID-19 lockdown. Harm Reduction Journal, 17, 1-8.

⑥ Salim S., Abdool Karim. The South African Response to the Pandemic, *The new england journal of medicine*, 382 (24), June 11, 2020.

三、南非灾难管理能力建设面临的挑战

"应急管理能力标志国家综合国力……国际实践表明，一个国家对公众的安全保护水平取决于三个维度要素：一是经济基础与生产力水平；二是科学与工程技术能力；三是执政理念、发展模式、价值观认同，特别是地方政府的宏观政策导向"。[①] 一个国家的应急管理能力同样依托于本国的经济、资源、技术水平能等基本能力。"有效的人、财、物等资源保障是突发事件应对工作的基础"。[②]《国际卫生条例》要求各缔约国应具备包括国家立法、政策和筹资，协调和国家归口单位间沟通、监测、响应、准备、风险沟通、人力资源和实验室等8项核心能力，其中的筹资、人力资源和实验室能力同样是对一个国家的资源保障能力所提出的要求。因此，考察一个国家的应急能力（或灾难管理能力）不能仅看其在预防、准备、响应及恢复各个环节的制度措施是否健全严密，或其体系运转是否顺畅高效，也应考察其实现应急体系运行的保障能力是否强大。脱离实现能力的应急管理是不切实际的，正如脱离硬件支持的软件无法运行一样。如对布隆迪和其他一些国家的调查表明，降低灾害风险的努力取得成功的主要绊脚石即为资金保障能力。[③]

尽管南非被广泛认为是灾害风险治理中的国际优等生，仍有大量研究表明其在落实降低灾难风险措施的过程中存在诸多不足，包括当地缺少恰当的技能和实现能力等。[④] 南非灾难管理能力建设所面临的挑战很大程度上源于其保障各项灾难管理方案、措施落实的能力不足。南非在抗击新冠

[①] 刘铁民，构建新时代国家应急管理体系，中国党政干部论坛，2019 (07): 6—11。
[②] 闪淳昌、周玲、秦绪坤、沈华、宿洁，我国应急管理体系的现状、问题及解决路径，公共管理评论，2020, 2 (02): 5—20。
[③] Kellett, J. and Sparks, D. (2012), Disaster Risk Reduction: Spending Where it Should Count, *Global Humanitarian Assistance*, Somerset, pp. 1 - 40. Kellett, J. and Sweeney, H. (2011), Analysis of Financing Mechanisms and Funding Streams to Enhance Emergency Preparedness, *Development Initiatives*, Somerset, pp. 1 - 142.
[④] Dewald, V. N. (2015). Disaster risk governance in africa. *Disaster Prevention and Management*, 24 (3), 397 - 416.

肺炎疫情的过程中一直面临着诸多压力，导致其应对疫情的诸多措施不具有可持续性。这些压力包括：病床、医生、医疗设备、防护物质等短缺；医疗物质生产能力有限，战略物质储备不足，可利用社会资源有限；低收入群体失业、贫民生活物质短缺；旅游、餐饮、交通等众多行业受到冲击，中小企业经营陷入困境；税收锐减，抗疫支出导致债务增加，政府财政压力增大等。上述种种压力是南非早期行之有效的抗疫措施难以持续的主要原因。本文认为南非在应急资源、民生保障与经济运行等三方面所面对的困难是其灾难管理能力建设所面临的主要挑战，这些挑战制约着南非灾难管理体系发挥出更好的作用。

（一）应急资源挑战

南非在此次新冠肺炎疫情应对过程中首先面对的难题便是医疗物质短缺。与多数国家一样，南非在疫情开始爆发时存在口罩、防护服等物资和呼吸机、监测仪等设备的严重不足。而由于缺乏生产能力，这些物资供应的短缺无法在短期内通过国内生产补足，其他国家对医疗物资的出口禁令与抢购行为更加大了南非获得这些物质的难度。南非总统拉马福萨积极推动医疗物质的本地化生产，并主导建立了"非洲医疗物资供应平台"[1]，南非贸易、产业与竞争部长同样认为非洲应该增加其经济韧性，减少对外部供应的依赖："非洲国家正在汲取痛苦的教训，即我们不能仅仅停留在原材料出口国及医疗用品和食品进口国的位置上"。[2] 然而远水解不了近渴，建立完善、可持续的医疗物资生产能力困难重重，远非一日之功。

南非在应对此次新冠肺炎疫情所面临的应急资源难题还体现在其收治

---

[1] South africa : President ramaphosa launches the africa medical supplies platform to help fight COVID-19 coronavirus pandemic. (2020). MENA Report, Retrieved from https: //search. proquest. com/docview/2415712921 · accountid = 13855.

[2] Coronavirus-south africa: Building african economic resilience is key for continental prosperity, says minister patel in briefing african union ministers: The disruptions caused by covid - 19 to global supply-chains has come at an enormous economic cost to countries across the world, including those in africa. (2020, Jul 28). African Press Organisation. Database of Press Releases Related to Africa Retrieved from https: //search. proquest. com/docview/2427496927 · accountid = 13855.

能力不足上。南非长期面临艾滋、结核等传染性疾病威胁，公众对医疗服务的需求巨大。而根据《柳叶刀》2018 年 5 月发布的对 195 个国家和地区进行的调查，南非的医疗可及性及质量指数得分为 49.7，低于全球平均值（54.4），在所有调查对象中排在第 127 位。[①] "严重的能力不足和结构性问题削弱了南非卫生系统及其工作人员满足公众服务要求的能力"。[②] 此外，由于有限的医疗资源被集中用于应对新冠肺炎疫情，大量其他传染病和基础疾病患者难以获得基本的医疗服务。类似的能力不足还表现在"专业技能及研究能力有限导致无法开展疾病传播及疫苗研究，也无法进行针对本地病例的疗法研究"。[③] 医疗资源的不足清晰地揭示出南非灾难管理能力建设所面临的应急资源保障方面的挑战。

（二）民生保障挑战

南非政府在灾难管理中必须面对的另一个难题是如何保障贫困人口的生活。南非大约 1/4 的人口生活在贫民窟中，多数没有固定工作和收入，在疫情或其他灾难到来前无力储备食品和日用品。他们住所简陋，没有自来水供应，卫生状况堪忧。此外，南非还有大量的流浪者和难民，新冠肺炎疫情中，他们的脆弱性暴露无遗。严格的隔离措施使他们失去了生活来源，窘迫的居住条件也使他们不可能保持社交距离或进行自我隔离。为控制疫情而实行的"封城"措施同时导致了较多中小企业破产，大量工人失业且生活陷入困境。一份就新冠肺炎疫情对夸祖鲁—纳塔尔省经济与商业的影响的评估报告显示，45.7% 的雇员受疫情严重影响，不得不接受降

[①] Measuring performance on the healthcare access and quality index for 195 countries and territories and selected subnational locations: A systematic analysis from the global burden of disease study 2016. (2018). The Lancet, 391 (10136), 2236 - 2271.

[②] Richard Downie, Sahil Angelo. (2015). Assessing South Africa's Ability to Meet Its Health Needs, in Counting the Cost of South Africa s Health Burden, 4 - 18. Retrieved from http: //www.jstor.com/stable/resrep23948.8, current as of day 1st September, 2020.

[③] Umviligihozo, G., Mupfumi, L., Sonela, N., Naicker, D., Obuku, E. A., Koofhethile, C., ... Balinda, S. N. (2020). Sub-saharan africa preparedness and response to the COVID-19 pandemic: A perspective of early career african scientists [version 1; peer review: Awaiting peer review]. Wellcome Open Research.

薪；29.7%的雇员被要求休带薪假，其工资的正常发放依赖政府补贴；另有部分员工被暂时解雇。[①] 让生活无着的人遵守严格的防控规定极为困难，因此，保障贫困人口的基本生活成为抗击疫情的关键环节。虽然南非政府采取了诸如发放免费食品、提供清洁饮水、建立流浪人员临时隔离点、减免税收、为中小企业提供资金补助等一些列措施，然而，由于近年接连干旱、资本外流、债务增加、经济发展缓慢等原因，政府能用于民生保障的资金十分有限。因此，民生保障能力不足对南非灾难管理能力建设构成了严峻挑战。

（三）经济运行挑战

灾难事件会拖累经济的正常运行，而经济运行不畅又将反过来制约减灾、救灾、灾后恢复等各种努力的效果。Marc Suhrcke 等人的研究表明，经济危机将会导致社区传播疾病的扩散情况变得更糟。[②] 新冠肺炎疫情中，严格的"封城"措施意味着经济运行的部分停滞。在经济缺乏韧性的南非，南非政府在进行抗疫决策时不得不考虑经济运行能在多大程度、多长时期内承受严格的抗疫措施带来的干扰。事实上，高度依赖大宗商品出口和消费拉动的南非经济已经受到疫情的重创。根据联合国开发计划署发布的报告，南非 2020 年的 GDP 可能倒退 8%，且可能需要 5 年时间才能恢复到 2019 年的水平。[③] 经济崩溃是比灾难事件本身更大的灾难。为避免顾此失彼，南非政府不得不在疫情防控与经济运行之间进行危险的平衡。这是其在疫情未取得根本好转的情况下逐步放松管控措施的重要原因，同时也折射出其在灾难管理中的两难境地。受制于经济运行压力而改变抗疫策

---

① South africa : MEC nomusa dube-ncube on coronavirus covid - 19 KwaZulu-natal economic and business impact assessment report. (2020). MENA Report, Retrieved from https: //search. proquest. com/docview/2415058531・accountid＝13855.

② Suhrcke, M., Stuckler, D., Suk, J. E., Desai, M., Senek, M., McKee, M., ... Semenza, J. C. (2011). The impact of economic crises on communicable disease transmission and control: A systematic review of the evidence. PLoS One, 6 (6), 1 - 12.

③ U. N. development programme: South africa's GDP could plunge 8% this year because of pandemic. (2020, Sep 01). Targeted News Service Retrieved from https: //search. proquest. com/docview/2438960820・accountid＝13855.

略并非南非政府所愿，却深刻揭示出经济基本面对灾难管理能力建设的深远影响。

四、结　　语

南非建立了一套完善且行之有效的灾难管理体系，这一体系在新冠肺炎疫情前期发挥了关键作用，延缓了疫情高峰的到来，避免了医疗系统的崩溃。然而灾难管理能力与完善的管理体系与强大的保障能力息息相关，缺一不可。在实行35天的封锁措施后，南非不得不逐步放松疫情管控措施的事实表明，其灾难管理能力建设仍然面临严峻挑战，这些挑战主要包括应急物资保障压力、民生保障压力与经济运行压力。当然，其灾难管理能力建设不可避免会受到社会文化因素的影响，这方面有待进一步研究。

学术书评

《巴西与金砖国家：贸易与政策》书评：回顾历史，挑战未来

刘梦茹[*] 童雪莹[**]

摘　要： 本文围绕《巴西与金砖国家：贸易与政策》[①] 一书对书中观点进行总结与评价。该书以经贸领域的各项数据、指标为依据，对比分析了金砖国家的历史发展、现存问题与未来建议。本文分为四个章节，主要对书中的内容进行简要介绍；对重要观点进行说明、再进行思考与评价。第一章主要对书中内容进行简要介绍，第二章概括作者书中所表达的主要观点；第三章对书中各章节主要内容与重要观点展开论述；第四章结合书中的主要观点与当今世界局势，得出启示，以期为未来金砖国家的发展与合作共赢提出一些建议方向。

关键词： 金砖国家；贸易；政策；市场竞争

---

[*] 刘梦茹，四川外国语大学葡萄牙语专业教师、讲师，四川外国语大学金砖国家研究院研究员，长期从事葡萄牙语语言教学、葡语国家相关研究。

[**] 童雪莹，四川外国语大学葡萄牙语专业学生，长期参与区域国别研究相关科研工作。

[①] 《O Brasil e os demais BRICs: Comércio e Política》，由巴西经济学家 Renato Baumann 汇编而成，笔者自译为《巴西与金砖国家：贸易与政策》，此后同一引用以《巴》表示。

一、《巴西与金砖国家：贸易与政策》内容简介

近年来，金砖国家[①]不仅受到学术界密切关注，而且在国际上占有重要战略地位，具有一定的国际影响力。金砖国家作为世界新兴市场国家的代表，多年来在重大国际和区域问题上共同发声，积极推进全球经济治理改革进程，大大提升了新兴市场国家和发展中国家的代表地位，并争得了更多的发言权。如此以来，金砖国家更多地是以一个集体的形象出现在国际舞台上，但同时，各国之间的差异性及其自身特点反而容易被忽略。巴西作为成员国之一，有必要提高对其他金砖国家的认知，建立合作伙伴关系，发现潜在机会，共同应对可能面临的挑战。在此背景下，巴西拉加经委会[②]与巴西应用经济研究所[③]合作出版了本书，旨在讨论金砖国家的特点，将巴西与其他金砖国家的贸易进行对比，并在此基础上探讨金砖国家共同合作的更多可能性。

本书依据大量的数据信息，从不同方面作出分析，以期以较为直观的方式展现各国不尽相同的现实国情，为商务策略提供构架。该书分为七个章节，分别为：1. 基于国情事实，通过对比金砖各国贸易结构及可能存在的竞争等方面，分析巴西与其他金砖国家的贸易关系；2. 着重分析巴西与中国在北美市场的贸易竞争，并根据中、巴两国在贸易竞争中的表现给出发展建议；3. 分析中、印、巴三国国际市场开放度并给出了相应建议；4. 通过分析中、巴、印三国的在经济改革中采取的政策法规，探求三国的国际贸易参与度；5. 基于中国经济发展事实，分析中国直接对外投资情况，重点阐释中国于拉美的外资投资；6. 分析金砖国家等新兴经济体在当前世界局势上的情况以及新兴国家面对美国霸权所面临的问题。7. 从巴西角度出发，分析巴西与包含金砖国家在内的其他新兴经济体合作现状与未来发展。

[①] 本书写于2010年，笔者认为撰稿期间南非还未被纳入金砖国家。作者主要是从此前金砖四国的角度出发所写，因此本书大部分内容涉及的是2010年之前中国、巴西、俄罗斯与印度的相关内容及具体分析。

[②] Comissão Econômica para a América Latina e o Caribe. (CEPAL)

[③] Instituto de Pesquisa Econômica Aplicada. (IPEA)

二、本书章节观点述评

本书主要围绕金砖国家展开对比分析。中国、巴西、印度、俄罗斯均属于新兴经济体，但在世界经济竞争中，由于各国定位不同，发展方向也存在差异。这些差异因多方面因素产生，主要包含地理位置、人口数量及不同的国家政策。书中从各国的基础人口、地理位置入手，对比金砖国家贸易关税、贸易相似指数、对比优势指数、市场渗透率等相关数据，以及固定资本形成总额、国内储蓄、名义汇率与国际储蓄等相关指标，分析金砖国家之间的贸易关系，得出各自发展轨迹的异同之处，并以此探究各国贸易流量构成。通过分析历年贸易表现，发现中国是金砖国家中前景最为可观的发展中大国，在国际贸易竞争中占有领先优势。面对中国的贸易竞争优势，作者从不同方面对其进行了剖析，将中国、印度、巴西三国经济体制与历史政策进行对比，给出各国应结合自身"要素禀赋"① 进行未来发展的建议。本书着重探讨中国与巴西的贸易合作与竞争关系，以两国在北美市场的贸易表现为依据，分析近年来在北美市场的竞争状态，给出了未来合作的可能性，最终将金砖国家的发展与新兴国家经济体的发展密切地联系在一起，共同探索在全球化局势下巴西与新兴国家经济体的发展潜力与发展方向。

（一）巴西与其他金砖国家的贸易关系

1.1 金砖国家基本国情

本章节通过列举金砖国家的基础人口与人口分布情况，介绍各国国情，揭示了人口因素对本国出口产品和生产方式的影响与决定性作用。中国与印度基础人口使其劳动力成本远低于巴西与俄罗斯，同时较高的人口密度也增加了市场需求：1990—2008 年间，通过比较金砖国家的

---

① 要素禀赋是指一国拥有各种生产要素的数量，而生产要素一般包括土地、劳动和资本三要素，也有人把生产技术、经济信息当作生产要素。根据要素禀赋理论，一国的比较优势产品应作为出口产品，是其使用该国相对充裕而便宜的生产要素生产的产品，而进口的产品应该是该国相对稀缺而昂贵的生产要素生产的产品。

GDP 数据，可以看出中国 GDP 是巴西的三倍、印度是巴西的两倍，而俄罗斯还不到中国的 1/10。这在一定程度上反映了基础人口对经济发展的影响。

从世界范围来看，金砖国家的 GDP 总和在世界 GDP 上所占的比例从 1990 年的 7.5% 增长到 2008 年的 11.7%。此外，金砖国家进出口贸易总额也翻了一倍，其中表现最为突出的仍然是中国，同期的巴西表现并不突出，这与当时巴西的多边贸易开放度有一定的关系。20 世纪 90 年代，巴西与印度的市场开放度相当，但由于市场发展不一致，巴西在此之后的发展表现不如印度。

文章通过对比进口渗透率和出口倾向指数来对比金砖国家的贸易表现，巴、印、俄进口皆大于出口，而中国反之，作者认为，只有出口大于进口才是参与国际市场的积极表现。

在各国各领域生产结构的改革方面，金砖国家改革的最大区别集中在农业和工业领域。一方面，在农业领域，早在 20 世纪 90 年代，巴西农业占比就已经减少了 6%，但将最近几年的数据和 20 世纪 90 年代的数据相比较，其余国家也呈现出一定比例的减少，如中国和印度也减少了 10%；另一方面，在工业领域，巴西和俄罗斯呈现出明显的减少，而中国和印度的表现虽未呈现大规模的增长，但仍然保持上升状态。书中指出，巴西的生产结构与发达国家更为相似，即服务业占比更高，中国和印度还处在加强巩固自身工业化的过程中。

1.2 双边贸易关系

本节通过贸易伙伴重要程度指数和贸易强度指数，分析了巴西与其他金砖国家的双边贸易密切程度与强度。21 世纪初期，中国进口巴西豆类食品占总进口的一半，且贸易伙伴重要程度指数显示，中国相对于巴西的贸易重要性呈逐年增加的趋势。但自 2004 年起，中巴进出口关系发生变化，此前一直作为贸易出口大国的巴西于该年起变为进口大国，即巴西进口中国总量反而大于巴西向中国出口总量。相对于中巴贸易而言，俄罗斯与巴西的双边贸易呈稳健型，增幅不大，增速较缓。与中巴、巴俄双边贸易相比，印度与巴西之间的双边贸易变数较大，巴西向印度的出口不稳定，但进口量有所增加。

除了贸易伙伴重要指数之外，在贸易强度指数方面，中国与巴西的贸易表现得也比其他国家好。对比巴西与世界其他国家的现有贸易往来，巴西与其他金砖国家的双边贸易发展也表现得相对积极。当然，金砖国家之间的贸易也并非绝对乐观：巴西与印度、俄罗斯的贸易强度指数有所衰退，即使是处于领先地位的中国，在面临 2002 年和 2008 年的经济衰退时，贸易上也出现了些许不乐观的情形。

作者指出，分析贸易伙伴重要程度和贸易强度有助于巴西调整与其他金砖国家进出口贸易的政策与方向，同时对其他国家的贸易调整也具有一定的借鉴意义。

1.3 贸易关税对比分析

该章节通过赫分达尔—赫希曼指数（HHI）[1]、出口多样性指数和相对熵[2]，对巴西与中国、印度和俄罗斯的贸易作出分析，得出巴西出口中国的产品贸易结构更为集中，而进口结构的集中度较小且更为多元化的结论，并指出巴西从中国的进口指数最贴近世界标准指数。而无论是在 HHI 指数还是相对熵上，巴西与印度、俄罗斯两国的上述贸易相关指数都呈现出一定程度的相似。

1.4 贸易组成相似度[3]

文章指出，巴西与其他金砖国家相比，进口结构均呈现一定程度的相似，而其中与中国最为相似。除贸易组成相似度指数外，两国贸易竞争还应考虑产业内贸易指数，该指数相似度低则竞争小。为寻求利益最大化、避免恶性竞争，文中建议各国可以加强自身的优势领域进行贸易活动。

1.5 对比优势

本节通过显示性比较优势指数（VCR）、Lafay 指数、出口比较表现指数和出口专业化指数[4]对金砖四国贸易情况进行分析，并列举出各国对应的优势领域。中国的优势领域数量最多，印度次之，巴西相对较少。在

---

[1] 反映贸易结构集中度，HHI 值越大，市场集中度越高，说明垄断程度越高。
[2] 相对熵值越接近"1"，贸易税集中度越小。
[3] 贸易相似指数是指两国出口同一产品到第三个国家，该产品占本国出口总额的比例。
[4] 出口比较表现指数：Índice de Desempenho Exportador Comparado；出口专业化指数：Índice de especialização das exportações。

上述三国中，中国优势产品多为手工业制品，同样作为人口大国的印度较为突出的也是手工制造业，而巴西具有优势的 200 多类产品大多属于 0 类、2 类、5 类、6 类和 7 类。① 俄罗斯优势产品在所处同一时期数量不增反降。

根据上述分析，得出以下结论：中国是较其他各国而言优势产业更多的大型经济体，其优势集中于制造业，同样以制造业为优势的印度位居第二，俄罗斯作为欧洲国家反而在这一领域的竞争力较弱。

1.6 市场竞争下的得与失

本节重点在于对中国和巴西在拉美及其他主要贸易地区的市场占有率做出对比。在中国强有力的竞争下，巴西在美国、墨西哥等国家市场份额逐渐减少，尽管巴西在南方共同市场、中美洲和大洋洲地区因中国的贸易领域的介入而流失了一定的市场份额，但在其他地区仍处于盈利状态。但巴西的盈利与中国的盈利相比仍然具有明显差距，尤其是在重要贸易地区这一差距表现得更为明显。

1.7 思考与建议

本章节介绍了金砖国家的基本信息，指出了各国之间双边贸易的特点，对各国的贸易关税进行对比分析。同时还对比各国的贸易相似指数，对比优势指数和市场渗透率，通过对固定资本形成总额、国内储蓄、名义汇率及国际储蓄等指标的对比，分析了巴西同其他金砖国家的关系，列举各自发展轨迹异同，从而加深对各国贸易流量构成的了解、以期利用各方优势寻求未来贸易合作的更多可能性。总体来说，金砖国家作为整体在世界经济中的比重逐渐增大，但它不是一个"霸权集团"，并且巴西和其他金砖国家的双边关系也不尽相同。相比中国，巴西与印度在产品数量上不占优势，且巴西主要受益于拉美市场，近年来随着中国在拉美市场的拓展，巴西逐渐在拉美市场失去地位。该章通过分析金砖国家贸易方面的异同，提出了巴西所应集中发展领域的建议，以加强与其他金砖国家的贸易

---

① 国际贸易标准分类（Standard International Trade Classification，简称：SITC）为用于的统计和对比的标准分类方法。文中提到的类别分别为：0 类：食品和活畜；2 类：非食用原料；5 类：化学成品及相关产品；6 类：按原料分类的制成品；7 类：机械及运输设备。

联系，提高巴西自身产品竞争力。

（二）中国与巴西在北美市场的竞争

本章节以2000—2008年间中国与巴西的出口产品数量、产品质量、产品种类及两国出口贸易结构相似度为分析对象，通过对比分析，探究两国的贸易竞争情形。2000—2005年，中巴两国出口相似度逐渐增加，2005年后，由于中国产品强大的市场竞争力，巴西向北美市场出口产品呈减少趋势，从而导致两国的出口相似度有所下降。此前，在1992—2004年间，由于中国参与市场竞争，巴西失去了北美1/3的市场。20世纪末到21世纪初期，中国出口产品以"薄利多销"与"量大从优"的优势迅速占领外国市场。在2000—2008年间，巴西为应对这一竞争危机，采取提升出口产品质量的措施来与中国产品竞争，这反映了巴西出口商在面对中国的竞争压力下必须做出改变以提高自身的竞争力。

总体来说，对北美出口贸易方面，中国比巴西更具优势，并且中方增长趋势也更为明显。根据赫克歇尔—俄林模型①，在中国与巴西的贸易竞争中，巴西最具竞争力的是自然资源类，竞争力有所下降的是鞋履类；而中国除了矿产品以外均有所增长，其中较为突出的是机械设备、皮革及纺织服装类。在美国市场上巴西与中国的竞争中，尽管巴西总体出口种类数有所增长，但在部分产品领域已失去了出口垄断地位，不得不与中国进行竞争，还存在一部分产品完全失去竞争力甚至可能完全由中国取代的情形。在这种情形下，巴西面临市场占有率减少、甚至完全失去产品市场的局面与困境。对此，作者指出，面对中国的明显竞争优势，建议巴西积极探索不同领域的出口产品，增加出口产品的多样化，减少出口结构相似度，从而避免同中国的直接竞争。

（三）中国、印度和巴西三国的贸易开放度

一直到80年代市场，中、印、巴三国都是相对封闭的状态，直到最

---

① 赫克歇尔—俄林理论模型理论认为：一国出口的应是使用本国相对丰裕生产要素生产的产品，进口的应是使用本国相对稀缺生产要素生产的产品。

近的20年才进行了改革。1994年印度成为第八条款国，卢比被列为可兑换货币；中国的人民币和巴西的雷亚尔被列为可兑换货币的时间分别是1996年和1999年。① 实现货币自由兑换的国家可获得更多益处，其中包括但不限于：一方面，政府可以赚到更多铸币税，促进国际贸易伙伴关系的建立；另一方面，私人领域的运输成本更低。货币可兑性降低了汇率蒸发对国内生产和对外贸易的影响。克鲁格曼指出，回滞现象②在这些货币可自由兑换国更显著。因此，如果要获得益处，仅通过外汇立法保证货币可兑换是不够的，还需要在区域整合中确保海关保护。

总体来说，巴西在外汇立法方面做得比中印两国更好，但中、印的贸易政策比巴西更为合理。由于各国技术标准和要素禀赋之间存在差异，各国的发展优势领域不同，平衡点也不同，因此，克鲁格曼认为，"了解世界经济运转的最好方法是搞清楚各国内部的情况"，这为中、印、巴三国未来提高本国贸易开放程度指出了调整方向。

(四) 中、印、巴三国在国际贸易中的参与度

近年来，新兴市场国家在国际舞台上大放光彩，不仅表现在经济实力大幅提升上，而且在国际政治方面也有所体现，主要指的是新兴经济体对全球多边关系决策的影响力也有一定增加。但就中、巴、印内部来看，三个国家的国际地位影响力增长却是不同步的，各自的贸易量增长也非并驾齐驱，三国中表现最好的是中国。1999年巴西金融危机爆发后，巴西对其战略计划做了部分调整，其中包括给予出口经济奖励，而印度一直到2002年采取的都是较为保守的改革策略。

20世纪70年代，中国的"改革开放"政策对国内生产结构进行了重塑。值得一提的是，中国出口额占全球贸易总额在1980年还不足1%，截

---

① 按照国际货币基金组织的定义，一国若能实现在经常账户下实现货币自由兑换，该国货币就列为可兑换货币。由于自由兑换的条款集中出现在基金组织协定第八条，所以货币自由兑换的国家被称为"第八条款国"。

② "回滞"是一个物理学概念，如果将回滞现象应用于经济学，那么其经济含义为：一个处于均衡的经济初始状态在受到外在的冲击后，不能再回复到原来的均衡，而达到了与原均衡状态的经济变量不一致的另外一种均衡（来源《回滞现象及其在西方经济学中的应用》：https://www.1xuezhe.exuezhe.com/Qk/art/221277·dbcode=1&flag=2）

至 2007 年已经攀升至 9%，进口额也从 1% 增长到了 7%。

巴西的大宗商品占进出口的主要地位，但巴西进口偏向于中高强度科技产品。巴西在历经 1991—1999 年间一段时间的大规模进口自由化后，尽管还依旧维持着进口自由化的机制，但仍试图通过改变汇率机制和实行出口奖励手段来改变贸易开放的战略。

印度的出口结构基本维持不变，在 2002 年国际贸易自由以后，贸易分配仍未发生明显变化。除了减少关税和某些数量限制外，印度还重新改革了部分对于进口控制的特定计划，其中包括扩展特许进口许可证、重组进口许可证等。印度最初实施了缓慢的进口自由化与边际出口激励计划，在第二阶段，深化了自由化改革，减少了进口的关税和非关税壁垒，提高了价格，实施出口促进计划，以提高国家的对外竞争力。印度商工部外贸总局 2009 年 8 月 27 日公布了《2009—2014 年对外贸易政策报告》[1]，明确未来 5 年印度对外贸易政策目标和具体措施。报告指出：目前，全球经济正面临二战后最严重挑战，世贸组织预计全球贸易将大幅萎缩 9%，虽然印度经济在危机中表现相对较好，但出口额已连续 10 个月大幅萎缩。报告对 2004—2009 年的对外贸易进行了总结，指出印度 5 年内完成了两大目标，一是印度在全球货物贸易中的份额翻了一番；二是对外贸易为经济增长和促进就业起到了重要作用。

新外贸政策的总体目标是挖掘出口潜能、提升出口表现、鼓励对外贸易和促进贸易平衡。报告指出，印度政府将采取包括财政刺激、改革机构、简化程序、加强全球市场准入、出口市场多元化、完善与出口相关的基础设施建设、降低交易成本、出口间接税全额退税等方式，扭转出口下降的趋势，2011 年 3 月前完成出口增长 15%，出口额达 2000 亿美元，2011—2014 年，出口额年增长 25%，到 2020 年，使印度在全球贸易中的份额翻一番。

---

[1] 印度商工部外贸总局《2009—2014 年对外贸易政策报告》，http://in.mofcom.gov.cn/article/ddfg/waimao/200909/20090906513018.shtml

（五）中国在拉美的外资投资

5.1 中国的经济实力

中国实现了改革开放以来30年[①]经济持续快速发展，创造了年均增长近10%的历史奇迹。中国于2009年成为世界最大出口国，1980年经济改革时中国以出口增值税低的产品（如纺织品和服装）为主，后逐渐出口高新科技产品，近年来中国达到可与美国抗衡的地位。2004—2008年，中国对外投资额从55亿美金增长到521亿美金，翻了10倍。据高盛公司2003年发布的全球经济报告[②]中所预测，中国将在2041年超过美国，从而成为世界第一大经济大国。

5.2 中国对外直接投资

中国在早期并非是对外投资大国，而是理想的投资对象国。在发展中国家投资可以取得优势资源且发展中国家的市场更具投资潜力，在发达国家投资是为了追求更高的效益，而中国是作为"世界工厂"的人口大国，自然吸引了大量外资来投资。1990年初，中国还只是发展中国家中最大的外资直接投资对象国，至2007年，已成为世界上仅次于美国的第二大外资直接投资对象国。1999年，中国政府提出的"走出去"战略促进了中国实现全球化的脚步，随后中国于2001年加入世贸组织，逐步登上世界舞台。文中作者提出中国大力发展对外投资的原因分为三个方面，首先，中国年均GDP增长保持在8%—10%，经济快速发展需要自然资源的输入来保障；其次是为了提升中国企业在国际市场的竞争力；最后，投资工业国可以将所学技术应用到本国产业中。比如联想、华为、TCL都曾采用这样的方式进行发展。

5.3 中国对拉美直接投资

中国在拉美的直接投资于2000年开始增长，起初该地区外资直接投资以欧美为主，包含中国在内的亚洲国家对其投资占比很少。一方面，中

[①] 该书完成时距离中国改革开放只有30年时间。
[②] 指2003年10月高盛公司发布的名为Dreaming with BRICs: The Path to 2050 的全球经济报告。https: //world. huanqiu. com/article/9CaKrnJngEX）。

国与拉美地区是一个购买者和提供者的关系，中方从拉美各国进口矿产资源、石油和天然气来保障自身经济的快速发展，方式包括但不限于直接购买和并购公司。另一方面，中国与拉美地区还存在和本地商户联结的合作模式，如由中国制造汽车配件再发到阿根廷进行组装，这样的模式可以大大减少运输成本。此外，近年来中国和拉美国家还存在贷款债权人的关系，其中一些企业向中国出口原材料作为贷款保证金，而另一些企业，如中兴则运用供应商融资的方法进行资金周转。

加拿大亚太基金会的一项研究表示，中国未来对外投资无疑会有所增长，但就当时而言只有27%的企业实现了对外投资，且大部分都是依靠"走出去"的战略得以实现，而只有不超过6%的公司对外投资额达到了1000万美金。对此作者建议中国企业若有意走出国门、走向世界舞台、打响国内品牌，少走收购并购线路，而应该设立自己的工业计划或者寻找合资公司。

作者认为中国在拉美的直接投资应朝三个方向发展：1）为中国自身的发展提供原材料、能源和食物；2）强化中国工业，使其在国际贸易中更具竞争力；3）在与美元相比的明显货币劣势下增加自身投资领域多样性。

（六）金砖国家与霸权更替

对于金砖国家面对的质疑，作者表示，金砖国家在初期只是一位经济学家依照各类数据而建议的一个国家集团，是不会对世界格局产生太大影响的。尽管如此，作者对中国发展持积极态度，认为中国是唯一有可能跻身世界经济体前列的国家，并预测中国会在2040年超越美国。

就金砖国家而言，无论中国、巴西、印度、俄罗斯在其他领域表现力如何，最终对国家发展、国际地位起决定作用的是谁会是"最后贷款人"，但目前在这几个国家之间还没有任何一个国家有这个能力。不过，其中最有潜力的依然是中国，中国政府正在朝这方面努力，但目前只处于缓慢发展阶段，距离实现这样的目标还有很长一段路要走。对此，中国应从两方面着手将"在努力"变为"做成功"：一是从财政赤字方面着手，二是要将人民币变为可自由兑换货币且为合作的国家或组织提供基金支持。

书中多次将同为人口大国的印度与中国进行比较，主张中、印两国是更可能成为领导金砖国家发展的潜力大国。对于印度来说，消极的方面是：印度基建条件很差、居民幸福指数较低、文盲率很高。但这些消极面并未使印度的"全球化"停滞不前，从某种程度来讲，如果印度变得过于规范，反而会对商业起到一定的约束作用。对于中国来说，其最大的优势是人口基数大，并且近年来在科技创新方面的重大影响也是不容忽视的。近年来，中国自身技术的发展很成功，在很多方面取得了主导地位，也对其他国家产生了一定的影响。一方面，中国技术的高速发展会促进部分发达国家进行技术革新，另一方面，也会造成另一部分发达国家和像巴西这样的发展中国家的失业情况愈发严重。

作者表示，尽管单纯地对金砖国家贸易体量进行定量分析并不能反应出对经济外交抑或是国际经济的影响，但总的来说，将人口、经济和军事情况和目前金砖各国的技术发展状况考虑在内也可以得出结论：未来金砖国家在国际市场上产品出口和GDP会在目前基础上进一步扩大。另外，作者认为不应将G7和金砖国家在国际上的重要程度分开讨论，而应将其对实现全球化的重要性归为一体。G7和金砖国家的人口基数综合占世界人口的1/2，经济体量占世界的2/3，可以说这两个集团在某些方面超过了G20。巴西外交部长塞尔索·阿莫里姆在圣保罗州报上表示，"如果不听取金砖国家的意见，G7作决定将会很艰难。尽管现在这种'咨询'还未发生，但并不代表未来就不会发生"。

文中指出，目前中国在"全球化"进程中表现得最好，这体现在积极寻求新市场、引进技术、保证自身原材料及能源供应方面。20世纪上半叶，中国大力发展国内企业实力以提高国际竞争力，但反观巴西、俄罗斯及同样身为人口大国的印度，却未在市场竞争上采取强有力的措施。2008年全球金融危机下，中国经济也遭受了重创，出口锐减40%，但经过短期调整并于2010年初实现复苏。

最后，作者认为，若要实现国际地位的提升，金砖国家不应只将重心放在发展自身上，还应该关注世界上其他国家的发展及存在的问题，考虑某些地区受环境影响、或长期受到突发公共卫生事件的影响而导致的发展不平衡的问题。而就目前各项经济体量统计来看，若从重要性来看，

"Bric"这一命名应该将中国排在第一位,称为"Cirb"。

(七)巴西与世界新兴市场国家

文中将新兴市场国家分为第一代新兴市场国家和第二代新兴市场国家,新兴工业化国家正是属于第一代新兴市场国家,它与发展中国家不同:新兴工业化国家在经历了进口增长后,发展上更加重视出口。文中指出,"金砖四国"的概念是冷战末期伴随全球经济格局深刻演变、第二代新兴经济体实力壮大的产物。但20世纪90年代,在华盛顿共识[①]的霸权理念下,新兴市场国家之间并不存在任何实质政治含义或是内部合作。作者指出,金砖国家的联合与第三世界联盟大有不同,尽管同南南合作关系相比,存在许多一致的方面,但也不能将其同等对待。

对于巴西与新兴市场国家之间的关系,作者认为,一方面,政府现有的经济政策为国家参与二代新兴市场创造了条件,另一方面,国家的外交政策旨在使其与这些新兴世界大国在政治上紧密相连。对此,作者对巴西进入国际市场及其对外政策指出了两个方向,一是加大全球化力度,加深全球经济相互依赖性;二是为大众创造消费市场,比如卢拉政府推崇的"家庭基金项目、提高国家最低工资和其他收入相关项目"。文中指出,巴西与其他新兴市场国家在外交政策上愈发亲近,但在贸易方面还是和中国的交往最为密切。与此同时,2005年来,与印度贸易往来也逐渐频繁。对比中巴和印巴贸易,巴西与印度之间贸易往来有政治因素的影响,中巴贸易增长迅速、贸易量大则是由于中国贸易本身实力强大。除了与巴西之间的贸易往来可观,中国还于2009年成为南非以及印度的重要贸易合作伙伴。

文中讨论了金砖国家的金融、贸易、环境、外交政策等相关问题,其中最为紧急迫切的是保护环境节能减排的问题。金砖国家中,俄罗斯因自身生产需求对《京都协定书》表现出较少兴趣。不过,尽管中国也需要发展高强度经济,但对于《京都协定书》的签署持积极态度。需要承认的

---

① 华盛顿共识(Washington Consensus)是1989年出现的一整套针对拉美国家和东欧转轨国家的新自由主义的政治经济理论。

是，印度在总碳排放量上增长了10%，是增长最多的国家，而这与协议书中减少排放的内容背道而驰。相比之下，巴西在环境保护与自身发展这方面平衡得最好，近20年来碳排放量基本维持不变。

三、启　　示

国际上对于"金砖国家"的存在一直有质疑的声音，认为BRICs只是根据数据统计结论而临时起意的团体，但自叶卡捷琳堡首次峰会以来，金砖国家多次就国际金融危机冲击、二十国集团峰会进程、国际金融机构改革、粮食安全、气候变化等国际重大紧迫问题交换看法。金砖国家在国际舞台做出的实际贡献已不可忽视，人民网评价道，"从2006年中、俄、印、巴四国外长在联合国大会期间举行首次会晤，到2017年金砖国家领导人厦门峰会，过去十年，金砖国家逐渐实现了由概念到实体的转变"[①]。我们认为，金砖国家是基于金砖概念而形成的，具有一定的代表性，可以推动并促进金砖各国的外交往来与贸易交流，这是具有重大战略意义的。

作为新兴经济体代表的金砖国家得以如此迅猛的发展离不开他们自身的条件优势，中国与印度人口数量排名世界第一、第二，俄罗斯具有辽阔的土地，巴西独享得天独厚的自然资源与环境。中国与印度享受"人口红利"，分别被称为"世界工厂"和"世界办公室"，俄罗斯与巴西则具有自然资源优势，分别被称为"世界加油站"和"世界原料基地"。与其他金砖国家相比，中国的规模和贸易增量贡献最大，超过其他四国总和。随着技术发展，中国不仅在金砖国家中处在领头羊的位置，在世界范围内的影响力逐渐增加也已成为不争的事实。

文中作者对中国的经济实力表现和国际地位作出了充分肯定，认可了人口基数对于国家经济发展的影响，但笔者认为，单纯从人口基数的因素出发分析GDP具有一定的局限性。文中主要对于中国和印度的贸易体量给予肯定而忽略了俄罗斯，但如果将尖端科技和军备实力考虑在内，俄罗斯

---

① 金砖国家在全球治理中的地位和作用．http://theory.people.com.cn/n1/2017/1012/c40531-29583869.html.

的相对重要性将会提升。而通过采用计量经济模型进行 GDP 影响因素实证分析，可以发现，GDP 增长将受到货币供应量、进出口差额、财政收入等影响。

金砖国家中，与中国贸易往来最密切的当属巴西，通过书中对比优势及贸易相似度分析，以及对中巴两国双边贸易的竞争与互补性研究可以得出以下启示：两国应根据自身资源禀赋的差异，加强本国有明显优势的产品出口，与此同时，两国可利用双方的互补性加强贸易往来，发现两国之间更多的贸易合作机会。此外，作者认为中国在早期发展阶段并未大力对国内市场进行投资，反而是加大对外直接投资力度。对此，笔者认为该观点不尽全面。回顾中国对外投资 40 年的发展历程可以发现，1979 年至今，中国对外直接投资发展经历了四个阶段：中华人民共和国成立以后中国着力于进行内部调整实现经济复苏，80 年代中国才开始有了对外发展的良好势头，直至 20 世纪末期中国就外汇管理、国际经济合作等具体事项进行调整，事实显示，中国一直处于契合国情、稳健发展的状态。

尽管新兴经济体发展迅猛，但当今世界还是以美国为霸权主导的经济体制，任何新兴经济体想要捍卫或者更替该国所处霸权地位都是不现实的。一般认为，一个国家衰落的同时，另一个国家正在崛起，但面对美国这样的一个霸权国，现有的大国兴衰理论也难以给出有力的解释。美国远未达到霸权衰退期，新兴大国也远未崛起到可取代美国霸权的程度。

书中提到巴西承诺到 2020 年依然维持和 2007 年相同的碳排放量，中国也宣告到 2020 年减少 40%—45% 的碳排放量。但联合国环境规划署《2019 年排放差距报告》指出，"我们几年的减排努力是失败的"。[①] 对于金砖国家而言，国际影响力及地位的提升不应只专注于国家自身的经济发展，更要参与到国际事务中，如环境保护、打击恐怖主义、解决世界贫困问题等。

需要注意的是，金砖国家在金融危机后实现了率先复苏，并且实现了较快的经济增长，各国之间存在相似性和互补性，那么，如何平衡好竞争

---

① 联合国环境规划署，https://www.unenvironment.org/interactive/emissions-gap-report/2019/report_zh-hans.php。

与合作之间的关系将是金砖国家共同面临的难题。如今，在美国霸权打压下，中国处境愈发困难，如何与金砖国家保持良好关系、实现贸易增长是中国面临的新挑战。

2020年初暴发的新冠肺炎疫情对全球经济产生了极大冲击，中国作为疫情防控速度最快、效率最高的国家，不仅可以在疫情防控方面为金砖国家提供支持与帮助，而且可以在贸易领域与金砖国家主动加强联系，开拓新的合作机会。机遇与挑战并存，在面对挑战的同时，也是寻找机遇的最佳时机。把握这一良好的时机，一方面有助于进一步加深、加强金砖国家之间的联系，正所谓"患难见真情"；另一方面有助于减轻各国经济下滑压力，发现更多的合作可能性，从而"共渡难关"。

Studies on BRICS Cooperation

Intra-BRICS Trade and Investment Cooperation: Overcoming the COVID - 19 Crisis

Svetlana Gusarova[*]

Abstract: BRICS countries over the next 50 years could become the driving force in the world economy. They have the huge joint potential and wide opportunities. Further growth of their economies requires creation of their closer partnership in trade and investment. China is playing the leading role in this process, as a main investor and importer of FDI and trade partner in BRICS group. Trade and investment cooperation of BRICS countries is a new paradigm of the formation of their economic growth. For the first time, author developed and tested the methodology of the determining the Intra-BRICS potential of trade and investment cooperation and getting the synergistic effect of the economic interaction of BRICS countries. Trade and investment cooperation of China with other BRICS countries exerts very strong impact on the development of their economies. China continue to deepen its economic ties with other BRICS countries and open up its financial market to serve as a cushion against rising

---

[*] Svetlana Gusarova, Doctor of Economics, Associate Professor, Chief Researcher Plekhanov Russian University of Economics.

global uncertainty. Development of Intra-BRICS trade and investment cooperation is very important in the context of overcoming the COVID-19 crisis. The obtained results of the research should be taken into account when developing the "Made in BRICS" program.

Keywords: BRICS Countries; FDI; Trade and Investment Cooperation; Economic Potential; Synergistic Effect

Ⅰ. Introduction

In 2020, all countries of the world have found themselves in very difficult conditions, fighting against the coronavirus pandemic. Many states were forced to introduce lockdown, suspending the work of some industries.

According to forecasts of the International Monetary Fund, the global economic downturn in 2020 will be 3%. The coronavirus pandemic will affect the economies of all countries of the world, including the BRICS states. Credit rating agency Fitch believes that no country in the world can avoid the devastating consequences of the coronavirus pandemic.[①] According to the Asian Development Bank, the volume of the world economy due to the coronavirus pandemic will decrease by $ 5.8 - 8.8 trillion in 2020.[②] In 2020, China's GDP is expected to grow by 1.2%, while the Indian economy will expand by 1.9%. The volume of GDP of the rest of the BRICS countries in 2020 will be significantly reduced-in Russia by 5.5%, in Brazil-by 5.3%, in South Africa-by 5.8%.[③] The decrease in the growth rate of China's GDP will be influenced not only by the

---

[①] Fitch rezko ukhudshil prognoz dlya rossiyskoy ekonomiki na 2020 god // Interfaks. https://www.interfax.ru/business/705548.

[②] Aziatskiy bank razvitiya otsenil ushcherb mirovoy ekonomiki ot virusa // RBKhttps://www.rbc.ru/economics/15/05/2020/5ebe145c9a79475ca82eaac8?utm_source = RBC&utm_campaign = 7908d8 1fld-EMAIL_CAMPAIGN_2020_05_15_03_02&utm_medium = email&utm_term = 0_140f28 82c5 - 7908d81fld - 50810719.

[③] World Economic Outlook 2020 // International Monetary Fund. https://www.imf.org/en/Publications/WEO/Issues/2020/04/14/weo-april - 2020.

suspension of the activities of many enterprises as a result of the pandemic, but by the "trade war" between China and the United States.

BRICS countries help each other to cope with the pandemic problems, they providing economic, expert and humanitarian assistance. Development and deepening of Intra-BRICS trade and investment collaboration allows BRICS countries to import high technologies and other goods. Now there is a gradual transition in BRICS countries from bilateral foreign trade to a multilateral trade and investment paradigm of the development of their economic relations aimed at the formation and improvement of mutually beneficial, open, equal, multilateral relations, to increase the economic growth and competitiveness of their national economies. Development of mutual Intra-BRICS trade and investment interaction promotes the obtaining of synergistic effect from the expansion of this cooperation, their further integration.

Ⅱ. Intra-BRICS Trade Cooperation

BRICS states are working on the creation of the "Strategy for the economic partnership of the BRICS countries until 2025". The new Strategy will include issues related to joint approaches in combating the epidemic and overcoming the economic consequences of crises, as well as supporting the multilateral trading system, unlocking the potential of the digital economy, sustainable and inclusive development in the context of the coronavirus pandemic.

The share of BRICS countries in global merchandise exports has increased from 8.1% in 2001 to 18.5% in 2018, including China - 13.2%, Russia - 2.1%, India - 1.7%, Brazil - 1.3%, South Africa - 0.5%. In 2001 - 2018, merchandise exports of China increased 8.5 times to US $ 2487 billion, of Russia - 3.5 times to US $ 452 billion, of India - 6.8 times to US $ 322 billion, of Brazil - 3.7 times up to US $ 240 billion, of South Africa - 3.4 times up to US $ 94 billion.① The value of Intra-BRICS merchandise exports in 2018 was nearly 11 times as high as in 2001.

The share of BRICS in global merchandise imports has increased from 6,8% in 2001 to 16.1% in 2018, including China - 10.9% (second place in the world), India - 2.6% (eleventh place), Russia - 1.2% (twentieth place), Brazil - 0.9% (twenty-eighth place), South Africa - 0.5% (thirty-fourth place). In 2018, China was the world's leading both exporter (first place in the world) and importer (second place in the world) of goods.

The volume of Intra-BRICS trade turnover increased in 2001 - 2018 by 10 times. For comparison, we point out that the foreign trade turnover of the BRICS countries with other countries of the world increased during this period only by 6 times, and the volume of global trade increased only by 2.6 times. The share of Intra-BRICS trade turnover in the total volume of foreign trade turnover of BRICS countries increased from 6.2% in 2001 to 10.5 % in 2018. The above data confirms the presence of significant potential for trade cooperation of BRICS countries.

China is one of the Top 10 trading partners of more than 100 economies that account for about 80% of world GDP. The largest share in merchandise exports by BRICS countries belongs to China (70.3% in 2018), second was Russia (11% - 6.4 times less, than Chinese share), third-India (9.3%), fourth-Brazil (6.8%) and on the fifth place was South Africa (2.6%). The largest share in merchandise imports among BRICS countries also belongs to China (66.1%), second was India (16.1%), third-Russia (8.5%), fourth-Brazil (5.6%) and on the fifth place was South Africa (3.7%).

BRICS economies have unique comparative advantages of merchandise exports specialization. There are a lot of ways in which BRICS countries can collaborate with each other. For example, Brazil specializes in mineral resources, iron and steel, agricultural products, foodstuff, chemicals and the aircraft equip-

---

① UNCTADSTAT. http: //unctadstat. unctad. org/wds/TableViewer/tableView. aspx.

ment; Russia-in fuels and mining products, military production and weapon, chemicals, industrial equipment, dual-use technologies; India-in high-tech production, chemicals, pharmaceutical goods, software, textiles; China-in high-tech production, telecom equipment, chemicals, automotive products, consumer goods; South Africa-in various ores, jewels. The share of Intra-BRICS merchandise exports in the total value of foreign merchandise exports of BRICS countries has increased from 4.2% in 2001 to 10% in 2018. The biggest share in Intra-BRICS merchandise exports belongs to China (56.2%).

China is one of the main trade partners of BRICS countries. *China and India* have been tapping the potential of cooperation more often since USA trade protectionism damaged the global trade system. China and India try to boost bilateral trade and attach more importance to building up bilateral relations with one another. Chinese merchandise exports to India in 2018 was the biggest in Intra-BRICS exports. China and India have strong complementarity in trade and economic development. The main export products from China to India were digital processing equipment, specialized industrial equipment, electronic chips, laboratory industrial equipment, medical equipment (44.1%), chemicale (20%) and other goods. China also exported to India electrical machines, motors and generators (6.9%), the electrothermal equipment (0.6%), television, radio-receiving and sound recording devices (4.3%), transistors (1.5%), optical equipment (1.1%), equipment for the mining industry (0.3%), home electrotechnical devices (0.5%) and other goods. China hoped to the resumption of Chinese dairy, apple and pear exports to India, thanks to the constantly improving investment environment in the country. On the other hand, the value of *Indian merchandise exports to China* was US $ 12.5 billion in 2018 (the biggest value of Indian merchandise exports to BRICS countries). Main positions of Indian exports to China were electronic chips, medical equipment, laboratory industrial equipment, cotton (25.2% of Chinese imports from India), metal ores (28.1%), diamonds (10.1%), textiles (4.5%), iron and steel (2.2%) and other goods (UNCTADstat). China intend to enhance imports of rice, sugar, soymeal and rapeseed from

India.

Amid the pandemic, India and China celebrated the 70th anniversary of diplomatic relations, they announced the beginning of a "new era" in their interaction.

Russia and India are long-standing partners in the field of military-technical cooperation. A joint Russian-Indian development is the BrahMos supersonic missile system. In 2020, Russia and India agreed to increase the range of the supersonic cruise missile to 600 km. It was also planned to supply and organize licensed production in India of Igla-S MANPADS and additional delivery of the MiG 29 UPG. India will be armed with the Russian AK - 203 assault rifle, which will be produced in India for ten years from 2020. The plant's capacity in India is 75,000 AK - 203 assault rifles per year. India is the world's largest producer of hydroxychloroquine. 100 million tablets of this drug were supplied to Russia.

China has been the largest trading partner of Russia for eight consecutive years. *China and Russia* continued to maintain the high-frequency interactions, signing several important documents in 2018 to consolidate the strategic development of bilateral relations. Value of Chinese merchandise exports to Russia was US $ 47.7 billion in 2018 (the second place of Chinese merchandise exports to BRICS countries). The main export products from China to Russia were digital processing equipment, specialized industrial equipment, medical equipment, electrical machines, motors and generators, television and radio equipment, equipment for the mining industry, electrothermal devices, optical devices and equipment (34.8%) and others. The considerable share of Russian import from China took food (4.3%) and consumer goods: footwear (2.4%), clothes (1.8%), cars, spare parts to them and accessories (2.6%), textiles (0.8%), female and kidswear (1.4%), telephone sets and accessories (0.4%) and other goods. On the other hand, the value of *Russian merchandise exports to China* was US $ 56 billion in 2018. Russia exports to China oil (52.3% of the value of Russian exports to China), gaz (28.9%), coal (6.1%), iron ore (4.9%), high-tech industrial equipment (7.6%) .① China is a major importer of commodities. China's demand for oil and gas remained strong. One of the most important oil and gas projects for Russia and China is the Power of Siberia-a thirty-year contract for the supply of Russian gas to China in the amount of US $ 400 billion. The length of the gas pipeline through Russia is 3,000 km, and through China - 5.1 thousand km. The first part of the gas pipeline in China (the eastern Russia-China gas pipeline) between Heihe and Changling has already been built. Another part of it, Changling-Yongqing, has been commissioned in 2020. This allowed China to receive 5 billion cubic meters of gas from Russia in 2020. The remaining Chinese section of the Yongqing-Shanghai gas pipeline will be built in 2023, which will increase Russian gas supplies to China to 38 billion cubic meters per year.

Chinese President Xi Jinping noted that the strategic cooperation between Russia and China, having passed the test of the epidemic, will become even stronger, and the friendship of the peoples of the two countries will certainly continue to grow stronger day by day.② China and Russia intend to strengthen anti-epidemiological cooperation, exchange experience on the prevention and treatment of coronavirus, together with other BRICS countries to respond to common threats and challenges in the health sector.

In January-April 2020, trade between Russia and China increased to US $ 33.6 billion. Exports of Russian goods to China increased 1.1 times over this period to US $ 20.4 billion, Chinese exports to Russia slightly decreased to US $ 13.1 billion.③ Despite the drop in domestic demand for fuel as a result of the pandemic, in March 2020 the volume of oil exports from Russia to China

---

① UNCTADSTAT. http: //unctadstat. unctad. org/wds/TableViewer/tableView. aspx.
② Xi Jinping uveren, chto sotrudnichestvo Rossii i Kitaya stanet prochneye // RIA Novosti. https: // ria. ru/20200416/1570147658. html.
③ Tovarooborot Rossii i Kitaya v yanvare-aprele vyros do $ 33, 56 mlrd // Informatsionnyy portal BRIKS. https: //infobrics. org/post/30882/.

increased 1.3 times-up to 7.02 million tons, or 1.66 million barrels per day.[①]

The value of *Chinese merchandise exports to Brazil* was US $ 33.5 billion in 2018 (the third place of Chinese Intra-BRICS merchandise exports). The main export products from China to Brazil were digital processing equipment, optical tools, air conditioning equipment, electro-thermal devices, electronic chips, electric motors and generators (45.9% of Chinese exports to Brazil). Beside hi-tech goods, Brazil imported from China such consumer goods as spare parts and accessories for phones (4.6%), fabrics (1.7%), conditioners, converters, TVs, spare parts to them, accumulators (6.5%) and other goods. The value of *Brazilian merchandise exports to China* was US $ 64.2 billion in 2018. Brazil exports to China mineral resources, food (92%), electronic chips, electric motors and generators, automobile electric equipment (3.1%) and other goods.

China has been the largest trading partner *of South Africa* for nine consecutive years. Value of Chinese merchandise exports to South Africa was US $ 16.3 billion in 2018. The main export products from China to South Africa were digital processing equipment, specialized industrial equipment, laboratory industrial equipment, medical equipment, electrothermal equipment, diodes, transistors, equipment for the mining industry, electrical machines, motors and generators, cars (38.3%). China also exported to South Africa such consumer goods as footwear (4.9%), furniture (3%), tourist goods (2.3%), TVs, radio receivers and sound recording devices (4.3%), chairs (1.9%), home electro-technical devices (0.7%) and other goods. The value of *South African merchandise exports to China* was US $ 8.5 billion in 2018. China imported from South Africa mineral resources such as iron ores, platinum, diamonds, coal, copper (77.9%) and other goods.

In May 2020, Russia sent the first shipment of humanitarian aid to South

---

① Import nefti v Kitay iz Rossii v marte vyros na 31% // Informatsionnyy portal BRIKS. https://infobrics.org/post/30816/.

Africa.

In 2001-2018 merchandise exports of China to other BRICS countries has increased by 22 times-to Brazil-by 13.7 times, to Russia-by 5.8 times, to India-by 8.4 times, to South Africa-by 10.5 times. Shares of Chinese merchandise exports to other BRICS countries were: India - 43.9%, Russia - 27.4%, Brazil - 19.3%, South Africa - 9.4%.

Correlation coefficient is used to measure the degree of linear dependence between two variables (value of Intra-BRICS trade turnover and their GDP in 2001 - 2018). China have a perfect positive correlation between two mentioned above variables with all BRICS countries: with India (0.95), with Brazil (0.93), with South Africa (0.90) and with Russia (0.84).

Ⅲ. Intra-BRICS FDI Cooperation

The share of BRICS in world inward FDI stock in 2018 continued to be small, but rising to 11% from 3% in 2010, its share in world FDI inflows was 19%. In 2007, the share of Chinese investments in Intra-BRICS FDI was 72%, then in 2018 it decreased to 47%, which was associated with more active participation in Intra-group investment process of other BRICS countries. But still, China remains the main exporter of FDI to the BRICS countries. Important targets of FDI outflow from China were Russian Federation and South Africa. The services sector accounts for a major share of Chinese FDI stock in these two countries.

The inward FDI stock from China to Russia rose in 2011 - 2018 by 4 times. China is the fourth largest foreign investor in Russian economy. In 2001 - 2018, Russia's imports of Chinese current investments increased almost 116 times. The investments were made in such fields as mining, energy, oil and gaz, automotive industry, agriculture, infrastructure projects, trade and services. The joint projects of Russia and China are, for example, the construction of Moscow metro station, the creation of infrastructure — a high-speed railway between Moscow and Beijing, the creation of a railway bridge between Russia (Jewish Autonomous Region) and China (Heilongjiang Province) across the Amur River, the creation of the Free Port in Vladivostok, the construction of a floating nuclear power plant, the construction of new car assembly plants. State-owned China National Petroleum Corporation acquired a 20% stake in OAO Yamal SPG (US $ 1.1 billion). China participated in the financing of construction of the oil pipeline connecting Russia's east Siberian natural gas field with northeast China (joint project worth more than US $ 100 billion-nearly 4000 km natural gas pipeline). The development of energy will continue to be the main aim of economic and trade cooperation between China and Russia as one of the key areas of practical cooperation between the two countries. It is a manifestation of the comprehensive strategic partnership between the two economies. China will become the largest importer of Russia's natural gas. Among the Top 10 greenfield projects, five were made by Chinese investors in Russian economy: 《China Triumph International Engineering》 invested US $ 3 billion in the industrial machinery, equipment and tools (3000 jobs created); Chinese company 《Hawtai Motor Group》 invested US $ 1.1 billion in Automotive OEM (3000 jobs created); Chinese company 《Great Wall Motor》 started to build an automotive plant in the Tula region with an estimated value of US $ 520 million (2500 jobs created); Chinese company 《New Hope Group》 invested US $ 500 million in food and tobacco, animal food (1267 jobs created); Chinese company 《Dongfeng Motor》 invested US $ 500 million in Automotive OEM (2931 jobs created). Cooperation between China and Russia in aerospace, infrastructure, and other fields has been steadily gaining grounds. The total amount of bilateral trade was US $ 100 billion in 2018. Russia decided to invest in the National Wealth Fund in yuan and in Chinese government bonds.

In South Africa State-ownedBeijing Automobile International Corporation invested US $ 819 million in automotive plant in South Africa (Coega Development Corporation) to produce motor vehicles for the local and regional markets.

Chinese companies also invested in the energy sector of South Africa, in the development of its infrastructure. More than half of the projects implemented in the field of renewable energy sources (in hydropower).

The main Chinese investments in India were made in the development of the automotive industry, metallurgy, industrial engineering, energy, in the manufacture of electrical equipment. China is increasing its direct FDI in India, despite the relationship between the two countries was affected due to the construction of the China-Pakistan economic corridor-one of the main infrastructure projects of the "One Belt-One Road" Initiative (US $ 46 billion is allocated for its creation). Faced with rising labor costs (which are 1.5-3 times higher than in India) and pressure from slowing economic growth, Chinese companies are looking for alternative sources and new markets to expand and increase their efficiency. One of the promising countries of effective investment is India, which is currently the fastest growing economy in the world. In an effort to increase their competitiveness, Chinese companies are shifting their production to India (in the automotive industry, in the chemical field, in the development of electronics, in the field of information and communication technologies). China's CRRC Corporation invested in India-China joint-venture plant US $ 63 million to produce rail transportation equipment. Huawei Technologies plans to start in India manufacturing smartphones.

Brazil has the strongest bilateral economic relations with China, but they are mainly driven by trade (there was a boom in Brazilian exports of primary goods to China in recent years). The presence of Brazilian companies in China is limited, and their main business activity is in the field of service (such as finance, business consulting and trading), the sales and distribution of their products, and procurement. Chinese investments are made in the Brazilian electric power industry, in the mining industry, in the oil and gas sector, in infrastructure. The Chinese investments in Brazil have been carried out in M&A. For example, Chinese petrochemical corporation 《Sinopek》 invested in Brazilian sphere of exploration and production of oil and gas. According to the Chinese-Brazilian business council within five years 44 Chinese companies invested US $ 68.5 billion in 60 Brazilian investment projects. Brazilian investments in China are more diversified than elsewhere (financial service, food, metal, electronic components, aerospace).

Chinese FDI into BRICS countries are diversified, focusing on natural resources, automotive sector and other industrial consumer goods. The rapid growth of Chinese outward FDI is likely to continue, particularly in services, as well as in infrastructure-related industries, as the country's One Belt, One Road Initiative (referring to the Silk Road Economic Belt and the 21 Century Maritime Silk Road) starts to be implemented. In China FDI inflows growth in transport, storage and postal services has been continuing. These initiatives create a framework for increasing economic cooperation among BRICS countries.

The BRICS New Development Bank (NDB) is helping BRICS states to overcome the crisis consequences and fight the coronavirus. A credit lines of US $ 1 billion each were approved for China, India, Brazil and South Africa as emergency aid to fight the coronavirus. Emergency Fund for NDB member countries will be created.

Ⅳ. Synergistic Effect of Intra-BRICS Trade and Investment Cooperation

The synergistic effect of cooperation among countries is associated with an increase of its efficiency as a result of integration, the merging of individual elements of this cooperation into a single whole. Analysis of the synergistic effect obtained as a result of the cooperation of countries, the identification of measures to strengthen their positive component is important and relevant. One of the motives of the uniting BRICS economies into a group is the possibility of obtaining a synergistic effect from this process, contributing to their economic development.

To determine the synergistic effect of Intra-BRICS trade and investment cooperation, the author propose to use the Multiple Factor Correlationand Multiple Regression analysis. The analysis of multiple correlation (calculated on the basis of formulas 1, 2, 3, 4) made it possible to determine the dependence between three variables (the value of Intra-BRICS trade turnover, FDI and GDP.

$$R_{y/x_1x_2} = \sqrt{\frac{r_{yx_1}^2 + r_{yx_2}^2 - 2 \cdot r_{yx_1} \cdot r_{yx_2} \cdot r_{x_1x_2}}{1 - r_{x_1x_2}^2}} \qquad (1)$$

R_{y/x_1x_2} —Multiple Fctor Correlation of Intra-BRICS trade turnover, FDI and their GDP, coefficient;

x_1 — Intra-BRICS trade turnover, US $ billion;

x_2 — Intra-BRICS FDI, US $ billion;

y —GDP of BRICS countries, US $ billion;

r_{yx_1} — Correlation coefficient of Intra-BRICS trade turnover and GDP of BRICS countries;

r_{yx_2} — Correlation coefficient of Intra-BRICS FDI and GDP of BRICS countries;

$r_{x_1x_2}$ — Correlation coefficient of Intra-BRICS trade turnover and FDI.

The following formula is applied for calculation of correlation coefficient:

$$r_{yx_1} = \frac{\Sigma (x_1 - \overline{x_1}) \cdot (y - \overline{y})}{\sqrt{\Sigma (x_1 - \overline{x_1})^2 \cdot \Sigma (y - \overline{y})^2}} \qquad (2)$$

x_1 — Intra-BRICS trade turnover, US $ billion;

$\overline{x_1}$ — Average Intra-BRICS trade turnover in 2001 - 2018, US $ billion;

y — GDP of BRICS countries, US $ billion;

$\overline{y}$ — Average GDP of BRICS countries in 2001 - 2018, US $ billion.

$$r_{yx_2} = \frac{\Sigma (x_2 - \overline{x_2}) \cdot (y - \overline{y})}{\sqrt{\Sigma (x_2 - \overline{x_2})^2 \cdot \Sigma (y - \overline{y})^2}} \qquad (3)$$

x_2 — Intra-BRICS FDI, US $ billion;

$\overline{x_2}$ —Average Intra-BRICS FDI, US $ billion.

$$r_{x_1x_2} = \frac{\Sigma (x_1 - \overline{x_1}) \cdot (x_2 - \overline{x_2})}{\sqrt{\Sigma (x_1 - \overline{x_1})^2 \cdot \Sigma (x_2 - \overline{x_2})^2}} \qquad (4)$$

When selecting factors for the analysis, an analytical grouping, a comparison of the time series, the construction of linear graphs were carried out, which made it possible to determine the presence, direction and shape of the relationship between the considered parameters. Based on the analysis of multiple correlation coefficient, a very close Intra-BRICS relationship between trade and investment cooperation with GDP for 2001 - 2018 was determined: in Brazil (the coefficient of multiple correlation was 0.97), in India (0.93), in China (0.92), in Russia (0.92). The close relationship of the above indicators was identified in South Africa (0.78). The high multiple correlation coefficient confirms the prospects of trade and investment cooperation of BRICS countries and indicate that they have high potential for economic cooperation and synergistic effect.

The author has calculated the equations of multiple regression of Intra-BRICS trade and investment cooperation of each of BRICS countries and their GDP in 2001 - 2018:

$$\gamma = \beta_o + \beta_1 x_1 + \beta_2 x_2 \qquad (5)$$

γ —GDP of BRICS countries, US $ billion;

β_o — Free member, determining the value of GDP (γ) in case, if factorial parameters (X_1 and X_2) equal to zero;

β_1 — Regression coefficient of the first factorial parameter (X_1);

β_2 — Regression coefficient of the second factorial parameter (X_2);

X_1 —First factorial parametr (Intra-BRICS trade turnover of each of BRICS countries, US $ billion.);

X_2 —Second factorial parametr (Intra-BRICS FDI inflow of each of BRICS countries, US $ billion.);

The method of the smallest squares and a matrix method used for the solution of the regression equation. In determining the synergistic effect of trade and investment cooperation of BRICS countries, obtained the following results. The multiple regression equation of two factorial parameters (Intra-BRICS trade turnover; Intra-BRICS FDI inflow to each of BRICS countries) and a resultant parametr (GDP) in 2001 - 2018 have allowed to determine regression coefficients of each of BRICS countries and to draw the following conclusions:

a) Increase of trade turnover of Brazil with other BRICS countries by US $ 1 leads to the growth of average GDP of Brazil on US $ 17; increase of FDI inflow to Brazil from other BRICS countries by US $ 1 leads to the growth of average GDP of Brazil on US $ 55.9. FDI inflow to Brazil from other BRICS countries makes bigger impact on the growth of GDP of Brazil, than the increase of trade turnover of Brazil with other BRICS countries.

b) Increase of trade turnover of Russia with other BRICS countries by US $ 1 leads to the growth of average GDP of Russia on US $ 16.6; increase of FDI inflow to Russia from other BRICS countries by US $ 1 leads to the growth of average GDP of Russia on US $ 78.4. FDI inflow to Russia from other BRICS countries makes bigger impact on the growth of GDP of Russia than trade turnover of Russia with other BRICS countries.

c) Increase of trade turnover of India with other BRICS countries by US $ 1 leads to the average GDP growth of India on US $ 14.9; increase of FDI inflow to India from other BRICS countries by US $ 1 leads to the growth of average GDP of India on US $ 249.1. FDI inflow to India from other BRICS countries makes bigger impact on the growth of GDP of India than trade turnover of India with other BRICS countries.

d) Increase of trade turnover of China with other BRICS countries by US $ 1 leads to average GDP growth of China on US $ 36.5; increase of FDI inflow to China from other BRICS countries by US $ 1 leads to the growth of average GDP of China on US $ 488.6. FDI inflow to China from other BRICS countries makes bigger impact on the growth of GDP of China than trade turnover of China with other BRICS countries.

e) Increase of trade turnover of South Africa with other BRICS countries by US $ 1 leads to the increase of the average GDP growth of South Arica on US $ 1.6; increase of FDI inflow to South Africa from other BRICS countries by US $ 1 leads to the decrease of average GDP growth of South Africa on US $ 1.2.

The results of the multiple regression analysis confirm the synergistic effect of the trade and investment cooperation of BRICS countries. The obtained results led to the conclusion that Intra-BRICS trade and investment cooperation leads to a more significant increase in their GDP compared to their cooperation in this area with other countries of the world. This fact indicates a high potential and synergistic effect of further trade and investment cooperation between BRICS countries. Based on the use of quantitative methods (multiple regression analysis), it is shown that further trade and investment cooperation between BRICS countries is promising. The increase of Intra-BRICS FDI inflows leads to a faster growth of GDP of Brazil, Russia, India and China. The growth of FDI inflows to South Africa from other BRICS countries has almost no positive effect on the development of its economy.

Obtaining a synergistic effect of trade and investment cooperation of BRICS countries is associated with: expansion of types and forms, increase of the volume of trade and investment cooperation; formation of a joint platform in the field of trade and investment interaction; using regional links to ensure mutual development of countries; liberalization of Intra-BRICS trade and investment; using the capabilities of the New Development Bank in implementing joint projects; the transition from bilateral to multilateral joint investment projects; using the possibilities of complementarity in the development of economic cooperation between countries; expansion of the strategic partnership of the BRICS countries, which allows to obtain a synergistic effect and increasing their influence in the global economy. The analysis allowed to draw a conclusion about the prospects of trade and investment cooperation of BRICS countries as one of the important areas of their economic interaction, which makes it possible to obtain a synergistic effect from the expansion of cooperation. The obtained results should be taken into account when developing the program "Made in BRICS》.

V. Conclusion

Methodological guidelines for determining the potential of economic cooperation of BRICS countries were developed and tested. It is characterized by: a) synergistic effect of multilateral cooperation between the countries of BRICS; b) exceeding the intensity of the relationship of trade and investment Intra-BRICS cooperation over the intensity of their cooperation with other countries of the world, which is a quantitative measure (indicator) of the potential of economic cooperation of BRICS countries; c) possibility of increasing the intensity of their interaction due to the significant complementarity of their economies; d) expansion of the list of industries in which cooperation takes place between these countries; e) development of existing and creation of new common institutions of the BRICS countries; f) development of joint strategies of action in existing international multilateral economic institutions.

The author developed and tested the methodology of the determining the synergistic effect of trade and investment cooperation of BRICS countries. Based on the proposed methodology (multiple correlation and multiple regression analysis), it was found that the expansion of Intra-BRICS trade and investment cooperation has a strong positive effect on the growth of their economies. The phenomenon of the faster growth of Intra-BRICS trade and investment cooperation compared with their interaction with other countries of the world has not been fully explained by any theory of economic development. Author revealed a complex of factors that have a decisive influence on this process: high complementarity of the economies of BRICS countries; presence of significant potential of economic interaction in the form of the synergistic effect of cooperation among BRICS countries, which leads to their great interest in the development of Intra-BRICS trade and investment cooperation; the developing institutionalization of the BRICS countries.

The current crisis associated with the coronavirus pandemic confirms the importance of strengthening the strategic Intra-group cooperation of the BRICS countries, and is a catalyst for expanding their relations in various sectors of the economy. The study made it possible to identify the risks that many countries of the world may face in overcoming the crisis: the continuation of the coronavirus epidemic may affect the correction of the timing of the cancellation of quarantine measures in different countries and lead to an uneven recovery of the world economy; expansion of sanctions against many states (for example, against Russia, China); overflow of oil reserves in storage facilities of many countries of the world; aggravation of relations in the field of international trade ("trade war" between China and the United States); change in the intensity of stimulating economic policies of governments of different states and central banks.

Science Diplomacy of BRICS: Results and Perspectives

Anna Kurumchina[*]

Abstract: Today science plays an extremely important role in human lives. There are several dimensions of it. First of all, it serves to protect national interests inside and outside the state. On the other hand, every national science, technologies and innovations are making their input into the solving global problems that we facing nowadays in such spheres as health, environmental pollution, water resources, medicine, solar energy, ocean and polar science, etc. In the multipolar world new powerful states and its coalitions use science diplomacy to protect their regional and national interests and to declare themselves as new science, technology and innovations centers that can participate in solving global problems mentioned above.

One of such examples of regional cooperation is BRICS. In 2015 BRICS singed the Science, Technology and Innovation Framework Programme. During this 5 year 58 STI projects were realized under this framework. Most of them are in the realm of fundamental sciences such as physics, biology, space re-

---

[*] Anna Kurumchina, Associate Professor, Ural Federal University.

search and others. All of the projects are aimed at achieving national and global goals. The scientific infrastructure of each country of the group is shortly analyzed in the article. It demonstrates that BRICS countries have great potential in STI sphere.

This potential and opportunities of BRICS in the sphere of science diplomacy is at the very beginning. Everything is dependent on wisdom of state governments of the group members on how to use the given set of circumstances of BRICS. The cooperation among scientists and the usage of all three dimensions of science diplomacy inside and outside BRICS can lead to the overcoming of existing difficulties.

Keywords: BRICS; Science Diplomacy; Technology; High-tech; Cooperation

Today science plays an extremely important role in human lives. There are several dimensions of it. First of all, it serves to protect national interests inside and outside the state. On the other hand, every national science, technologies and innovations are making their input into the solving global problems that we facing nowadays in such spheres as health, environmental pollution, water resources, medicine, solar energy, ocean and polar science, etc. Article 3 of Vienna Convention on Diplomatic Relations says that the functions of sending state are protecting in the receiving State the interests of the sending State and of its nationals; promoting friendly relations between the sending State and the receiving State, and developing their economic, cultural and scientific relations[1]. This document describes the traditional international relations. The contemporary situation is differing in some cases because there is multipolar world today, there are some regional leaders appeared like China, India, Brazil, etc. Global problems demand solutions of all nations and its national science. That is why science was included into the agenda of international policymaking

---

[1] Vienna Convention on Diplomatic Relations 1961. p. 3. https: //legal. un. org/ilc/texts/instruments/english/conventions/9_1_1961. pdf.

and diplomacy.

According to the Royal Society concept there are three dimensions of science diplomacy: "informing foreign policy objectives with scientific advice (science in diplomacy); facilitating international science cooperation (diplomacy for science); using science cooperation to improve international relations between countries (science for diplomacy)"[1]. Harnessing a country soft-power tools or intangible assets such as culture, tourism, cuisine, cinema, or science, technology and innovation is a new way to act or be perceived as a decision maker in contrast to the use of coercive means, such as military power or payments, traditional hard power tools. Therefore, countries combine strategically hard- and soft-power tools in what can be framed as smart power[2].

In the multipolar world new powerful states and its coalitions use science diplomacy to protect their regional and national interests and to declare themselves as new science, technology and innovations centers that can participate in solving global problems mentioned above.

One of such examples of regional cooperation is BRICS. Its first official Summit was held 10 years ago in 2009 in Yekaterinburg, since that time the cooperation among the BRICS group is developing not only in political sphere but in culture, technology, innovation and education ones. In 2015 BRICS singed the Science, Technology and Innovation Framework Programme. It is aiming to support excellent research on priority areas which can best be addressed by a multinational approach. The initiative should facilitate cooperation among the researchers and institutions in the consortia which consist of partners from at least three of the BRICS countries.

Since 2016 coordinated calls for multilateral research projects are launched

---

[1] New frontiers in science diplomacy. Navigating the changing balance of power. January 2010. The Royal Society, 2010. p. 8. https: //royalsociety. org/topics-policy/publications/2010/new-frontiers-science-diplomacy/

[2] Lorenzo Melchor, Izaskun Lacunza, and Ana Elorza. 2020. What Is Science Diplomacy? S4D4C European Science Diplomacy Online Course, Module 2, Vienna: S4D4C.

under BRICS STI FP inviting researchers from BRICS member states to jointly carry out basic, applied and innovation research projects on multilateral approach"[①]. Every member of the BRICS appointed definite structures and institutes. From Brazil the National Council for Scientific and Technological Development (CNPq) and Brazilian Innovation Agency (Finep) participate in this Programme. Russian Foundation for Assistance to Small Innovative Enterprises (FASIE), Ministry of Science and Higher Education (MSHE), and Russian Foundation for Basic Research (RFBR) are delegates in it. Department of Biotechnology (DBT) and Department of Science and Technology (DST) of India were appointed too. Chinese Ministry of Science and Technology (MOST) and National Natural Science Foundation of China (NSFC) signed the Programme. And Department of Science and Technology, National Research Foundation (NRF), and South African Medical Research Council (SAMRC) joined the Framework Programme from South Africa. All these structures are the highest governmental level bodies that stresses the importance of understanding of science diplomacy by the BRICS group.

During this 5 year 58 STI projects were realized under this framework. Most of them are in the realm of fundamental sciences such as physics, biology, space research and others. All of the projects are aimed at achieving national and global goals. For instance, Boron and gadolinium nanoparticles for cancer diagnosis and therapy project is a great compliment into the global searching of cancer diagnostic tasks. "Chinese team (Head Prof. Zheyu Shen, Ningbo Institute of Materials & Technology Engineering, Chinese Academy of Sciences, Ningbo City, China) prepared gadolinium-based nanoparticles for MRI investigations. Russian team (Head Prof. Vladimir Bregadze, Institute of Organoelement Compounds, Russian Academy of Sciences, Moscow, Russia) focused on the synthesis of novel boronated lipids and their analogs, and the model study of lipid-bo-

---

① About BRICS STI Framework Programme. http: //brics-sti. org/index. php? p = about/About + BRICS + STI + FP.

ron cluster non-covalent interactions. Indian team (Prof. S. Mandal, Indian Institute of Science Education and Research, Kolkata, India) studied liposomal formation and encapsulation of the obtained boron compounds and MRI contrast agents into a lipid bilayer via supramolecular assembly. Further cell experiments and animal experiments will be carried out to verify the synthesized materials as potential agents for early diagnosis and boron neutron capture therapy (BNCT) for cancer"[1].

Green economy is an important part of global tasks that should be reached as soon as possible taking into account environmental problems of the humankind. The BRICS group makes its significant input into this aim as well.

The "LargEWiN" ——Design and Development of Large-Scale Ambient Energy Harvesting Wireless Networks project is about empowering "the large-scale wireless networks with the ambient energy harvesting and the emerging communication technologies to promote the green economy in a more efficient, reliable, and sustainable manner. It seeks to address the system performance, planning, and resource allocation problems by exploiting cooperation among available network resources with renewable and/or radio-frequency (RF) energy sources for implementation of Large-Scale Ambient Energy Harvesting Wireless Networks (LargEWiN). Especially, it intends to integrate the more appealing millimeter wave (mmWave) technology into LargEWiN for its potential futuristic deployment. Such developments will not only help in accommodating the increasing demand of information delivery, but also in reducing the operating expenditure of mobile operators, while protecting the environment and preserving the natural resources"[2].

As for the current COVID situation, BRICS countries compliment and solve this global extremely important challenge which damaged all countries in the

---

[1] "BGNCDT" -Boron and gadolinium nanoparticles for cancer diagnosis and therapy. http: //brics-sti. org/index. php? p = project/9/.

[2] "LargEWiN" -Design and Development of Large-Scale Ambient Energy Harvesting Wireless Networks. http: //brics-sti. org/index. php? p = project/57.

world. All BRICS countries joined together to research this virus and to find the vaccine. The project was announced on 1st of July 2020 and the deadline was on 18th of August 2020. "The following thematic areas are currently planned for the BRICS STI FP call as response to COVID-19 pandemic:

1. Research and development of new technologies/tools for diagnosing COVID-19.

2. Research and development of COVID-19 vaccines and drugs, including repurposing of available drugs.

3. Genomic sequencing of SARS-CoV-2 and studies on the epidemiology and mathematical modeling of the COVID-19 pandemic.

4. AI, ICT and HPC① oriented research for COVID-19 drugs design, vaccine development, treatment, clinical trials and public health infrastructures and systems.

5. Epidemiological studies and clinical trials to evaluate the overlap of SARS-CoV-2 and comorbidities, especially tuberculosis"②. And as known Russian Federation has patented the first vaccine on 11th of August③.

All these projects demonstrate that BRICS group has great potential in science diplomacy. The author would recommend to add the results of mentioned projects to this platform to demonstrate outcomes and outputs of them: quantity of publications with the links to the articles, number of national and international patents as a result of these projects, etc.

Speaking about science diplomacy of BRICS it is important to mention and analyze the scientific infrastructure of each country of the group.

---

① Artificial intelligence, Information and communications technology and High-performance computing.

② Pre-announcement BRICS STI Framework Programme Response to COVID-19 pandemic coordinated call for BRICS multilateral projects 2020. http://brics-sti.org/index.php?p=new/26.

③ Минздрав России зарегистрировал первую в мире вакцину от COVID-19. https://covid19.rosminzdrav.ru/minzdrav-rossii-zaregistriroval-pervuyu-v-mire-vakczinu-ot-covid-19/.

Russia

According to the Federal Service for Supervision in the Education and Science there are 1266 public universities and 622 private ones in Russia not to count their branches[1]. About 1696 national accredited laboratories[2], 177 startup incubators and accelerators[3], Federal Service for Intellectual Property and 7 public grant foundations. Main Russian innovation legislation is Federal Law No. 223 - FZ dated July 18, 2011 on the procurement of goods, works, services by certain types of legal entities (as amended on December 29 2015) that regulates the state policy in this sphere. The main forms of financial support in Russia are as follows:

— Subsidies-non-repayable benefits Subsidization has strictly specified areas related to the implementation of projects;

— subsidies-allocations from the budget to cover losses from innovation activities of the main participants, as well as to develop infrastructure;

— real investments-long-term investments of state capital in the creation of a scientific and technical reserve;

— financial investments;

— financial leasing.

Financial support should have certain boundaries and be based on the following principles:

— multichannel system for obtaining additional funding sources;

— priority of government funding;

— purposefulness of financing;

---

[1] Federal Service for Supervision in the Education and Science. https: //map. obrnadzor. gov. ru/application/university.

[2] Eurasian Economic Commission. https: //eaeunion. org.

[3] All business incubators and accelerators. https: //rb. ru/incubator/ · &page = 1.

— the integration of public funds with private investments.

In 2017 there were 21 037 patents, and more than 350 international patents (Skolkovo residents, 2018).

India

India identifies innovative development and innovations as a priority and has committed to catalyzing inclusive development. Policy action on education and improving the conditions for innovative entrepreneurship are critically spread benefits from innovation across Indian society. Today India is on 52nd position on the Global Innovation Index and gained nine position in the last three years, presenting better performance than expected based on GDP. Ministry of Science and Technology (MST) has the responsibility to negotiate conclude and implement S&T agreements between India and other countries in close consultation with the Ministry of External Affairs, Indian Missions Abroad, S&T counsellors, stakeholders in scientific, technological and academic institutions, concerned governmental agencies and with different industry associations in India. The main governmental actor is the Department of Science and Technology (DST) linked to MST. Forum for Indian Science Diplomacy is the major programme of DST promotes Indian potential by using such means as capacity building in science diplomacy; developing networks and Science diplomacy for strategic thinking. They are working with Indian diasporas around the world looking at them like at economic assets.

India invests a lot into the STI sector. There are 865 universities in the country. According to the report of Startup Ecosystem in India "India has the 2nd largest ecosystem of start-ups with over 20,000 start-ups and a year on year growth of 10% - 12%. There were 1,400 start-ups born in 2016 alone, implying that there are 3—4 start-ups born every day. Most of the start-up clusters are present in Bengaluru, the National Capital Region, and Mumbai"[1]. There are great amounts of investment in India. "Investors have invested over USD 33.62 billion into the Indian start-up ecosystem since 2014 and over half of the amount has been invested in 2017 (USD 13.7 Billion) and the first quarter of 2018 (USD 2.26 Billion)"[2]. A large number of incubators are established in cooperation with universities and educational bodies, they develop many star-ups in collaboration with partners from abroad[3].

Brazil[4]

Brazil consists of several subregions that are developed unequally. One of the most developed subregions is Sao Paulo. It contains the main national universities and research centres like University of Sao Paulo, Campinas State University (UNICAMP), San Paulo State University (UNESP), Sao Paulo State Technological College (FATEC SP); Federal University of Sao Carlos (UFSCar), Federal University of Sao Paulo (UNIFESP). There are 23 engineering laboratories, 15 agrarian and Biological Sciences; 15 laboratories focused on health; and 7 Social/Human Science institutions. There are 16 startup incubators and 10 accelerators in this subregion. In 2019 Sao Paulo got US $ 20 million as a public financing with/at private companies[5]. San Paulo has around 40% participation in patent system. From 2014 till 2018 Brazil has got about 2000 international patents per year. This region has 30% in high-technology and 26% in medium high-tech products from total exports of the region. In the sphere of Science and

---

[1] Startup Ecosystem in India: Incubators and Accelerators. https://www.s-ge.com/sites/default/files/publication/free/startup-ecosystem-india-incubators-accelerators-23-01-2019.pdf.

[2] Startup Ecosystem in India: Incubators and Accelerators. https://www.s-ge.com/sites/default/files/publication/free/startup-ecosystem-india-incubators-accelerators-23-01-2019.pdf.

[3] Chaturvedi, S. and Mulakala A. India's Approach to Development Cooperation. Routledge, 2016. p. 190.

[4] The data are taken from the Augusto G. F. Costa's presentation at InnScid SP 2020, August 4th.

[5] Secretariat for Economic Development. http://www.desenvolvimentoeconomico.sp.gov.br/.

Innovation diplomacy Sao Paulo has several programmes: Sao Paulo Research Foundation (FAPESP), Invest SP, Embrapa Labex Program for China, Europe, South Korea the USA, and Innovation and Science Diplomacy School. Brazil pays more attention to diaspora supporting around the world. They developed the Institutional Support for mapping the diaspora networks.

China[①]

China's STI infrastructure is like this. There were 2688 ordinary colleges and universities in China (including 257 independent colleges). China has 20 national laboratories, more than 2000 startup incubators and accelerators, they have State patent office, National Independent Innovation Demonstration Zone and High-tech Industry Development Zone. By August 2018 The National Guiding Fund for Transformation of Scientific and Technological Achievements has reached 24.7 billion yuan, and 161 scientific and technological achievements transformation projects have been invested. By the end of 2017 there were 5052 Sci-tech journals 1196 medical and health ones. 58990 national patent applications were in 2019. China's export of high-tech products account about 30% of China's total export. China has developed and implemented the "One belt One road" technological innovation cooperation plan. China strengthens international scientific and technological personnel exchange and cooperation.

South Africa

South Africa was deindustrialized practically at the same period of time as the USSR. Richard Grabowski from Southern Illinois University wrote an article

---

① The data are taken from He Zhou's presentation at InnScid SP 2020, August 6th.

devoted to this topic[①]. Nevertheless, South Africa does its best to rebuild and renovate the system. For this purpose, South Africa signed Southern Africa Development Community Protocol on Science, Technology and Innovation, and developed STI strategic plan 2015 - 2020. The UNDP adapted Global development goals to South Africa[②]. The innovation infrastructure of South Africa includes 26 public universities 8 of them are Universities of Technology, and 6 ones are comprehensive that is compile classic and technology approaches. There are 4 university collaborations in the country, for instance Cape Higher Education Consortium and Southern Education and Research Alliance. There are 20 accelerators and incubators for STI sector in South Africa[③]. According to South African Accreditation System there are about 120 blood banks in the country, and many other ones. More detailed information is on the official web-site of The South African National Accreditation System (SANAS)[④]. High-technology exports (% of manufactured exports) in South Africa was reported at 5.3197 % in 2018, according to the World Bank collection of development indicators, compiled from officially recognized sources[⑤].

So, as it is shown all BRICS countries have great potential in STI sphere, and some of them can compete the world leaders. It should be stressed that most of BRICS members belong to the South, and only Russian Federation is from the North. This peculiarity makes the group unique. The joined science, technology and innovation opportunities and potential might be used to develop

---

① Grabowski, R. Deindustrialization of Africa. https://scholarworks.wmich.edu/cgi/viewcontent.cgi? article =1041&context = ijad.

② Sustainable Development Goals. https://www.za.undp.org/content/south_africa/en/home/sustainable-development-goals.html.

③ Here are 20 accelerators, incubators for African startups to apply for in 2020 // VentureBurn, 2 Jan, 2020. https://ventureburn.com/2020/01/accelerators-incubators-african-startups - 2/.

④ The South African National Accreditation System. https://www.sanas.co.za/Pages/index.aspx.

⑤ Trading Economy. https://tradingeconomics.com/south-africa/high-technology-exports-percent-of-manufactured-exports-wb-data.html.

this type of cooperation to the regional leadership.

We have tried to make a SWOT analysis of the BRICS STI sphere.

Table 2-1　SWOT-analysis of STI BRICS

Strengths	Weaknesses
· Huge STI potential of BRICS members; · 43% of human resources, including intellectual of the world; · The biggest mineral and natural resources of the group; · Big agricultural experience and opportunity; · Nuclear potential of the group; · Big industrial and production infrastructure of some members of BRICS; · Development of independent financial system of BRICS;	· Low investment potential of some BRICS members; · Lower standard of living of BRICS population in comparison with the West; · Lower purchasing power of the BRICS population; · Environmentally polluted countries;
Opportunities	Threats
· BRICS countries can use national markets of each other to overcome sanctions from other countries; · The BRICS potential might be use to overcome mentioned weaknesses; · Reciprocal usage of STI infrastructures of BRICS members	· Sanctions from the US and EU as a reaction to global competition with some BRICS members; · Difficult access to global STI market for some BRICS members; · Armed conflicts between some BRICS countries; · US dollar dependent economies.

Source: Making by the author.

It is far from being ideal, of course, but it might be supplemented and it is thought-provoking by demonstrating that if we think about BRICS as a STI body it opens plenty of opportunities for development.

Conclusions

In conclusions the author wants to stress that the potential and opportunities of BRICS in the sphere of science diplomacy is at the very beginning. Everything is dependent on wisdom of state governments of the group members on how to use the given set of circumstances of BRICS. The cooperation among scientists and the usage of all three dimensions of science diplomacy inside and outside BRICS can lead to the overcoming of existing difficulties.

Cooperation and Challenges of Youth Exchange in BRICS[*]

You Han[**]

Abstract: With more and more cooperation mechanisms among BRICS, strengthening people-to-people and cultural exchanges has developed into the "third pillar" of BRICS cooperation, and youth exchanges have gradually become institutionalized under the framework of BRICS cooperation, which have increasingly become the main component of the social agenda. At present, there are distinct characteristics of youth exchanges in BRICS: multiple goals carried; platforms ever enriched; guided proactively by government. However, the different focus of the youth policies of the BRICS, the insufficient representativeness of youth, and the lack of consolidation of the effects of activities have hindered the further deepening of youth exchanges in BRICS. Therefore, only by continuing to attach importance to youth exchanges in BRICS, strengthening coopera-

---

[*] This is the phased outcome of "A Comparative Study of Global Governance Strategies between China and Russia" (Project Approval Number: 19CGJ021), a project of National Social Science Foundation.

[**] You Han, Associate Professor, School of International Relations, Sichuan International Studies University.

tion with civil society forces, and expanding the forms of exchanges can we draw on the wisdom of young people from all countries and promote the future development of the BRICS.

Keywords: BRICS; Youth Exchange; Youth Policy

I. The Development of Youth Exchanges in BRICS

According to the definition by the United Nations, "youth" are those who between the ages of 15 and 25. This category actually includes adolescents (between the ages of 13 and 19) and young adults (between the ages of 20 and 25), and this age group is the most vulnerable in society. Young people account for a very large proportion of the world's population who suffer from the newly added infection of HIV, dire poverty, and lack of literacy skills. Therefore, their voices are often unheard. Since the first BRICS Summit in 2009, youth issues have been paid attention to. In recent years, youth issues have increasingly become a major part of the social agenda.

1. Initial Stage

In 2010, the *Brasilia Declaration* issued at the 2nd BRICS Summit stated that in the field of poverty eradication, technical and financial capacity must be strengthened to promote social development and social protection. The disadvantaged groups, including the poor, women, youth, immigrants and the disabled are the key targets of development and protection. In the 3rd BRICS Summit in 2011, the leaders redeclare to "strengthen dialogue and cooperation in areas such as social protection, decent work, gender equality, youth, public health, and AIDS prevention and control." It can be seen that during this period, the BRICS mainly regarded youth as the disadvantaged groups in society, with the focus of cooperation being put on protecting youth.

In 2012, the "*Delhi Declaration*" issued at the 4th BRICS Summit formally proposed the "BRICS Youth Policy Dialogue" as a new cooperation project, aiming to include youth voices on the agenda of the BRICS and popularize the BRICS among young people in these countries, which is conducive to enhancing mutual exchanges among BRICS youths and consolidating the youth foundation for BRICS cooperation.

2. Transition Stage

The theme of the 2014 BRICS Summit in Brazil is "Sustainable Solutions for Inclusive Growth", where youth is the key to achieving inclusive growth and stabilized society. Therefore, creating employment opportunities for youth and promoting technical and vocational education among BRICS have become the focus of BRICS youth exchanges.

As the rotating presidency in 2014, Brazil, with the support of the International Policy Centre for Inclusive Growth of the United Nations Development Programme, released the research reports of "*Youth and Employment among the BRICS*" and "*Social Programmes and Job Promotion for the BRICS Youth*" before the BRICS Summit.[①] The two reports conducted a comprehensive analysis of the demographic structure, youth employment rate and unemployment rate, and informal treatment in the BRICS, and compared the youth-oriented employment promotion policies and programs of the BRICS. These researches have pointed the way ahead for cooperation. In the end, the BRICS Summit in 2014 proposed the idea of establishing a youth dialogue mechanism among the BRICS.

3. Institutionalization Stage

On July 4th, 2015, the BRICS Ministers of Youth Affairs Meeting was held

---

[①] MacLennan Michael, ed., Youth and employment among the BRICS, International Policy Centre for Inclusive Growth UNDP, Brasilia, April 2014, No. 28; PL de Arruda, AK Slingsby: Social programmes and job promotion for the BRICS youth, International Policy Centre for Inclusive Growth UNDP, Brasilia, Oct. 2014, No. 130.

in Kazan, Russia. After the meeting, the BRICS Ministers of Youth Affairs signed the *Memorandum of Understanding and Cooperation on Youth Affairs*, which speculates that the main areas of youth cooperation include mutual exchanges of countries' experience in the youth policies in international youth exchanges, business, research, and innovation activities. In addition, the *Memorandum* also envisages annual technical meetings on youth affairs.

From July 4th to 7th, 2015, just before the 6th BRICS Summit, the first BRICS Youth Summit was held in Kazan, whose main goal is to further develop the BRICS youth dialogue, enhance the interaction of youth among different civilizations and promote people-to-people exchanges. More than 200 youth representatives from the five BRICS countries held a three-day meeting in Kazan, Russia. The participants signed the *Youth Action Plan* under the framework of groups that are dedicated to the areas in political, economic, humanitarian, informational, and scientific and technological cooperation. The *Plan* unanimously approved the affairs including the reform of the United Nations, the development of an international internship program within the BRICS, and the establishment of the BRICS United News Agency. The participants believe that the BRICS should create an economic and social environment conducive to young people then can provide equal opportunities for them, incorporate youth issues into the activities of other BRICS forums such as academics, parliaments, and diplomacy, and call for the expansion of the proportion of youth representatives in all BRICS meetings so as to ensure that youth can participate in the decision-making process and strategy formulation of BRICS policies. The *Youth Action Plan* is constructive in nature and aims to make leaders of BRICS understand the concerns of youth groups, so it was submitted as an official document to the Ufa Summit.

Since 2015, the BRICS Youth Summit has become the annual fixed agenda of BRICS activities, and the continuous deepening of youth exchanges from 2016 to 2019 has made it an important topic in people-to-people exchanges. During Russia's presidency in 2020, the 6th BRICS Youth Summit and the BRICS

Ministers of Youth Affairs was held in Ulyanovsk from Nov[30th] to Dec[2nd] 2020, whose main topic is the role of young people in expanding cooperation in the BRICS Space.

II. Characteristics of Youth Exchanges in BRICS

With the continuous development and institutionalization of youth exchanges in BRICS, the objectives, methods, and topics of their exchanges have gradually been enriched. Youth exchanges in the BRICS have unique "BRICS" characteristics: First, the composition of the population of the BRICS is generally different from that of Western developed countries, with a relatively high proportion of youth. More than 60% of young people in the world live in the Asia-Pacific region, totaling up to approximately 750 million. In 2010, India alone had 234 million young people, accounting for 19% of its total population, and this proportion will continue to rise, while China has 225 million young people, accounting for 17% of its total population;[①] secondly, the BRICS are representatives of emerging market countries and developing countries who are the important participants and contributors to the international system, and thus their demands for reform and improvement of the current global governance system are relatively consistent. Therefore, the special composition of BRICS makes young people have different demands of interests.

1. Multiple Goals Carried

Firstly, protecting youth is the initial goal of youth exchanges in BRICS. From the outset of the establishment of the BRICS, the discussion of youth issues was based on the United Nations standard of the age group between 15 and 25. Therefore, young people were considered as completely disadvantaged

---

[①] Regional Overview: Youth in Asia and the Pacific. United Nations Youth. https://www.un.org/esa/socdev/documents/youth/fact-sheets/youth-regional-escap.pdf.

groups for discussion. Strengthening the protection of youth is one of many key areas of BRICS promotion of social development and social protection, which also conforms to the basic setting of the United Nations on youth issues.

Secondly, the establishment of the BRICS mechanism is to build a cross-regional economic cooperation and joint action mechanism. Therefore, promoting youth employment and development and making youths promote innovation and economic growth in BRICS become another goal of BRICS youth exchanges. Based on the different judging criteria for age characteristics, social status, and values in BRICS, they adopt respective youth age ranges that are different from those of the United Nations. For example, Brazil's youth policy targets people from 15 to 29 years old, while Russia's being 14 to 30 years old, India being 10 to 35 years old, China being 15 to 30 years old, and South Africa being 15 to 35 years old. Young people is an important linking group, and only when the young population is healthy, educated, and employed can the country realize the demographic dividend and promote innovation and economic growth.

Finally, youth issue is an important approach for BRICS to participate in global governance. 2014 was the year when the United Nations Sustainable Development Agenda was under formulating. At that time, the international community was assessing how to get rid of the global financial crisis and promote global economic growth and social development. As the main driving force for the steady growth of the world economy, BRICS are actively increasing the discussion of youth issues as well as the formulation of effective youth policies. On the one hand, it will contribute to the international community for achieving the Sustainable Development Goals. On the other hand, participating in the setting of the global agenda will help BRICS increase their voices when participating in global governance.

2. Platforms Ever Enriched

The BRICS utilize the multi-party participation of the state, educational institutions, enterprises and students to build a multi-field, multi-level, and multi-subject interactive platform in the development of youth exchanges. The main mechanisms for youth exchanges in BRICS are:

(1) BRICS Youth Summit. After its first summit was held in Kazan, Russia in 2015, it has become an important part of the BRICS Summit every year thereafter. The focus of the summit is to unite the young people of BRICS to expand cooperation among the BRICS countries in a number of areas, including the economy, politics, information, science, technology and humanitarian sphere.

(2) BRICS Young Diplomats Forum, which was firstly held in Moscow, Russia on October 29, 2015, aims to establish direct contact among young diplomats of BRICS and promote their recognition and understanding of the importance of cooperation among BRICS.

(3) The BRICS Young Scientist Forum, which includes a series of special forums on scientific and technological issues and their impact on society, covers sub-projects such as Youth Innovation and Entrepreneurship Competition, aiming to jointly promote scientific progress and contribute to innovative growth.

(4) BRICS Youth Energy Agency was established in 2015 according to the action plan of the first BRICS summit held in Kazan, with the purpose of enhancing youth's understanding and research on energy development and providing constructive suggestions for the energy transition of the BRICS. The agency regularly publishes the *BRICS Youth Energy Outlook*, holds the BRICS YEA summit, and establishes the BRICS YEA network.

In addition, the youth exchanges platforms among BRICS also include the BRICS International Youth Forum, the International BRICS Young Leaders Forum, and the Shanghai Summer School Fudan University BRICS program as well as a series of other activities. In 2020, in Russia was held events such as the BRICS International school and the Contest for BRICS Young Leaders as supporting projects of the BRICS Summit.

3. Guided Proactively by Government

With the formation of the three major cooperation pillars of BRICS, that are, political security, economics and finance, and people-to-people exchanges, the scope of people-to-people exchanges and cooperation has gradually expanded, and youth exchanges, as a part of people-to-people exchanges, have also been gradually institutionalized. At present, the specific forms and themes of the BRICS youth exchanges are implemented based on the "action plan" of previous summits. The major methods include: one is to hold youth dialogue forums and conferences in various fields during the BRICS summit, and the other is to use cooperation in the field of higher education to increase mutual visits and exchanges among students. Therefore, the BRICS youth exchange fully reflects the countries' top-level design and strategic planning for the BRICS youth exchange.

Ⅲ. Challenges and Responses

In recent years, considerable results have been achieved in the field of BRICS youth exchanges. Through exchanges and cooperation, young people from various countries have deepened their understanding of each other, and the public foundation for BRICS cooperation have truly been laid. The future of BRICS cooperation lies with the younger generation. A series of in-depth exchanges and cooperation have a profound impact on the younger generation of BRICS, which has improved the young people's understanding and support of the BRICS mechanism and encouraged them to think about and make suggestions in related fields. It also has played an important role in promoting the practical cooperation and long-term development of BRICS.

However, at the same time, youth exchanges in BRICS are also encountering many challenges, which need countries to make timely adjustments to the difficulties in the exchanges so as to further promote their exchanges and cooperation. The main challenges are as follows:

1. Different Countries Have Different Focus on Youth Policies

Although BRICS are representatives of emerging economies and developing countries, they belong to different regions, and thus their countries' political and economic development models, population proportions, and social security systems vary a lot from each other. Therefore, the focus of youth policies in every country is also very different. For example, in its National Youth Policy - 2014 [1], India plans an overall vision for Indian youth, that is, "to empower the youth of the country to achieve their full potential, and through them enable India to find its rightful place in community of nations". Therefore, the Indian Youth Policy focuses on strengthening young people's skills and empowering and enhancing their participation in governance; China has pay much attention to the youth education, protection innovation in its national youth policy[2]; Russia focuses on the socialization of its youth, emphasizes youth services in country's public institutions and shapes the important role of youth in national development and social transformation[3]; due to the intensification of crime and violence in Brazil, youth policies there focus on promoting youth's social integration through education, career development and digital inclusion, and fostering a culture of peace[4]; because of the high unemployment rate in South Africa, the

---

[1] National Youth Policy - 2014. Ministry of Youth Affairs and Sports Government of India, Dec 2014. http://yas.nic.in/sites/default/files/National - Youth - Policy - Document.pdf.

[2] The Medium and Long Term Plans for Youth Development (2016 - 2025), issued by Central Committee of CPC and State Council on April 13th, 2017, http://www.gov.cn/zhengce/2017 - 04/13/content_5185555.htm#1.

[3] Основы государственной молодежной политики Российской Федерации на период 2025 года. Правительство Российской Федерации. Москва: 29 ноя 2014. №2403 - p. http://static.government.ru/media/files/ceFXleNUqOU.pdf.

[4] Guia das políticas públicas de juventude / Secretaria Nacional de Juventude.. Brasília : SNJ, 2010. p. 24. https://www.youthpolicy.org/national/Brazil_2010_National_Youth_Policy.pdf. Last visit on September 10th, 2020.

issue of labor and employment has always been its focus[①]. As early as 2013, South African President at that time, Jacob Zuma, pointed out that promoting youth employment and development was the focus of South Africa's participation in the BRICS cooperation.

The differences in the youth policies of various countries will inevitably increase the difficulty of setting the agenda for youth exchanges in BRICS. Some initiatives proposed can hardly receive positive responses from other BRICS. For example, at the Fifth BRICS Summit, in order to solve the problem of youth unemployment, South Africa proposed to set up a BRICS Youth Fund to encourage and support youth entrepreneurship. Unfortunately, this initiative has not yet been realized.

2. Insufficient Representativeness of Youth

The current youth exchanges among BRICS are mainly carried out under the overall framework of the BRICS Summit. All youth representatives are selected by the respective government agencies of the BRICS. Those who can participate in the BRICS Youth Summit or Dialogue Forum are some outstanding college students, young entrepreneurs and young scholars. In other words, those who participate in the BRICS youth exchanges are the elite representatives of every country. For example, there were only 8 people in the Chinese delegations to participate in the BRICS Youth Summit in 2018, which was held in South Africa[②]. Some people criticized the BRICS youth activities that "participants just wear business casual attires" and "it emphasizes too much on formality lacking substantive content", and they pointed out "The language spoken by the youth representatives of the BRICS is different from that of young people... their discussions

---

[①] National Youth Policy 2015 - 2020. The presidency republic of South Africa. https: //www. gov. za/sites/default/files/gcis_document/201610/nationalyouthpolicy. pdf.

[②] Xinhuanet: "Eight Chinese Youth Representatives Participated in the 2018 BRICS Youth Summit in South Africa". July 24, 2018, http: //www. xinhuanet. com/gongyi/2018 - 07/24/c_129919660. htm. Last visit on September 14, 2020.

only reflect the priorities of the government, never the priorities of the youth."[①] This means that if youth policies are constrained to the official and academic levels, only a small number of youth groups will benefit, which will still be difficult to obtain the support of young people from various countries for the BRICS.

3. Lack of Consolidation of Activities' Effect

When the BRICS summit is held annually, activities for the youth of the BRICS are also held as scheduled. However, most activities have relatively weaker sustainability. The main mode of communication is youth forums in various fields. In addition, there may be some short-term cultural experience activities, which are often held on a grand and spectacular scale but once the BRICS summit ends, the communication among the youths cannot be found anymore, resulting the failure to reaching the desired effect of building "people-to-people bond". Therefore, a long-term mechanism must be established to effectively consolidate the results of exchanges.

Although various challenges still exist in youth exchanges in BRICS, youth is undoubtedly the main force in people-to-people exchanges. They are not only the most direct beneficiary of BRICS education cooperation, but also important participants in the culture, science, technology, health, sports and tourism of BRICS. On June 9, 2018, the 2018 BRICS Think-tank International Symposium and 21st Wanshou Forum were held in Chongqing. Hosted by the China Council for BRICS Think-tank Cooperation and undertaken by Sichuan International Studies University, the forum is themed with "BRICS People-to-People Exchanges: Government's Leading Role and People-to-people Interaction". Many of these measures to promote cultural exchanges are related to young people. For example, Jiang Shixue, a researcher from the Institute of European Studies of the Chi-

---

① Brics Youth: Everything about us without us? https: //mg. co. za/article/2018 - 06 - 21 - 00 - brics-youth-everything-about-us-without-us/. Last visit on September 15th, 2020.

nese Academy of Social Sciences and a distinguished professor of Shanghai University, proposed "BRICS universities should set up BRICS scholarships to specifically fund young students in BRICS". Huo Weidong, president of Beijing Geely University, suggested that "BRICS college student art exhibitions, scientific and technological competitions, sports competitions innovation and entrepreneurship competitions should be carried out." Hou Xiaochen, project director of the Center for BRICS Studies of Fudan University, proposed to "establish the BRICS course to help young students learn more about BRICS and global governance" and so on[1]. In short, youth is a group distinguished by age, so it overlaps with various fields of humanities exchange.

The promotion of youth exchanges in BRICS requires improvements in the following aspects:

First, it is to continue to attach importance to youth exchanges in BRICS, which is an important approach to realize the "people-to-people bond" in BRICS. The development of youth is basically in line with the development of BRICS. They are an important force to promote the development of the country, and sooner or later will become the midstream of social development. Only by recklessly deepening youth cooperation in various fields and enabling more young people to participate in and benefit from it, can achieve the recognition and support of the BRICS from the majority of young people.

Second, it is to strengthen cooperation with civil society forces. In addition to be guided by government, BRICS youth exchanges must also deepen people-to-people cooperation. At present, many youth organizations of BRICS play the role of cohering and connecting young people[2]. The BRICS should set up corresponding institutions to develop contacts and cooperation with youth organiza-

---

[1] Wu Peibin: The People-to-People Exchanges of BRICS Build Bridges Among the People in This Five Countries: A Summary of 2018 BRICS Think-tank International Symposium and 21st Wanshou Forum, issued on July 17th, 2018, http://world.people.com.cn/nl/2018/0717/c187656-30152590.html.

[2] Gong Aiguo, XU Yanling. "Path of Youth Organizations in BRICS to Contact and Unite Youth". *China Youth Study*. Issue 3, 2014. pp. 115 - 119.

tions in various countries and create more platforms for in-depth understanding, assistance and guidance to youth.

Third, it is to expand the forms of communication. Nowadays, the Internet plays an increasingly important role in the daily lives of young people. Traditional offline forums and summit not only increase the cost of activities, but are also not conducive to spreading BRICS activities among young people. Therefore, it is necessary to open public accounts in the software commonly used by young people in the BRICS, increase new media's spreading of BRICS' information, and actively construct the common concept of BRICS. Only by doing so can help deepen young people's identity with BRICS.

Current Status and Challenges of Public Health Cooperation among the BRICS

Pu Gongying[*] Cai Jiafei et al.[**]

Abstract: The total population of the BRICS accounts for 42% of the world's population. Public health cooperation among the BRICS is a guarantee for the lives and health of the people of the BRICS, and it is also a scientific answer to the ongoing globalization. In recent years, the cooperation of the BRICS as to public health has developed and expanded its fields, and has made certain achievements in combating communicable and non-communicable diseases. During the critical period of the global fight against the COVID-19 epidemic, the BRICS, as representatives of emerging market countries and developing countries, actively cooperate in the field of public health. With an effort to take the initiative to assume responsibility for global health governance, new ways of health public cooperation have been explored among the BRICS such as high-level network meetings, vaccine R&D cooperation, and loans provided by the

---

[*] Pu Gongying, Phd. Associate Professor, Russian Department of Sichuan International Studies University.
[**] Cai Jiafei, Wu Yawen, Huang Yue, Luo Dan and Xu Hanrui, Students of Russian Department of Sichuan International Studies University.

New Development Bank, etc. In the future, BRICS public health cooperation will face much more challenges due to the emergence of public health incidents and the series of inherent problems among the BRICS.

Keywords: the BRICS; Public Health; Coronavirus Epidemic (COVID-19)

Ⅰ. Current Status of Public Health Cooperation between the BRICS

Public health is an important field of cooperation for the BRICS. In recent years, the BRICS have flourished in the development of cooperation in the field of public health, and they have gradually cultivated their own characteristics.

1. BRICS Continue to Expand and Deepen Public Health Cooperation

Since 2011, the BRICS have held 9 Health Ministers meetings. In order to closely meet the common needs of "improving the level of public health and the health care system" within the framework of medical and health cooperation, the BRICS are discussing new topics in the field of public health each year, such as disease prevention and control, drug development and accessibility, vaccine development and technology transfer, etc. Meanwhile, the possibility of cooperation in wider range of fields has witnessed a constant increase. (Table 4-1)

The BRICS have deepened cooperation in the field of public health. Take tuberculosis as an example. The BRICS account for 40% of the global burden and mortality of tuberculosis, and account for at least 50% of cases in the global MDR and drug-resistant tuberculosis. In the past ten years, the prevention and control of tuberculosis has always been the key target of BRICS health cooperation. The BRICS have invested at least US $20 billion in tuberculosis control.[①]

[①] Global tuberculous report 2017, pp. 160, 162, 170, 186, 188. https://www.who.int/tb/publications/global_report/gtbr2017_main_text.pdf·ua=1.

In response to the formidable challenges of tuberculosis, the BRICS have gradually deepened their cooperation in this field and strived to make phased progress. In 2012, the BRICS proposed in the "Delhi Communiqué" that "resolved to collaborate and cooperate for development of capacity and infrastructure to reduce the prevalence and incidence of tuberculosis through innovation for new drugs/vaccines, diagnostics and promotion of consortia of tuberculosis researchers to collaborate on clinical trials of drugs and vaccines, strengthening access to affordable medicines and delivery of quality care." In 2014, at the 4th BRICS Health Ministers Meeting held in Brazil, the BRICS agreed to cooperate in tuberculosis research and innovation and strive to achieve technology sharing. Drug manufacturing capabilities and tuberculosis financing are key cooperation items. In December 2016, the Ministers of Health of the BRICS proposed "agreed to the setting up of a BRICS network on TB Research and creation of a research and development consortium on TB, HIV and Malaria including the possibility of international fund raising". In 2017, the BRIC countries stated in the "Xiamen Declaration" that they would establish a tuberculosis research network. As of August 2020, the BRICS have held 6 tuberculosis research network technical meetings.[①]

Table 4-1 Relevant Information of Previous BRICS Health Ministers Meetings

Time	Location	Announced Document	Fields of Cooperation
2011	Beijing	Beijing Declaration	Public health, health service, drug's accessibility, technology transfer, export of medical products, health protection technologies
2012	New Delhi	Delhi Communiqué	Non-communicable diseases, traditional medical science, drug research & development, technology transfer, telehealth

---

① BRICS TB Research network. http: //bricstb. samrc. ac. za/.

Continued Table

Time	Location	Announced Document	Fields of Cooperation
2013	Cape Town	Cape Town Communiqué	Health surveillance system, universal health coverage, communicable and non-communicable diseases, medical technology, drug development, health of pregnant women, women in delivery and children, bio-technological application and cooperation
2014	Brasilia	Brazilian Communiqué	Prevention and control of Ebola, TB, and Neglected Tropical Diseases (NTD), medicine's accessibility, drug resistance of antibiotics, chronic non-communicable diseases
2015	Moscow	Moscow Declaration	AIDS, NTD, surveillance of non-communicable diseases, tabaco control, universal health care
2016	New Delhi	Delhi Communique	Medical product development, challenges of communicable diseases, TB research network, health surveillance, drug resistance of antimicrobial drugs, drug availability, child and women's health, mental illnesses
2017	Tianjin	Tianjin Communique	Traditional medicine, R&D of medical products, reduction of maternal and newborn mortality, disease surveillance, and access to health services
2018	Durban	Durban Declaration	Universal health coverage, medical technology, strengthening of medical system, drug's accessibility, vaccine R&D and cooperation, drug resistance of antimicrobial drugs, non-communicable diseases, tabaco control
2019	Curitiba	Declaration of Curitiba	Primary health care (PHC), progressive reduction in the maternal mortality, neo-natal mortality, infant mortality, vaccination, regulation of medical products, technology transfer, BRICS TB research network, non-communicable diseases, rare diseases, telehealth, digital health

Source: http://brics.utoronto.ca/docs/index.html#health.

2. Strengthened Development of Work Division in Public Health Collaboration of the BRICS

In the early stage of health cooperation, the BRIC countries began to adopt a system of division of work in the field of public health. During the 66th World Health Assembly (WHA) of the World Health Organization in 2013, the BRIC countries emphasized the need to commit to five areas of thematic cooperation: India will strengthen cooperation in the construction of health surveillance systems; South Africa is mainly responsible for reducing the risk factors of non-communicable diseases as well as its prevention, health promotion, and universal health coverage; Brazil utilizes its advantages to focus on strategic health technologies for communicable diseases; Russia fosters research on medical technology, and China puts an emphasis on drug research and development.① The clear division of work and concerted efforts of the five countries have improved the effectiveness of cooperation, and undoubtedly enhanced the exchange and sharing of experience.

In addition, taking the advantages as a hosting leader, the system of rotating presidency of the BRICS allows the five countries to better consider the needs of national development in the setting of the agenda, and to maximize their respective advantages. In September 2016, BRICS wellness workshop themed "BRIC's Cooperation in the Area of Traditional Medicine" was held in Bengaluru, India. Under the framework of the seminar, the Arroyyan Expo functioned to provide a platform for the exchange of a large number of traditional medicines and communication between raw material manufacturers and importers, which are conducive to the other four countries to approach Indian traditional medicine products and manufacturing facilities. In 2017, the "promotion of traditional Chinese medicine" was listed on China's agenda of BRICS health cooperation.

---

① BRICS Nations to Establish Extensive Human Milk Bank Network. https: //www. who. int/bulletin/volumes/92/6/14 - 141051/zh/.

In July of the same year, the BRICS Health Ministers Meeting and the High-level Meeting on Traditional Medicine was held in Tianjin, China. The BRICS issued a joint statement on strengthening cooperation in traditional Chinese medicine. The statement called for the integration of traditional medicine in the national health care system and its importance as a valuable means to promote and encourage the practice, education and training of traditional medicine, therapies and medicines, which helps to encourage traditional medicine practitioners to systematically improve the quality of health care services and outreach service.[1] As a global breast milk bank leader, Brazil has 230 of the 550 breast milk banks in the world[2], which is considered the most effective breast milk bank system in the world. With such an advantage, Brazil has helped 32 countries in Latin America, Africa and Europe establish breast milk banks. The breast milk bank system of Brazil is gradually developing towards a global mode.[3] At the 2019 BRICS Brasília Summit, Brazil proposed the establishment of a BRICS breast milk bank network. The BRICS promised in the summit declaration that "mobilize efforts, within the framework of the international technical cooperation of our countries, for the creation of the BRICS Network of Human Milk Bank in order to expand sharing of knowledge and Technologies focused on food and nutritional security in neonatal and nursing infant care, with the right to health as its central value."[4] It can be seen that on the basis of establishing an agreed health cooperation agenda, the BRICS innovate topics for cooperation according to their respective situations and advantages, so as to broaden the scope and depth of cooperation, and effectively enrich the BRICS public health coopera-

---

[1] Tianjin Communique of BRICS Health Ministers Meeting. http://en.nhc.gov.cn/2017-07/17/c_71977.htm.

[2] The Surprisingly Simple Way To Save Babies' Lives. https://storytracker.solutionsjournalism.org/stories/the-surprisingly-simple-way-to-save-babies-lives.

[3] BRICS Nations to Establish Extensive Human Milk Bank Network. https://eurasiantimes.com/brics-nations-to-establish-human-milk-bank-network/.

[4] Declaration of thr First BRICS Meeting on Human Milk Bank. http://brics2019.itamaraty.gov.br/images/documentos/Declaration_of_thr_First_BRICS_Meeting_on_Human_Milk_Bank.pdf.

tion.

II. Public Health Cooperation among BRICS under the COVID-19 Epidemic

Commonly inflicted upon dense population distribution and underdeveloped medical and health systems, the BRICS are facing a high risk of the outbreaks of communicable diseases. The current outbreak of the coronavirus (COVID-19) epidemic around the world has brought severe challenges to the BRICS response mechanism for public health emergencies.

Among the BRICS, China's prevention and control of the coronavirus disease has achieved good results, but Russia, Brazil, South Africa and India are still enshrouded by the shadow of the epidemic. As of September 14 2020, the number of confirmed cases of coronavirus disease in India has reached more than 5 million and Brazil has more than 4 million. This figure goes up to more than 1 million in Russia and more than 650,000 in South Africa, and China has confirmed more than 80,000 people.[1] Being the first country to detect coronavirus, China has given full play to its own institutional advantages to mobilize people around the country to support the hardest-hit areas of the epidemic, and adopted effective measures such as lockdown and quarantine, which has contributed to the phased success in handling the epidemic. Currently, China has been actively engaging in foreign aid by sharing its experience in combating this global epidemic. As to Russia, early preparation work for epidemic prevention and control included the establishment of the epidemic prevention and control headquarter, communication center and other institutions at the end of January 2020, and effective measures were also taken to prevent and control imported cases from China. However, the number of confirmed cases witnesses a dramatic

[1] Worldometer. https://www.worldometers.info/

surge due to various negative factors like the influx of large numbers of European cases in the middle of the epidemic, slack law enforcement and low public cooperation, which led to a worrying situation for Russia. South Africa established a national command committee in mid-March 2020 and implemented a travel ban. In the early stages of the epidemic, the military was used to assist the police in maintaining public security. However, since May 2020, the anti-epidemic lockdown restriction has been gradually relaxed in stages, leading to a sharp rebound of cases. Brazil is a major country stricken by the epidemic in South America, and it is also suffering from its struggling dilemma against epidemic combating. On the one hand, President Bolsonaro has a negative attitude towards the prevention and control of the epidemic. On the other hand, the fact that more than 5.1 million Brazilians living in slums with unfavorable living conditions is also a huge pressure for the work of prevention and control of the epidemic. The situation in India, which is also struck in the dilemma of managing its people in slums during the prevention and control stage of fighting the epidemic, is far from being optimistic. The Indian government began to "lock down the country" since March 2020, and adjusted its regulations to relax and gradually unlock the country in May considering the economic development of the country. As to many local cities, policies and regulations for prevention and control of the disease keep constantly changing between lockdown and relaxation.

The trial of the epidemic is regarded as a solemn challenge against mechanism of coping with public health incidents for the BRICS. In this sense, Minister of Foreign Affairs of the BRICS propose to highlight the cooperation in the field of public health at the video conference of BRICS combating COVID-19 in April. 2020[①] To jointly combat COVID-19, the BRICS can work together in the field of public health cooperation as below:

[①] Statement by Wang Yi at the Extraordinary Meeting of BRICS Ministers of Foreign Affairs, http: //www. chinanews. com/gn/2020/04 - 28/9170943. shtml Log-in time: Sep. 14, 2020.

1. BRICS Summit: New Voice for Collaboration in Combating COVID-19

On April 28, 2020, in order to mobilize joint efforts to combat COVID-19, the BRICS held an extraordinary meeting of BRICS Ministers of Foreign Affairs in discussion with the coronavirus. The agenda of meeting focused on the impact of the coronavirus disease and the response measures of the BRICS. At this meeting, the five foreign ministers had an in-depth exchange of views on issues such as adhering to multilateralism, joining hands to fight the epidemic and deepening BRICS cooperation. It is stated that the BRICS must stand firm by multilateralism, uphold unity and coordination, and step up the sharing of information and experience with BRICS. Moreover, conduct joint research and development of drugs and vaccines which enables a more effective response against the virus in order to maintain world public health security and work hard to mitigate the negative impact of the epidemic. Most BRICS members condemned the politicization and stigmatization of the epidemic and opposed the undercut of the role of the WHO. They believed that discrediting the WHO or even cutting off its funding would seriously undermine the cooperation and effort of the international community to respond to the epidemic, especially to help African countries to fight the epidemic. To sum up, all parties should firmly support the WHO and other UN agencies to play a leading role in global anti-epidemic cooperation.[1]

In order to further discuss cooperation between the BRICS to counter the outbreak of the COVID-19, the Meeting of the BRICS Health Senior Officials under the Russian BRICS chairmanship was held via video conference on May 7, 2020. The conference summarized the major achievements of the five countries in combating COVID-19. Among the central topics of discussion were providing mutual support in activities to prevent and treat the novel coronavirus infection

---

[1] Statement by Wang Yi at the Extraordinary Meeting of BRICS Ministers of Foreign Affairs, http: //www. gov. cn/guowuyuan/2020 - 04/29/content_5507226. htm Log-in time: Sep. 14, 2020.

as well as searching for effective methods of creating a favorable environment for the provision of medicines, diagnostic tools, immunobiological drugs and medical equipment. In addition, the proposal of the Russian Side on the need to set up a comprehensive early warning system for the risks of biological threats within BRICS was agreed as a consensus. The partners also welcomed the proposal of the Russian Side to compile an overview of the advanced measures taken by BRICS to counter the spread of COVID-19 for further use not only by the five countries, but also by specialists from other countries. The New Development Bank will play the role of financing these joint projects. Representatives of the BRICS reached a consensus on the call for concerted action in the field of communicable disease prevention and treatment. "We must strengthen our cooperation in developing inexpensive and sustainable methods for testing infectious diseases, address the issue of vaccination and conduct global research in the field of treatments," Deputy Minister Oleg Gridnev pointed out in his opening remarks.[①]

2. New Development Bank (NDB): New Guarantee for Cooperation in Combating COVID-19

The BRICS New Development Bank (NDB) was established in 2015 to finance the construction of infrastructure and sustainable development projects in BRICS as well as other emerging economies and developing countries. The declaration of the Ninth BRICS Health Ministers Meeting in 2019 stated that the BRICS "agree to explore the feasibility of the New Development Bank to support the financing of health projects to ensure the health and well-being of the people." The outbreak of the coronavirus epidemic in 2020 has become a real driving force for the implementation of this consensus.

---

① Минздрав России провел встречу старших должностных лиц стран БРИКС по вопросам здравоохранения. https: //brics-russia2020. ru/news/20200508/395195/Minzdrav-Rossii-provel-vstrechu-v-formate-videokonferentsii-starshikh-dolzhnostnykh-lits-stran-BRIKS-po. html Log-in time: Sep. 14, 2020.

On April 22, 2020, the NDB Board of Directors issued a statement on the response to the COVID-19, stating, "We welcome the New Development Bank to establish an emergency assistance fund to meet the urgent needs of member countries." Since the outbreak of the COVID-19, the NDB actively supports countries in responding to the epidemic by issuing loans and bonds.

Since March, the NDB has issued approximately US $1 billion in emergency assistance loans to China, India, South Africa, and Brazil (Table 4-2) to support countries in fighting against COVID-19. The rapid response of the NDB has reduced the social and economic losses of the BRICS to a certain extent and mitigated the negative impact of the epidemic on the BRICS.

Table 4-2 The New Development Bank's Loan Disbursement to the BRICS since the Outbreak of the Coronavirus Epidemic
(Statistics collected till August 2020)

Time	Received Country	Loan
2020. 3	China	RMB7 bn (approx. USD 1 bn)
2020. 5	India	USD1 bn
2020. 6	South Africa	USD1 bn
2020. 7	Brazil	USD1 bn

Source: https://www.ndb.int/.

In addition to issuing emergency assistance loans, the NDB also helped the BRICS fight the epidemic by issuing bonds. On April 2 2020, the New Development Bank issued RMB 5 billion worth of bonds to fight COVID-19 among the Chinese inter-bank bond market to help the Chinese government fight the epidemic. The funds raised are available for the emergency assistance loan projects in the fight against the epidemic in China, specifically as a financial support for emergency public health expenditures under the epidemic. Hubei, Guangdong, and Henan, which are the three Chinese provinces that are hit the hardest by the outbreak of COVID-19, will be especially financed.[1]

On September 4, 2020, Wang Yi pointed out at the BRICS Foreign Ministers' Meeting: "As the NDB is a representative project of BRICS economic cooperation, it has played a positive role in the economic and social development of the five countries and has become a useful supplement to the international financial framework. We should strive to achieve substantive progress before this year's leaders' meeting, expand the international influence of the bank, and enhance the voice of BRICS' global financial governance."[2] At present, the NDB has assumed its important responsibility of jointly fighting the epidemic in the field of public health cooperation. Meanwhile, it has also expanded its service. In the future, the NDB is expected to increase the special loan for anti-epidemic to US $10 billion.[3] The NDB will continue to provide support to the BRICS and other developing countries in the field of building and improving public health prevention and control as well as emergency response capabilities, and continue to contribute to the BRICS public health cooperation.

3. Collaboration of Medical Technologies: A New Way of Anti-epidemic Cooperation

Since the sudden outbreak of the coronavirus, the BRICS has put forward the crucial task of medical and health technology cooperation, that is, to carry out technical research and development projects within the framework of the BRICS, promote the research, development and production of vaccines, and contribute to well-being of humankind.

---

[1] NDB Issuing Bonds to Support China to Combat COVID-19, http: //www. xinhuanet. com/politics/2020 - 04/03/c_1125811913. htm.

[2] Statement of the State Councilor and Foreign Minister Wang Yi at the BRICS Ministers of Foreign Affairs Video Conference (full text), http: //new. fmprc. gov. cn/web/wjbzhd/t1812434. shtml.

[3] Meeting of BRICS Ministers of Foreign Affairs/International Relations. http: //www. brics. utoronto. ca/docs/190926 - foreign. html.

In the context of the prevalence of the epidemic, the science and technology departments of the BRICS jointly organized the selection of cooperative research projects for the Science and Technology Innovation Framework Program. This event is helpful for the promotion of technical exchanges and research cooperation among BRICS in a wider range of fields in order to find better solutions to global challenges. Themes for the project collection center around research and development of new technologies and equipment for COVID-19 diagnosis, research and development of available drugs, SARS-CoV-2 gene sequencing and epidemiology and mathematical model research of the COVID-19 virus, development of COVID-19 drugs and vaccines oriented by artificial intelligence and communication technology and the assessment of SARS-CoV-2 and its comorbidities in order to conduct epidemiological research and clinical trials.[1]

In addition, the outbreak of the COVID-19 has strengthened the determination of the BRICS to jointly establish a vaccine research and development center. As early as the 2015 BRICS Summit, the BRICS proposed in the Ufa Declaration about the task of establishing a joint vaccine development and employment mechanism. The 2018 BRICS Summit in Johannesburg focused more specifically on this task and initiated the establishment of a BRICS vaccine research and development center for the first time.[2] After the outbreak of COVID-19, at the special foreign ministers meeting of the BRICS in response to the coronavirus epidemic in April, the foreign ministers of China and Russia stated that the BRICS should expedite the implementation of this initiative and carry out drug

---

[1] BRICS STI Framework Programme Response to COVID-19 epidemic coordinated call for BRICS multilateral projects 2020. http: //brics-sti. org/files/BRICS_STI_Framework_Programme_Call_2020. pdf.

[2] Zhang Qingmin. COVID-19 Tests Global Health Governance. Northeast Asia Forum, 2020 (4): 57.

and vaccine research and development cooperation.[①] Minister of Foreign Affairs Wang Yi stated at the meeting of BRICS Ministers of Foreign Affairs in September that "now that BRICS countries have their respective advantages in different perspectives of vaccine such as research and development and production, the key is to make joint contributions to vaccine affordability and accessibility in developing countries and press ahead with the BRICS vaccine R&D center and information sharing. The lead in establishing a virtual research and development center can be taken into consideration, which helps to pave the way for further actions such as joint research and development, joint overseas phase III clinical trials, authorized production and mutual certification of vaccine standards, etc. Most importantly, the collaboration of COVID-19 vaccine development is a valuable opportunity to promote the communications and exchanges between drug regulatory and R&D institutions among the BRICS."[②]

4. Media and People-to-people Exchanges: A New Kind of Anti-epidemic Cooperation

As the general prevalence of COVID-19 epidemic has changed the way of communication between people, the BRICS have adopted a flexible way in encouraging cultural exchanges. By focusing on information exchanges online, experience of fighting the disease and recent updates about disease are constantly shared among the BRICS, which is regarded as an important message for the people of the BRICS to jointly overcome the epidemic.

As news media is a major tool for people-to-people exchanges and information promotion, the BRICS and the "United Television Channel of BRICS"

---

① Statement by Wang Yi at the Extraordinary Meeting of BRICS Ministers of Foreign Affairs, https: //www. fmprc. gov. cn/web/ziliao_674904/zt_674979/dnzt_674981/qtzt/kjgzbdfyyq_699171/t1774233. shtml.

② Statement of the State Councilor and Foreign Minister Wang Yi at the BRICS Ministers of Foreign Affairs Video Conference (full text), http: //www. chinanews. com/m/gn/2020/09-05/9283146. shtml.

(TV BRICS) have jointly launched the program of "Special Information Exchange Channel of COVID-19 Combating of the TV BRICS International Media Network". TV BRICS was proposed to be established during the BRICS Xiamen Summit in 2017, and currently broadcasts in five languages of the BRICS to provide quick access to information for the people of the BRICS. The "Special Information Exchange Channel of COVID-19 Combating of the TV BRICS International Media Network" reports the latest news about the BRICS fighting COVID-19 during the epidemic, including quarantine, prevention measures and diagnosis methods, and shares the stories of ordinary people in the BRICS combating the virus.①

As to people-to-people exchanges, an online seminar with the theme of "The Global Scenario of COVID-19: BRICS and Other Countries" was held by young people from BRICS. Jointly organized by BRICS Research Committee and BRICS Russia Expert Committee, the conference mainly discussed topics around "What are the social, economic and political impacts of the COVID-19 pandemic in your country?", "What is the role for BRICS in the changing reality?", and "What can the youth do to help?".②

Chinese Foreign Minister Wang Yi stated at the BRICS Foreign Ministers' Meeting on September 4 2020, "People matters most as to BRICS cooperation. Under the special situation of the epidemic, we must continue to try every means to promote cultural exchanges in a flexible manner." In this sense, media cooperation and people-to-people exchanges among the BRIC countries have worked to effectively promote the information exchange of epidemic prevention among the people of the BRICS, and further deepen the understanding of different groups in the BRICS in fighting the epidemic together.

---

① Международная сеть TVBRICS запустила информационный обмен материалами о борьбе с COVID-19. https://news.rambler.ru/other/44093704-mezhdunarodnaya-set-tvbrics-zapustila-informatsionnyy-obmen-materialami-o-borbe-s-covid-19/ Log-in time: Sep. 14, 2020.

② International youth webinar "The Scenario of COVID-19 across the Globe: BRICS and beyond". http://www.nkibrics.ru/posts/show/5ee8d9466272695143170000 Log-in time: Sep. 14, 2020.

Ⅲ. Problems and Challenges in Public Health Cooperation between the BRICS

At present, especially in the context of the prevalence of COVID-19, there are still many possibilities for improvement in the field of public health cooperation between the BRICS. The following problems and challenges as to the public health cooperation of the BRICS deserve our attention.

1. Inequity of Basic Conditions of the BRICS

Although the BRIC countries are all emerging market countries with many common features, as reflected in public health, there are relatively large differences in the level of pharmaceutical industry and burden of disease among the member states.

As is known, the development level of a country's pharmaceutical industry can be judged by its competitiveness in the international pharmaceutical market to a certain extent. According to the competitiveness index of BRIC countries' pharmaceutical trade from 2013 to 2017, only India's competitiveness index has always been positive and maintained at around 0.75 during these five years, while the pharmaceutical trade competitiveness index of the other four countries is all negative each year. This shows that only India has a relatively competitive advantage in international pharmaceutical trade among the BRIC countries currently. The other four countries have their respective advantage products in their pharmaceutical industry (such as China's raw medicine, etc.)① with different degree of competitiveness and priority of directions of developing pharmaceutical products, which is unfortunately difficult to forge a joint force.

The BRICS have certain commonalities in the burden of high-incidence dis-

---

① Liu Xiaohui. Analysis of Competitiveness of Pharmaceutical Trade of the BRICS, Economic & Trade Update. 2018 (25): 37.

eases, but the differences among countries with regional features cannot be ignored. Main diseases affecting China, Russia and Brazil are non-communicable diseases such as tumors, chronic respiratory diseases, and cardiovascular diseases; while those affecting South Africa and India are mainly communicable diseases such as AIDS and tuberculosis. In India and China, chronic respiratory infection is one of the main factors for fatality. In Brazil, however, more than 1929 deaths per 100,000 people were due to mental illnesses in 2017, which is 1. 18 - 1. 22 times that of the BRICS. Russia, which goes differently, is being gradually perplexed by cardiovascular diseases which is affecting the health of more and more people and it is becoming one of the most prominent major diseases in addition to tumors. In 2017, the number of deaths from cardiovascular diseases in Russia was 2. 2 - 4. 9 times that of other BRICS and 2. 9 times the world average; the number of deaths from chronic respiratory diseases in India is 3. 52 times that of Russia; South Africa is stricken by the prevalence of AIDS transmission, and the number of deaths due to AIDS far exceeds that of other BRICS by nearly a hundred times[①] (Picture 4 -1).

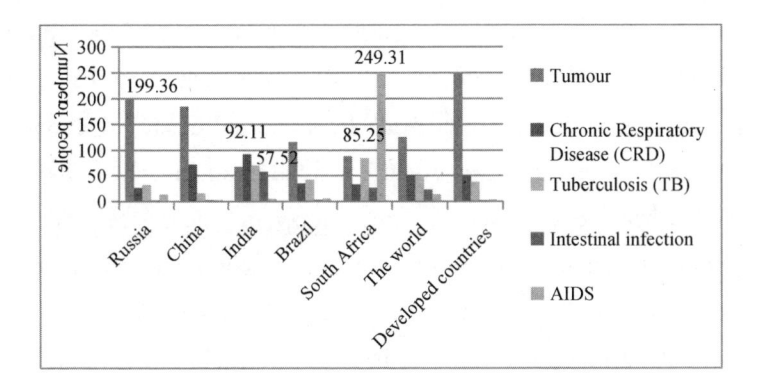

Picture 4-1 Comparison of the Number of Deaths Due to Various Diseases Per 100, 000 People in BRICS, Developed Countries, and the World in 2017
Source: GBD Viz Hub.

---

① GBD Viz Hub. https: //vizhub. healthdata. org/gbd-compare/.

The imbalance of medical development and the differences in the burden of high-incidence diseases of the BRICS have made it difficult for the BRICS to reach a consensus on the priority of public health cooperation. By now, working together to fight against the COVID-19 has been prioritized to be a major task of public health for the BRICS due to its abrupt and invasive prevalence. In the future, the BRICS as a whole will be confronted with more topics to work through, such as the best way to deal with internal differences among itself and how to realize overall development and common progress of the BRICS in the field of public health cooperation.

2. Discordant Disruption in Bilateral Public Health Cooperation among the BRICS

It is acknowledged that the deepening of the BRICS public health cooperation is a general trend in the interests of the BRICS. However, the negative effects of internal discordance and bilateral dispute in the process of fighting against the epidemic counter the effort of the BRICS in the field of public health cooperation.

Bilateral cooperation within the BRICS in the context of the epidemic is regarded undoubtedly as an important effort to realize united combat against the epidemic. The stigmatized remarks made by some politicians of certain countries, however, has not only adversely affected the development of bilateral relations, but also become an obstacle to the cooperation under the epidemic. For example, some Brazilian congressmen made an inappropriate remark on social media, suspecting that "China deliberately concealed the epidemic, which has a negative effect on the global fight against the epidemic." This remark quickly caused an uproar in all walks of life in Brazil. In response to this, the Embassy of China in Brazil also issued a statement stating that the congressman's "words caused harmful influences, seen as a serious insult to Chinese national dignity, and not only hurt the sentiment of 1.4 billion Chinese, but also damage Brazil's good image in the hearts of the Chinese people. They also generate unnecessary interference in our substantial cooperation."① On April 27, 2020, the Indian Council of Medical Research, after conducting a field test on the rapid antibody test kits imported from China, expressed dissatisfaction with the test results and requested all states to stop using these reagents and ask for refund. In view of this incident, Counselor Ji Rong, the spokesperson of the Chinese Embassy in India, commented, "China not only sincerely supports India in its fight against COVID-19, but also takes concrete actions to help. The quality of medical products exported from China is prioritized. It is unfair and irresponsible for certain individuals to label Chinese products as 'faulty' and look at issues with preemptive prejudice. Regarding the current issue occurred, we hope the Indian side could respect China's goodwill and sincerity, strengthen communication timely with relevant Chinese companies based on facts, and resolve it reasonably and properly."②

As the Chinese Ambassador to India Sun Weidong said, "Viruses respect no borders, and epidemics do not distinguish between races. They are common enemy of mankind. We are all in the same boat. Only by working together can we win this battle. In a crisis like this, complaining, finger-pointing or scapegoating is not the way to get countries to stay focused on their battle against the virus. Such moves will very likely divide the international community, lead to prejudice against specific ethnic groups and ultimately hurt the shared interests of the world. We advocate to reject ideological biases and attempts at labeling the virus, politicizing the response and stigmatizing any specific country." As the BRICS countries are facing the challenge of preventing and controlling the epidemic together with other countries in the world, it is critically significant to properly handle the problems encountered in bilateral cooperation and exchanges and maintain good bilateral relations. Only by achieving this goal can the public health cooperation of the BRICS be further strengthened.

---

① http://br.china-embassy.org/chn/gdxw/t1758511.htm.
② https://www.fmprc.gov.cn/ce/cein/chn/sgxw/t1773984.htm.

3. Imbalance in the Implementation of Public Health Cooperation

At present, there is a dire need to expect a more advanced improvement as to the institutionalization for the public health cooperation among the BRICS, and the general insufficiency in terms of the implementation of cooperative initiatives also calls for improvement. To be specific, the common goals for the development of health cooperation have not yet been designated among the BRICS except for the establishment of cooperation in the five thematic fields as proposed in 2013. What is more, there is a lack of a clear definition of the rights, duties and benefits of each member.[①]

Larionova, director of the Institute of International Organizations and Cooperation of the Russian National Research University Higher School of Economics, and some scholars quantified the process of BRICS participation in global governance into five steps, namely: meeting discussion, determining the course of action, passing resolutions, implementing resolutions, and global governance has made progress. By adopting a quantitative and qualitative method to analyze the BRICS documents in the field of health from 2008 to 2014, it is found that the proportion of discussions about "passing resolutions" continues to increase while the "global governance has made progress" is gradually shrinking, and discussions on the "implementing resolutions" that are truly put into action have actually decreased year by year.[②]

After experiencing pandemic such as Ebola virus in 2014 and Zika virus in 2016, the BRICS Health Ministers Meeting and High-level Meeting on Traditional Medicine held in July 2017 proposed "jointly strengthen education and training of traditional medicine; give full play to the clinical advantages of traditional medicine; jointly regulate the production of traditional medicine products;

[①] Construction of Cultural and People-to-people Exchange Mechanism in BRICS: Roles, Challenges and Strategies, http: //theory. people. com. cn/n1/2018/0823/c40531 - 30246463. html.

[②] М. В. Ларионова, М. Р. Рахмангулов, А. В. Шелепов, А. Г. Сахаров Формирование повестки дня БРИКС в сфере здравоохранения//Вестник международных организаций, 2014, №4.

scientifically explore and innovate traditional medicine; and promote exchanges between traditional medicine practitioners." However, the BRICS have not yet established effective mechanism for cooperation in terms of traditional medicine education and training and practitioner exchanges.

It can be seen that although the BRICS confront common public health challenges, the results of cooperation are mostly reflected in the signing of statements and various documents, and actual implementation of cooperation often is mostly below expectation.

Conclusion

Strengthening public health cooperation is not only conducive to ensuring the well-being of the people and deepening mutual trust between countries, it is also an effective plan to resolve public health emergencies for all mankind. In the face of the coronavirus epidemic in 2020, multilateral cooperation in the field of public health has become the expectation and consensus of people all over the world. After nearly ten years of hard work, the BRICS have reached many consensuses in the field of public health cooperation and achieved certain results. In particular, they have made timely joint responses and concerted efforts in combating the coronavirus epidemic. These efforts have contributed to the formation of "BRICS attitude" in global health governance and the positive "BRICS voice" to be heard. Also, "BRICS plan" as proposed to solve its own problems sets as a model for the world to jointly respond to public health threats. Due to various internal reasons of the BRICS and the emergency of the public health crisis, there is still much room for improvement in the effectiveness of the cooperation of the BRICS in fighting the epidemic. In addition, it is equally important for the BRICS to explore further about the realization of a more concrete and effective declaration of cooperation, and come up with ways to abandon prejudice and help each other in major emergencies.

Studies on BRICS Countries

The Russia's Agricultural Development Orientation and Its Influence[*]

Cui Zheng[**]　Yang Yueming[***]

Abstract: This paper takes the changes and influence of Russia's agricultural strategy as the core issue, and sorts out the agricultural policies, main adjustment of directions and prospects of China - Russia's agricultural cooperation in various stages of Russia after the Cold War. Russia's agricultural strategy is of long - lasting importance. With the development of the country and the adjustment of national interests, the goals of agricultural development demonstrate phased changes in different periods. The fundamental reason for the growth of agriculture against the economic downturn is the long - term national strategic

---

[*] This paper is a phased research result of major project of Liaoning University's Humanities and Social Sciences Key Research Base of Ministry of Education During the "13th Five - Year Plan" Period, namely, the "Major adjustments and consequences of Russia's internal affairs and diplomacy after Putin's re - election as president" (LNUJD201702), and of the 2017 Liaoning Provincial Social Science Planning Fund Project, namely, "Study on the Role of Russia in the China - U. S. Co - opetition Relationship During the Trump's Administration" (L17BGJ004).

[**] Cui Zheng, Associate Professor, the Supervisor of Graduate Students and the Vice Director of Research Center for the Economies and Politics of Transitional Countries (RCEPTC), Liaoning University.

[***] Yang Yueming, Graduate Student, School of International Relations of Liaoning University.

subsidies and support. At present, Russia's agricultural productivity has been greatly improved, and new adjustments have taken place in the agricultural strategy. The new development plan is issued so as to cope with the constraints caused by economic structural imbalance. The new strategy will deepen the reform of the agricultural industry structure and ensure the development of this field to become an innovative and sustainable one. Among them, actively developing agricultural cooperation is an important part of the reform process. Russia's agricultural cooperation focuses on national interests and aims at attracting foreign direct investment. It can improve the passive situation of diplomatic isolation while expanding trade markets. The upgrading of the China - Russian partnership will also deepen bilateral cooperation in the agricultural field.

Keywords: Export - oriented Agriculture; Economic Structure; Multilateral Cooperation; Technological Innovation

Since the outbreak of the Ukrainian crisis in 2014, Russia - US relations have reached the lowest since the end of the Cold War. The United States and its allies have utilized economic advantages to implement a series of sanctions against Russia through the way they deal with the Ukrainian issue, such as "crackdown" on Russia in the fields of finance, credit and foreign trade. In a series of anti - crisis policies issued by Russia, the agricultural sector, as an important area for the implementation of the "import substitution" policy, has achieved remarkable results. At present, agriculture is a key area of Russia's economic transformation, and new agricultural strategies have been introduced one after another. Actively expanding industrial cooperation, promoting the construction of related infrastructure, enlarging product exports, improving product processing capabilities and improving related cooperation mechanisms have become new elements of the Russia's agricultural cooperation mechanism.

Ⅰ. A Review of the Development of Russia's Agriculture

Stage I: The period of import quotas. After the collapse of the Soviet Union, Russia implemented powerful de‑collectivization and marketization in the agricultural sector during the transition to a market economy. A large number of collective farms were transformed into private farms and agricultural companies. In 2000, only about a quarter of producersmade profit, and the proportion of agriculture in GDP fell from 15.4% in 1990 to 6.5% in 1997. At the same time, due to the long cycle of agriculture, a large number of loans had placed a huge burden on the national banking industry. Against this background, imported meat began to flood into the Russian market. In addition to the people's daily needs for meat products, Russia's open market also faced severe challenges from fully functional agricultural enterprises in developed countries, especially in terms of market trade, which Russia had very limited capability to respond to. Russia has obtained targeted loans and humanitarian assistance from the International Monetary Fund for "high‑priced" food purchases, which has caused a heavy blow to the Russian poultry industry while American chicken was delivered at dumped prices, so there is no opportunity at all for domestic products to join the price competition. Putin's "Russia at the Turn of the Millennium" published on December 30, 1999 pointed out that one of Russia's basic projects is to promote modernized agriculture. The goal is to organically integrate state support and state regulation measures with the market reform implemented in rural areas and land ownership. When Putin came to power, he pointed out clearly the specific development direction with Russian characteristics for the agricultural policies. Through the orderly guidance from the national plan, a new mechanism for the coordinated development of various agricultural organizations that strengthen the production vitality of the agro‑industrial combination is formed. He emphasized that the development of agriculture is a necessary condition for Russia to return to the world stage and an inevitable requirement for implementing the strategy of building a strong country and delivering a better life for people. In 2003, the government of the Russian Federation officially proposed that the annual import volume of poultry meat should be reduced by 25%, while the import volume of beef and pork should be reduced by 20%. The import quota is carried out for poultry meat (import volume cannot exceed the quota), and the tariff-rate quota is implemented for pork and beef. Beef that exceeds the quota is subject to a 60% tariff, and a 80% tariff for pork. By comparing the annual growth rate of domestic meat production with the annual growth rate of national demand, it shows that the increase of domestic production is slightly faster than residents' living needs, which directly reflects the positive trend brought about by the quota system during this period.

Table 5-1 Demand and Output of Meat Products and Their Growth Rate (unit: thousand tons)[1]

	2003	2004	2005	2006	2007	2008	2009
Domestic production	4936	—	4972	5259	5790	6268	6688
Growth rate compared to the previous year	105.6%	—	—	105.8%	110.1%	108.3%	106.7%
Domestic individual consumption	7464	—	7871	8287	8774	9353	9545
Growth rate compared to the previous year	103.6%	—	—	105.3%	105.9%	106.6%	102.1%

Data source: according to the report "Agriculture, Animal Husbandry and Forestry" of the Russia's Federal State Statistics Service.

Stage II: The period when long-term agricultural strategy was formed. The food security strategy adopted by the Russian Federation in 2010 means

---

[1] 《Сельское хозяйство, охота и лесоводство в России-2004г》《Сельское хозяйство, охота и лесоводство в России-2011г》、доклад《Ресурсы и использование мясо и мясопродуктов》, https://gks.ru/bgd/regl/b04_38/Main.Htm.

that the state will maintain reasonable consumption standards for residents based on economic conditions, and ensuring the accessibility of material and economy is the main condition for ensuring food independence. Generally, food security ensuring is assessed by the state based on the level of food self-sufficiency. Although import quotas have stimulated the production capacity of domestic producers, nearly 30% of food still needs to be imported. Reliance on imports has seriously threatened Russia's food security. Therefore, if the state fails to strengthen the supporting role for this most important economic area, it is impossible to further develop agriculture under the conditions of market relations.

From the economic perspective, Russia's high dependence on imports of certain foods has greatly reduced its own economic security. Against the background of foreign debt increase, the large purchases of foreign food and food raw materials have further increased the pressure on limited foreign exchange resources. In addition, the increase in food imports is ever forcibly being paid with non-renewable natural resources and has thus weakened Russia's role in the global economy. Therefore, Russia puts forward the main goal of food security: timely prediction, identification and prevention of internal and external threats to food security: the sustainable development of domestically produced food and raw materials should be sufficient to ensure the country's food independence. For this end, the state proposes that the market share of various domestic foods is: cereal products account for at least 95%, sugar to be at least 80%, vegetable oil to be at least 80%, meat and its products to be not less than 85%, milk and dairy products to be not less than 90%, fish products to be at least 80%, potatoes to be at least 95%, and salt to be at least 85%. This principle can be regarded as an upgrade of the agricultural protection policy from the previous stage, which has upgraded the reduction of imports to the level of protecting food security.

Stage III: the period of stalled agricultural development. Russia's negotiations for its accession to WTO lasted for 18 years, and it was until 2012 that

Russia has formally become a member of the WTO. There are different opinions on the impact of joining the WTO on Russia. Most experts and scholars believe that joining the WTO may not bring obvious positive effects in the short term, and may even hit the domestic fragile manufacturing industry due to tariff reduction. In the past ten years, Russian agriculture has gradually resumed its production with the support of a number of national protection policies, but it still lacks competitiveness compared with a large number of cheap imported agricultural products. The domestic voices hold a negative attitude towards the agricultural market that has been opened after joining the WTO. In the process of reaching the agreement, opening up the agricultural market has become one of the important conditions for WTO accession. Russia has long been a major importer of agricultural products from European and American countries. The domestic agricultural productivity is far from reaching the level of food security. And the opening up of the domestic market definitely will hit the agricultural production that has just developed. In the final agreement, the main restrictive provisions include: cancellation of pork quota (before January 1, 2020) and beef quota and the amount of "amber box subsidies" should be reduced in accordance with the agricultural agreement within the framework of the organization.

Joining the WTO exerts a curial impact on participating in the redistribution of world resources and integrating into the world order. It may take longer to obtain this strategic advantage than negotiations for accession to the WTO. At that time, the domestic agricultural productivity was far from reaching the level of food security, and the results of lowering tariffs and controlling the "amber box" subsidies would definitely give a major blow to the newly developed agricultural production. At the same time, during the negotiations, Russia also secured a transition period of 5 to 7 years for the agricultural sector. In the final agreement, it was determined that the import quota system for meat products could be retained, but the imported pork within the quota should be exempt from tax, with additional tariffs on imported pork that surpasses the quota having a drop of 10 percentage points. In 2013, the state's subsidies for domestic producers should not exceed 9 billion U. S. dollars, and will be gradually reduced to 4. 4 billion U. S. dollars by 2018.①

Stage IV: import substitution stage. In response to sanctions imposed by Western countries, Russian leaders announced the implementation of an import substitution policy. Faced with a severe economic situation, one of the goals of the import substitution policy is to promote the diversified Russian economy. From the development of domestic production to innovative development, it is necessary to gradually get rid of dependence on foreign technology and products. Strengthening the country's management in the field of foreign trade and formulating a standard mechanism for effective implementation of import substitution can become a rare opportunity for Russia to promote economy growth, develop technology, overcome technological gaps, and improve the investment environment.

In August 2014, Russia formally implemented counter - sanctions and retaliatory measures against U. S. and European sanctions, imposing restrictions on certain types of food imported from EU countries and the U. S., Australia and Canada. Restrictions involve the import of beef, pork, poultry, fish, seafood, cheese, milk, fruits, vegetables and many other types of agricultural products and food. This has promoted the growth of domestic agricultural production and replaced imported products in some areas. After restricting the access of imported products into the market, domestic agricultural producers have gained opportunities for development. Importers' share has been replaced by domestic agricultural producers. Domestic agricultural foods have begun to dominate the Russian market, and the agricultural sector has almost become the only growing filed in Russia during the economic downturn.

According to a report released by the Ministry of Agriculture in August 2017, the support from state budget for agriculture has increased by 27%:

---

① "Процесс присоединения России к Всемирной торговой организации (ВТО)," РИА, https: //ria. ru/20130614/94315318 4. html.

from 190 billion rubles in 2014 to 242 billion rubles in 2017. Russia has also introduced a series of subsidies and loan policies. Among them, the Ministry of Agriculture has introduced an individual regional subsidy, which allows each region to independently determine the focus of supporting various industries according to the specific conditions of the region. The combined effects of these measures have led to the successful implementation of import substitution policies in agriculture: the meat industry has achieved the most significant results. The import share of pork consumption fell by 2/3 (from 26% in 2013 to 8% in 2016), while poultry meat fell by 3/5 (from 12% in 2013 to 5% in 2016). The import volume of vegetables fell by 1/2 (from 866,000 tons in 2013 to 463,000 tons in 2016), while domestic vegetable production has increased year by year. In the past three years, the production of greenhouse vegetables has increased by 30%.

As a result of the construction of a new greenhouse complex and the reclamation of new arable land, in 2017, even encountering adverse weather conditions (frost, rain, hail, and flood), the fruits and vegetables will still be harvested at the previous year's level.[1]

Table 5-2 Production and Consumption of Vegetables and Dairy Products in the Past Five Years (unit: thousand tons)[2]

Vegetables

	2014	2015	2016	2017	2018	Proportion % 2017	Proportion % 2018
Domestic Production	14352.1	14967.8	15064.4	15426.7	15655.0	61.2	61.5

---

[1] "Минсельхоз России подвёл итоги реализации программы импортозамещения за 3 года," Министерство сельского хозяйства Российской Федерации, http://mcx.ru/press-service/news/minselkhoz-rossii-podvyel-itogi-realizatsii-programmy-importozameshcheniya-za-3-goda/.

[2] "《Потребление основных продуктов питания населением Российской Федерации》," Федеральная службагосударственной статистики, https://www.gks.ru/compendium/document/13278.

Continued Table

	2014	2015	2016	2017	2018	Proportion % 2017	Proportion % 2018
Export	2952.5	2643.6	2356.7	2669.9	2484.6	10.6	9.7
In Total	24161.1	24632.0	24608.4	25195.2	25471.0	100	100
Loss	483.2	509.3	510.4	511.5	472.2	2.0	1.9
Export	76.4	197.5	269.1	248.0	282.2	1.0	1.1
Individual Consumption	14833.4	14918.3	14946.9	15219.4	15651.0	60.4	61.5

Dairy Products

	2014	2015	2016	2017	2018	Proportion % 2017	Proportion % 2018
Domestic Production	29995.1	29887.5	29787.3	30185.0	30611.1	77.5	79.0
Export	9157.9	7951.3	7578.6	6996.9	6493.0	10.6	9.7
In Total	41134.8	39959.2	39313.6	38927.9	38743.0	100	100
Loss	35.2	33.7	30.3	29.4	31.3	0.1	0.1
Export	628.9	606.0	644.8	607.6	576.3	1.0	1.1
Individual Consumption	34953.1	34148.2	33832.9	33736.9	33552.0	86.6	86.6

Data source: According to the report of "The Population's Consumption of Basic Food in the Russian Federation in 2019" from the Russia's Federal State Statistics Service.

Ⅱ. Russia's New Agricultural Development Strategy under the Background of U. S. and European Sanctions

In the context that geopolitical factors and the macro economy have been challenged once again, Russia's agriculture has ushered in a new period of development after basically achieving food self-sufficiency. Although previously affected by multiple pressures, the overall trend during the import substitution is still positive - all products have maintained a high level of profit. In October 2018, Putin attended the Agricultural Conference held in the Stavropolskiy Kray. At the conference, the results of the agricultural sector were evaluated and the strategic guidelines for future industrial development in key areas were determined. Putin described the achievements of the agro - industrial combo as a breakthrough, pointing out that in the past five years, agricultural production has increased by more than 20%, and domestic producers can almost completely supply all necessary food products to its own countries, while foreign markets are actively explored. A large number of foreign trade activities have been carried out with China, India, Southeast Asia, Africa and the countries along the Persian Gulf. In 2017, the export delivery volume of food and agricultural raw materials increased by 21% to reach more than 20 billion U. S. dollars, which surpassed arms sales by more than 5 billion U. S. dollars and became the country's second largest export commodity.

As early as November 30, 2016, Russia approved the "agricultural export" priority project, which means that the agricultural sector is gradually shifting to be "export-oriented". At the Russia's Agricultural Export Conference in July 2019, Prime Minister Medvedev firstly affirmed the remarkable achievements in the agricultural sector in the past five years. The agro - industrial combo is developing rapidly, and the production and processing of grain, feed, milk and meat is increasing. The food security problem has been initially solved. In 2018, the export value of agricultural products and food was close to US $ 26 billion. It has even exceeded the goal of 23 billion U. S. dollars set in the federal project "Agricultural Export". Russia is one of the leading countries in grain exports. The regions for export continue to expand, with main partners including Asia - Pacific region, Africa and the Middle East.

It is estimated that by the next stage of 2024, Russia's agricultural exports will reach the goal of 45 billion U. S. dollars. First of all, the state will provide support for investment projects in the deep processing of agricultural products, alter the export structure, and transform the advantages in the raw materials to that in the deep processing products. Grain products have begun to follow this trend, and in the next stage, this development will accelerated in seafood products. At present, 90% of seafood is just frozen before being exported, and it is planned to increase the share of high value-added fish products to 40%. Second, the logistics infrastructure needs further development. The wholesale distribution center network required by exporters will continue to be improved. In 2018, eight centers were put into operation, and another 14 would be built within four years. In the comprehensive plan for the modernization and expansion of major infrastructure in 2024, taking into account the needs of farmers in the transportation of agricultural products, part of the cost of railway transportation of agricultural products will be compensated to agricultural producers through preferential tariffs. Third, in order to boost exports, quarantine standards will be unified for domestic products to reduce the doubts of importing countries about the quality of Russian domestic food.[①]

1. Conditions for the Transformation of Agricultural Strategy

First, the geopolitical environment is still complicated. First of all, the West is still an unavoidable factor affecting Russia's national security. In June 2019, the European Union announced the extension of sanctions on certain economic sectors of Russia, including: restricting five Russian financial institutions controlled by the state and their subsidiaries established outside the European Union from entering EU's primary and secondary capital markets, and restricting three large Russian energy companies and three defense companies; prohibiting the import and export trade of arms; prohibiting the export of dual-use goods for military purposes or for the Russian army; and restricting Russia's access to certain strategically significant technologies and services that can be used for oil development and production. Russia has also issued a corresponding Anti-Sanctions Law and decrees, confirming the right of the Russian President and the government to impose counter-sanctions against "unfriendly behaviors" of other countries.

[①] "О стимулировании экспорта сельскохозяйственной продукции," Правительство России, http://government.ru/news/37430/.

Although there are huge conflicts in the bilateral relations between Russia and Europe, both sides have gradually realized the economic and trade ties that have been formed over a long period of time. At the same time, the United States' "unilateral" approach also disappointed European countries, which brought opportunities for Russia and Europe to cooperate. Due to its superior geographical location and many other reasons, Russia has become an indispensable economic partner of EU countries. Therefore, the longtime cross-border cooperation between Russia and EU countries has never ceased. As far as the EU is concerned, it has the longest land border with Russia, and terminating cross-border cooperation will violate the policy of good-neighborliness, and the friendly relationship between the two sides will change to be hostile. In 2014, the European Commission decided to continue implementing the cross-border cooperation program, and dozens of small joint projects continued to be implemented. These all help to alleviate political conflicts, encourage officials from both sides to meet regularly and maintain contact with local authorities and law enforcement agencies.

Secondly, as an important strategic space for Russia, the CIS countries have always been Russia's top priority in maintaining its special status and Russia's diplomatic work. This is the bottom line for Russia to maintain its status of "big power." On the basis of the "Eurasian Partnership", a multi-level and multi-field cooperation mechanism has been established in this region. The main idea that Russia needs to convey to its partners is that the goal of the integration in the post-Soviet space is not limited to the establishment of a customs union and a common economic space, but also to establish a vast Eurasian cooperation zone. The most important condition for achieving this goal is the economic integration of the post-Soviet space. At the same time, this integration is Russia's strategic goal in the CIS countries. For Russia, the need for the integration of post-Soviet Union space is mainly related to its geopolitical goals and the long-term prospects of its economic development. Russia hopes to keep its products competitive in the Eurasian market, and also hopes to establish a friendly cooperation zone with its neighboring countries. Cooperation between Russia and the CIS countries can be developed through payment and customs unions, the establishment of inter-continent industrial associations, international financial centers and industrial companies.

The sharp relationship between Russia and the United States have the risk of continuing to deteriorate, which will inherently last for a long term and is determined by the ideology of the American political elites. It features the continuous strengthening of neo-conservatism, which has led to the idealism and realism of American foreign policy. The formulation of a new US strategy in the ever-changing world structure reflects the US's realistic understanding of power boundaries and determines the turbulence and instability and deterrent factors in US-Russian relations. Russia-US relations have always been at the lowest level. The "imbalance" of pivotal international security may lead to the emergence of direct military conflicts between the United States and Russia. The most sensitive and fundamental strategic stability and security issues in bilateral relations have greatly affected the state development of Russia.

The complex and tense geopolitical environment puts forward urgent requirements for Russia's economic development, and provides the opportunity for the transformation of the agricultural sector and the strengthening of agricultural cooperation. Cereals enjoy an important strategic position as a food crop. Russia can access to the world market by virtue of its status as an exporter, which is of great political significance for boosting the country's development momentum. The advantage of the cereal industry will help increase the investment attractiveness of Russia's national economy. In September 2019, the Deputy Minister of Agriculture of the Russian Federation led a Russian delegation to participate in the ninth conference of the Ministers of Agriculture of the BRICS countries. During the conference, all parties emphasized the priority of implementing goals of the *2030 Agenda for Sustainable Development*. The meeting also emphasized the sharing of experience among member states and strengthening international cooperation among professionals. In the report of the conference, Russia talked about the digital transformation of the domestic agricultural sector and the national plan related to the development of rural areas. Later on, the joint declaration signed in the BRICS ministerial conference covers topics related to the use of new technologies in the communications sector in the BRICS countries, the development of agricultural innovation companies, trade and regionalization, as well as the sustainable development of agriculture.[1]

Second, the country's macroeconomic development is unstable. In 2018, the World Bank predicted in its Russian Economic Report that Russia's economic growth prospects for 2018 -2020 will be moderate, with an estimation of 1.5% to 1.8%. At the beginning of 2019, the Russian Ministry of Economic Development, the Central Bank and the State Statistics Services successively announced the results of 2018 economic growth. The State Statistics Services estimates that the GDP growth of the Russian Federation is 2.3%, which is higher than the forecast of the Ministry of Economic Development and the Central Bank. The Ministry of Economic Development estimates economic growth to be 1.8% (later increased to 2%), and the Central Bank forecasted the growth to be between 1.5% and 2%. However, the annual growth rate is only due to short-term reasons such as rising oil prices, and does not reflect the effective use of basic elements such as labor and capital.

Increasing the economic growth rate above the global average level is a key task for the further development of the national economy. This will ensure the living standards of Russian citizens, ensure the country's food security, and improve the competitiveness of Russia's agricultural products and food in markets at home and abroad. The state is considering developing export products to achieve this goal. The development of the deep processing export of grain, flour, oil products, sugar, starch, and confectionery industries has received further at-

---

[1] "На встрече министров сельского хозяйства стран БРИКС обсудили трансформацию российского АПК," Министер ство сельского хозяйства Российской Федерации, http: //mcx. ru/press - service/news/na - vstreche - ministrov - selskogo - khozyay stva - stran - briks - obsudili - transformatsiyu - rossiyskogo - apk/.

tention from the state. The export of poultry, pork and beef also sees a positive tendency. The main export regions of Russian products are located in the Azov Sea-Black Sea, the Caspian Sea Coast and the Asia - Pacific region. The report prepared by the United Nations Conference on Trade and Development specifically pointed out the following: "Under the circumstance of low global demand, world trade is very likely to fail to achieve widespread growth. In addition, the hope of the rapid breakthrough in the largely development-oriented multilateral trade negotiations is gradually disappearing." This situation in the global economy brings certain risks to development. "Under the situation of low global demand, except some individual countries and certain special circumstances, world trade is unlikely to provide widespread growth. Russia's agricultural exports are a prioritized development project to realize long-term goals, so the state needs to adopt reasonable trade protectionism. This policy should implement necessary institutional and infrastructure support to promote the agricultural products to foreign markets.

2. The Role of Russia's Agricultural Policy in the Context of Sanctions

The first is at the international level: it is conducive to the implementation of economic diplomacy and attracting foreign investment. After Russia faced setbacks in its relations with the West, its strategic goal paid more attention to the "East". The Asia-Pacific region is related to Russia's major strategic interests in economy, geopolitics, state relations and many other aspects. The Asia-Pacific should become one of the most important regions for Russia's overall development. Among them, cooperation in the agricultural field has become an important fulcrum for the implementation of the "eastward" strategy. First, under the trend of globalization, the role of developing countries in the world's agricultural product market is increasing: economic growth, poverty reduction, increased consumption and imports have prompted Western partners to gradually adopt east-orientation in its world trade, which is obviously good for Russia's agricultural development. Compared with the energy sector or the entire industry, the global agricultural market is less sensitive to changes in investment policies and has limited dependence on fluctuations in the political situation. Population growth and climate change in certain parts of the world have become favorable factors for Russia's agricultural exports. According to data from the Food and Agriculture Organization of the United Nations, the world's largest agricultural importers are the European Union, the United States, China, Japan, Canada and Mexico. The largest exporters are the European Union, the United States, Brazil, China, Canada and Argentina[①]. The most promising markets for Russia's agricultural exports are countries in the Asia-Pacific region where consumption continues to grow, including China, Japan and South Korea.

One of the representative manifestations of this is the economic cooperation between Russia and Japan in the Far East, mainly in the fields of agriculture and energy. Taking advantage of the opportunity of Russia's eastward movement, Japan actively engages in the contact with Russia, with the goal of negotiating territorial disputes with Russia and the bottom line to be the initiation of dialogue and cooperation with Russia through economic cooperation. In May 2016, Japan formally announced the "new approach" to its relations with Russia. Its plans include eight elements, such as extending the average life expectancy, developing urban modernization, providing convenient and clean life and convenience, interaction between small and medium-sized enterprises, expanding cooperation, energy, the diversification of Russia's industry, the increase of productivity, the development of the Far East's industry, the establishment of export bases, cooperation in the field of advanced technology, as well as strengthening non-governmental exchanges between Russia and Japan. On the sidelines of the Fifth Eastern Economic Forum held on September 4, 2019, the Deputy Minister of Agriculture of Russia and the Deputy Ministers of Agriculture, Forestry and Fisheries of Vietnam and Japan held a working meeting, focusing on the imple-

---

① "The state of agricultural commodity markets," *(FAO)*, http://www.fao.org/3/I9542EN/i9542en.pdf.

mentation of the Russian-Japanese joint project, which aims to improve the productivity of agriculture and fisheries in the Russian Far East, and to establish greenhouses and pig farms that can adapt to the climatic conditions of the Far East.

Apart from the Asia-Pacific region, Russia is also actively developing trade relations with the Middle East, Africa and other regions. Russian Deputy Minister of Agriculture Sergey Levin stated at the session of "Sustainable Partnership in Agriculture: Institutions, Tools, and Guarantees" at the Russian-Africa Economic Forum in October 2019 that Russia believes that Africa is a reliable partner for constructive cooperation established in the agricultural sector. Since 2016, Russia's exports to countries in this region have increased by 73%, reaching 4.6 billion U.S. dollars by the end of 2018, and it has considerable trade potential. In the next few years, Russia plans to double the supply of agricultural products to the Africa. The growth is expected to exceed US $ 5 billion.[①] Currently, most of Russia's agricultural exports go to North Africa, and it plans to expand cooperation with other regions. Russia is ready to meet Africa's growing demand of food. Deputy Minister Levin emphasized that wheat and barley, as well as sunflower oil, poultry, confectionery and fish products, possess huge growth potential for exports to countries on the African continent. Participants also discussed the establishment of logistics infrastructure to develop partnerships with African countries, the issue of mutually beneficial partnerships in the trade of agricultural products and food and the prospects of Russia's investment in the region's agricultural infrastructure. In November 2019, the Russian Minister of Agriculture visited Jordan, where they expanded the level of bilateral agricultural cooperation. Jordan has long needed to import Russian barley, beans and vegetables. The two countries have agreed on quarantine standards and proce-

---

① "Россия удвоит поставки продовольствия в Африку," Министерство сельского хозяйства Российской Федерации, http://mcx.ru/press-service/news/rossiya-udvoit-postavki-prodovolstviya-v-afriku-/.

dures for the supply of Russian meat and finished meat as well as milk and dairy products, and have prepared to increase the export volume of cereals.

The second is at the state level: it is conducive to solving the structural contradictions of the national economy. Agriculture is one of the most important sectors of the Russian national economy. It provides food for the people, becomes the source of raw materials for the processingindustry and meets various other needs of society. The population's living standards and well‐being, nutritional structure, per capita income, consumption of goods and services and social living conditions depend on the development of agriculture in many ways. Currently, Russia is pursuing "breakthrough development" in national economic and social development, and urgently needs to improve its economic structure. Agriculture is one of the pillar sectors in the national economy of all countries. Regardless of soil and climatic conditions, even the most developed countries are vigorously developing agricultural economies. Any powerful country in the world needs strong agriculture for support, so Russia must develop its own independent agricultural industry. Moreover, Russia enjoys the inherent advantages of developing agriculture, where it has vast, flat and fertile land for agriculture.

At the same time, the development of agriculture is conducive to the stability of rural areas and guarantees of national security. There is a huge gap between urban and rural areas in Russia. Most of the rural areas are located in remote areas. Many villages and towns lack basic living facilities such as running water, electricity and communications. This has caused a large number of rural laborers to migrate to cities. According to the regional quality of life rankings announced at the beginning of 2019, the highest‐ranking Moscow and the lowest Tuva region had a 25‐fold difference in per capita GDP. Promoting the development of the agricultural sector can effectively attract labor to move back, and its spillover effect can also facilitate the construction of related infrastructure.

However, "import substitution" as an economic strategy implemented by the country possesses a contradictory nature: On the one hand, it is one of the economic policies implemented to protect the economy; On the other hand, it is also a way of focusing on economic growth goals and integrating into the global economy. The current import substitution strategy is very important to Russia. Import substitution can be understood as a national policy aimed at increasing domestic demand for its products, while active measures are taken to reduce dependence on the consumption of similar foreign products, thereby creating globally competitive domestic manufacturers and products so as to reflect the necessity to implement innovative import substitution strategy. We should take two perspectives to judge the import substitution policy as a stimulus to the domestic economic development. Judging from the development trend of sanctions and retaliation measures, it may become an incentive measure to stimulate the development of domestic industries. However, it should also be recognized that its purpose is not only to substitute imported goods for domestic goods at the domestic market, but also to improve these goods and improve the quality of services so that they can compete with foreign goods in the world market. In consideration of this, more cautious attitude needs to be taken.

Table 5-3　Monthly Living Expenses of Russian Households (unit: rubles)[①]

	2011	2012	2013	2014	2015	2016
Average household monthly consumption	11715.1	13066.3	14153.8	15094.3	15295.4	16632.5
Average monthly food consumption	4078.1	4375.1	4694.9	5111.0	5707.8	6220.7
Rural household monthly consumption	8156.8	9305.4	9739.5	10611.9	11271.3	12070.4
Monthly food consumption of rural households	3579.3	3842.8	4073.8	4457.0	5100.5	5486.2

Data source: according to the report of "The Social Status and Living Standard of the Russian People" from the Russia's Federal State Statistics Service.

---

① Социальное положение и уровень жизни населения России-2015 г. доклад Состав расходов на конечное потребление домашних хозяйств различных социально - экономических категорий. Федеральная служба государственной статистики, https: //gks. ru/bgd/regl/b15_44/Main. htm.

3. Prospects for Future Agricultural Development

The first is the positive aspects: Organic agriculture is the "new label" for exports, which is one of the features of Russian agriculture. It satisfies Russia's requirements for the "clean and quality improvement" of its own agricultural products. It is also the biggest difference from other large agricultural countries that promote agricultural development with advanced industries and scientific and technological capabilities and establish large - scale intensive farms. Russia's development of organic agriculture has not only raised import standards, but also utilized this factor in its diplomatic practice to impose sanctions on some countries. The Russia's Ministry of Agriculture has obtained the exclusive right to trademarks for organic products. The Patent and Trademark Commission will issue the logo to the company. The law on organic products came into effect in 2020. At present, the Russia's Ministry of Agriculture is working with other competent authorities to formulate regulations including the maintenance of the registration of organic producers, and establish some national standards. The introduction of the single - label model will help improve the quality of products at the domestic market, and will generally help the development of the country's agricultural and industrial combo. Combining with other measures provided by the Russian government and the Ministry of Agriculture, creating the brands for the protected organic and environmentally friendly agricultural products in Russia will solve the task of increasing agricultural exports and improving food quality set by the President of the Russian Federation.

From May 16th to 18th, 2018, the 31st Session of the Food and Agriculture Organization of the United Nations for Europe was held in Voronezh, whose theme was e - agriculture, agroecology and organic agriculture. On the eve of the meeting, the IFOAM released the results of Russia's research in this region from March 2017 to April 2018. At the meeting, Acting Governor Alexander Gusev proposed to support the development of organic agriculture in the Voronezh region, and pointed out that the future challenge is to make it a short - term priority for agricultural development in the region.

Organic agriculture isa method of agriculture that does not use pesticides, herbicides, chemical fertilizers, growth regulators and genetically modified seeds in the process of agricultural production. There are a total of 70 certified organic agricultural companies in Russia. Among them, 53 companies meet international certification standards. Currently, there are 16 certified domestic manufacturers having exported their products (mainly grains, oil seeds and essential oils) to EU countries. When the State Duma passed the Organic Agriculture Act on first reading in January 2018, former Prime Minister Dmitry Medvedev once stated that Russia could occupy 10%-25% of the global organic agriculture market in the future. This will bring irreplaceability to Russia's agricultural products, stabilize the export market of Russian agriculture and also stimulate the development of agriculture - related science and technology. The only risk is the deterioration of the political situation. The development of organic agriculture is a highlight of Russia's agriculture, whose political significance lies in improving the disadvantages in Russia - Europe trade and increasing Russia's initiative under sanctions.

The second is the negative aspects: The domestic comprehensive agricultural production chain has not yet formed. One of the main trends in agricultural development is the technological modernization of the industry. Another important area is the guarantee of subsidies to agricultural producer. The state supports greenhouse vegetable cultivation, pig raising, seed production, etc. The high level of agricultural subsidies has attracted a large number of investors to enter the agricultural market. However, some problems are still pending, such as the unreasonable distribution of subsidies, where a large part of the subsidies is used to support animal husbandry production, while problems in areas such as feed production still wait to be resolved.

Ogunka, executive director of the Russian Federation of Phytochemical Manufacturers, said: "We are indeed behind the rest of the world in many industries. With the exception of cereal crops, almost all crops are highly dependent on imports of seed." Almost half of the seeds at the domestic market come from abroad, among which more than 50% of them are dependent on imports. The varieties of sugar beet even account for 90%. Under the background that agriculture in developed countries has become a high-tech industry, Russia's agricultural science faces scarce funds. Although the Ministry of Agriculture has formulated corresponding strategies and plans, they have not produced effective results so far. Russia has reached a cooperation intention with Bayer in response to the status of agricultural raw materials and underdeveloped agricultural science and technology. Bayer will provide Russian researchers with seed materials and teach production technologies that can accelerate agricultural development. The seed market in Russia is worthy of 50 billion rubles, of which 24.14 billion rubles are for imported ones. According to data from the Department of Science, Technology, Policy and Education of the Russian Ministry of Agriculture: The dependence on imports of vegetable seeds reaches 47%, while feed crops reach 90% and the breeding and nursery of fruits, berries and nuts reached 70%. The person in charge of the Bayer technology transfer project stated that Russian scientists will receive foreign seed materials for important crops such as corn, soybeans, rapeseed and wheat, and obtain information about the technology related to improve the productivity of vegetable crops such as tomatoes, cucumbers and cabbage. Researchers in the domestic agricultural science and technology research institutes can carry out localization improvements, use them for domestic research to obtain localized hybrids and sell the varieties. As part of the technology transfer, Bayer will also provide expert support, including educational activities and Russian representatives' training in the company's European research center. Bayer will also participate in the establishment of a plant biotechnology education and research center, which will focus on corn, canola, soybeans and wheat.

In the first two decades of the 21st century, Russia's agricultural policies have been continuously adjusted along with national development. Although Russia boasts certain geographical advantages in developing agriculture, there are still constraints such as a low starting point for development, lack of labor, poor weather conditions and dependence on imports of machinery technology. To truly achieve self-sufficiency in agricultural products, a large amount of national capital and technological input is required. Strong agricultural productivity relies on long-term investment and attention as the modernization of the industry has been a long process. Because the average investment payback period of the agricultural sector is about 4 to 5 years, it is difficult to attract external funds. An independent agricultural production chain needs the support of many factors such as manpower, technology and industrial modernization. The current agricultural development in Russia is only at the level of improving agricultural productivity, leaving the future of independent sustainable development in the agricultural sector to be still unclear.

Ⅲ. The Eastward Strategy's Influence and Prospects on China-Russia's Agricultural Cooperation

At present, Russia's foreign economic and trade relations are obviously changing. Russia is gradually developing economic and trade cooperation with Eastern countries. Given that the vibrant Asia-Pacific region has become one of the world's economic centers, establishing economic and trade cooperation with Eastern countries has become increasingly attractive to Russia. China is not only Russia's largest trading partner in the Asia-Pacific region, but their relationship is also one of Russia's most important bilateral relations. The 30-year development of China-Russian economic and trade cooperation has manifested similar phase features of two countries' political relations. Since the 1990s, with the continuous improvement of China-Russian political relations, economic and trade cooperation has gradually expanded. At present stage, both Russia and China are solving economic restructuring and transformation issues, and therefore, both sides are interested in finding new forms of interaction and cooperation. As the political relationship between the two countries comes into a "new era", which will stimulate the further development of China-Russian economic and trade cooperation as well as agriculture, as an important field of China-Russian economic and trade cooperation, also ushers in new opportunities for cooperation. In 2018, Dmitry Patrushev, Minister of Agriculture of Russia, and Han Changfu, Minister of Agriculture and Rural Affairs of the People's Republic of China, reached a consensus on the joint development of agro-industrial combo among the Far East, the Baikal region of Russia and Northeast China. Russia and China plan to develop cooperation in key areas of agriculture. Special plans have been made for cooperation in the construction of grain, livestock and fishery complexes. It intends to promote the plantation of soybeans and rice, the development of vegetable cultivation, breeding of dairy and beef cattle and cultivation of the pig and poultry. It is possible to establish unified nursery gardens and aquafarms, and jointly increase the output of high value-added products. The two sides will develop agricultural infrastructure and cooperate in terms of innovative agricultural technology and scientific development. The joint communiqué of the 23rd regular meeting between the Chinese premier and Russian prime ministers clearly stated that it is necessary to strengthen cooperation and exchanges between regulatory agencies and accelerate the process of food and agricultural products access so as to further expand the scale of agricultural product trade between the two countries, promote the implementation of investment and infrastructure cooperation projects in the agro-industrial combo and continue to carry out constructive cooperation on the formulation of the list of agricultural products that both sides are interested in and the list of major agricultural products and food production enterprises with export potential.[1]

  Due to the level of bilateral economic and trade cooperation is restricted

---

[1] http://www.gov.cn/guowuyuan/2018-11/07/content_5338172.htm. "Joint Communique of the 23rd Regular Meeting between Chinese Premier and Russian Prime Minister", Xinhua.net, Nov. 7th, 2018, http://www.gov.cn/guowuyuan/2018-11/07/content_5338172.htm.

by the industrial structure and economic model of the two countries, economic and trade cooperation is obviously lagging behind the political mutual trust between the two countries. Taking 2018 year as an example, the total bilateral economic and trade volume exceeded US $ 100 billion, reaching the highest level in history. However, it just accounts for a small proportion in China's total foreign trade of US $ 4 trillion. At present stage, the focus of China-Russia's agricultural cooperation is still trade, and its low level is mainly due to the large gap between the economic scale of the two sides. There is a certain degree of complementarity in the agricultural trade structure between China and Russia. In the agricultural sector, Russia can cooperate with China in terms of its shortcomings such as seed cultivation, agricultural machineryproduction and labor. Russia has shown obvious results in strengthening its own agricultural productivity, which is conducive to further promoting the increase of China-Russia's agricultural trade. Based on this, for the expansion of China-Russia's agricultural cooperation, it is more important to innovate cooperation models at the national level. China-Russia's agricultural cooperation has a short history, and the trade of a large number of agricultural products is just an emerging area. Nowadays, cooperation zones have been established to reduce the operating cost of agricultural production and improve the efficiency of customs clearance. The establishment of free trade zones for agricultural products can eliminate long-standing obstacles hindering the development of China-Russia's agricultural cooperation and strengthen the basis for interaction between the two countries, thus greatly improving the efficiency and level of cooperation and at the same time strengthening customs cooperation and coordination. It is urgent to establish systematic and effective specific rules to simplify quarantine procedures of agricultural products.

Ⅳ. Conclusion

The Russia's agricultural sector has bucked the trend under the influence of sanctions. The country's long-term protection policies have provided conditions for the development of Russia's agriculture, which has shown a good momentum. After basically meeting the needs of the country's food security, the new agricultural strategy is shifting to an "export-oriented" one. It is, on one hand, to improve the country's economic structure and reduce the economy's dependence on fuel exports; And on the other hand, to combine the eastward strategy to use the advantages of agricultural trade and actively carry out diplomatic activities with countries in the Asia-Pacific region. Given the complex geopolitical situation and the prominent contradictions in the national economic structure, attaching importance to agricultural development is one of the important approaches for the country to deal with the challenges it faces.

However, Russia's agricultural development is also facing shortcomings and disadvantages. The key factors affecting agricultural development include uncertain macroeconomic prospects, shortage of labor, the still high rate of importing agricultural machinery and seeds, the training of agricultural talents, scientific research and other factors, which may require one decade or two to get improved. It is necessary to realize that many foods are not suitable considering Russia's geographical conditions. Excessive adherence to nationalism and conduction of comprehensive substitution will cause high costs. Only extensive participation in international cooperation is of the country's economic interests. Therefore, China-Russia's agricultural cooperation possesses huge development potential. As an important part of bilateral economic and trade cooperation, it is important to strengthen the top-level design of the two countries and solidly promote and deepen cooperation, so that the fruits of agricultural cooperation will benefit the people of the two countries.

BRICS Partnership for Global Stability, Shared Security and Innovative Growth

——Russia's Priorities as the rotating presidency of BRICS

Valeriia Gorbacheva[*]

Abstract: Russia announced the theme of the 2020 BRICS Summit as "BRICS Partnership for global stability, Shared Security and Innovative Growth" in November 2019, indicating the priorities of cooperation among Russia and other BRICS countries. However, due to the spread of coronavirus infection, Russia has to revise the contents of these priorities as to adjust the "Enhancing foreign policy coordination on multilateral platforms" to "taking joint action in response to the COVID-19 pandemic" in terms of global stability, which is conducive to coping with the epidemic and to stressing the role of BRICS as a "stable island" as well; to delay the common anti-terrorism strategy made by Russia for the BRICS countries later to the national plans in "Post-epidemic Era" in the field of security; as for the innovation and growth, to adjust the BRICS economic cooperation strategy in the next five years in light of the current world economic situation. Although the spread of coronavirus infection has

---

[*] Valeriia Gorbacheva, GR – Director, Russian National Committee on BRICS Research; Research Fellow of the Asian Strategy Center, Institute of Economics of the Russian Academy of Sciences.

greatly affected many a Russia's existing programs as the presidency, the BRICS mechanism is still the single to deal with global stability.

Keywords: BRICS Summit; Global Stability; Russia; Priorities

At the Summit of BRICS (Brazil, Russia, India, China and South Africa) held in November 2019, Russian President Vladimir Putin affirmed the importance of maintaining the continuity of the BRICS agenda and proposed the main purpose of the Russia's BRICS Chairmanship in 2020, will to promote BRICS cooperation in many major fields for the benefit of all BRICS member countries.

Russia put forward the theme of Russia's chairmanship as "BRICS Partnership for Global Stability, Shared Security and Innovative Growth", referring to three priorities of development that rank the top of issues discussed by Russia with other BRICS partners. However, due to the spread of COVID-19, Russia has to adjust initiatives of international affairs in its presidency.

Global stability has always been one of the key issues discussed by Russia with other BRICS partners. Russia firmly supports to enhance the foreign policy coordination among the BRICS countries' in some significant international occasions, in particular with the United Nations that has already accumulated positive experiences in cooperation among member countries. As confronted by the COVID-19 epidemic, many countries has been forced to refocused their domestic affairs, resulting in a series of international conflicts. It seems inevitable for all BRICS countries including Russia, to come up against the problem of taking sides given the ever escalating trade war between China and the United States; nevertheless, none of the BRICS member countries especially Russia, truly supports the confrontation against the United States or China, which means, despite of the thorough destruction of BRICS in this "epidemic crisis", the important role of BRICS in contributing to global stability and the sustainability of world order should be firmly stressed and strengthened. So that it is essential for Russia as the rotating presidency of BRICS grab this opportunity to formulate unified and coordinated action plans in cooperation with partner countries so as to meet the challenge of the epidemic and enhance the strength of BRICS as an "island of stability" in this current turbulent time.

Security-another eternal priority, in basis of which, Russia builds up cooperative relationship with BRICS member countries with a unified position on matters of the international security agenda, including peacekeeping, counter-terrorism, combating cross-border crime and jointly solving global and regional hotspot issues. And Russia always stands by the BRICS countries to play a more active role in promoting initiatives proposed by the UN which has been an important organization in ensuring peace and security. And one of the primary tasks for the coordination between BRICS and the United Nations is to formulate unified international standards for preventing terrorism and the spread of terrorist ideology (including network communication).[1] Russia will take over Brazil's chairmanship and step up to strengthen cooperation among BRICS countries in combating money laundering terrorist financing and taking back criminally obtained assets. Russia proposes to formulate BRICS Anti-terrorism Strategy[2] that will greatly accumulate the formation of a comprehensive convention against international terrorism and the completion of adoption in the UN General Assembly. However the restrictive measures taken to prevent the spread of the COVID-19 have been temporarily put off, giving way to national plans to combat the epidemic.

Many plans have been taken off. 2020 is the year for the upcoming 75th anniversary celebration of the end of the World War II and the foundation of the United Nations, so Russia, as the chair, has proposed to discuss with BRICS member countries on a possible joint statement on those events, since it seems to be very important for BRICS countries to firmly support the world order

---

[1] Speech by Russian President Vladimir Putin at the BRICS Summit in Brasilia on November 14, 2019. http://kremlin.ru/events/president/news/62045.

[2] Patrushev proposed to formulate the BRICS counter-terrorism strategy/ Rianov News Agency. https://ria.ru/20191018/1559938410.html.

based on international law and UN Charter. However, structural shift has happened in effect of the COVID-19 pandemic, so that nothing but the global order transformation in 'post-pandemic' time can be speculated.

The third focuses on innovative development, whichis able to open up new opportunities for BRICS countries, that is, to lead the international economic agenda, form a new model of world economic development and cooperation that will further be promoted to other developing countries. And its essence lies in equal cooperation, fair competition and docking of initiatives without sovereignty restriction so as to develop inclusive economy. However, BRICS countries make major adjustments in the further development of economic and trade, financial and investment cooperation considering the current situation of the world economy.

Nevertheless, Russia's main task in 2020 has still maintained to update the BRICS economic partnership strategy to 2025. The first "version" of the strategy, approved by BRICS in 2015, has made a positive effects on economic cooperation among BRICS countries in various fields.[①] However, the epidemic has made severe consequences on the world economy, so that Russia needs to adjust strategy for economic partnership proposals in the next five years.

Another task for Russia stepping after Brazil is to enhance BRICS cooperation. First to consolidate the existing organizations and financial mechanisms of BRICS, including the New Development Bank, the Foreign Exchange Reserve and under the framework of which, the Macroeconomic Information Exchange System. In 2020, Russia will continue to open the Europe and Asia Branch of the New Development Bank in Moscow. Russia together with the BRICS member countries intend to prepare for the foundation of the BRICS Local Currency Bond Fund. And Russia also prepares to launch a series of new initiatives to deepen cooperation with BRICS member countries on the tax, customs and anti-

---

① The BRICS Economic Partnership Strategy/ The official website of Russia during its presidency in 2015 July 9, 2015. http: //BRICS 2015. ru/documents/.

monopoly line agencies, aiming to achieve the strategic development goals of BRICS.

To boost the "BRIC Plus" mechanisms is also one of Russia's priorities during its presidency. The BRICS countries are marching forward to enhance cooperation with other countries and integrating alliances. At the same time, further consultations with the membership of shareholders of the New Development Bank are under discussion, which will help BRICS countries alleviate the urgency for the expansion of the membership.

In 2020, Russia's priorities of development during its presidency are as follows:

1. Strengthening the Multilateral Principles in Global Politics and Promoting the Shared Interests of the BRICS Countries in International Fora:

——Promote the unifying agenda on the basis of universally recognized principles and norms of international law and the interests of all countries;

——Consolidate the central role of the United Nations in international relations;

——Strengthen collectiveefforts to meet global and regional challenges and threats;

——Strengthen cooperation between the BRICS countries in combating terrorism, extremism, corruption, cross-border crime, illicit drug and arms trafficking;

——Further enhance collaboration in the peaceful use and research of outer space;

——Continue the dialogues on the security in the use of international information security (ICTs) and countering cybercrime;

——Strengthen BRICS coordination mechanism in key multilateral fora;

——Develop cooperation with partner countries in the "BRICS Plus" and "Outreach" dialogue format;

——Strengthen dialogue on the issues of international development cooperation;

2. Developing Cooperation in the Field of Economy, Trade and Finance:
　　——Renew the Strategy for BRICS Economic Partnership;
　　——Facilitate trade and investment between the BRICS countries;
　　——Promote the potential of New Development Bank;
　　——Enhance the BRICS Contingent Reserve Arrangement mechanisms;
　　——Develop and integrate the BRICS national payment system;
　　——Carry out the practical activities of the BRICS Woman's Business Alliance;
　　——Promote economic development in remote areas within BRICS;
　　——Strengthen cooperation among the BRICS tax, customs and anti-monopoly line agencies;
　　——Deepen cooperation in the field of energy;
　　——Promote collaboration in the digital economy and innovation;
　　——Strengthen ties in health care including taking joint-preventing measures for infectious and non-infectious diseases;
　　——Engage in dialogue among the BRICS countries on agriculture and food security;
　　——Strengthen communication in the field of prevention and the eliminationthe consequences of emergencies and natural disasters;

3. Cooperation in People-to-people and Cutural Exchange:
　　——Develop inter-parliamentary ties;
　　——Expand Cultural cooperation;
　　——Strengthen cooperation among BRICS educational institutions;
　　——Further develop the BRICS Network University activities;
　　——Strengthen youth contacts;
　　——Promote cooperation within public diplomacy formats;
　　——Develop the contacts among representatives of the BRICS journalism

community.

One of the main issues for Russia remains to promote the development of the BRICS energy agenda. Russia will continue work to promote the initiative of establishing the BRICS energy research and cooperation platform for joint research in the fields of oil, gas and energy efficiency.

Another important direction for BRICS cooperation oriented to people-to-people and cultural exchange, so that particular attention should be paid to develop youth contacts among the BRICS countries.

To deepen cooperation with the other four countries in the field of higher education, Russia will pay attention to the development of Network Universities, the establishment of academic and research centers (an increasing effect has grown in academic field during the Russian presidency), the cooperation between research institutions and universities. A number of Russian universities have proceeded the BRICS student exchange program. And the first international student exchange program was launched at the Far East Federal University which admitted 150 students from other four countries in February 2020.

The cooperation and communication in the private sector has gradually developed as well. In 2015, Russia launched the initiative to create a platform for cooperation and development of non-governmental organizations form the BRICS countries, under which, BRICS parliaments and woman's work have pressed ahead a lot.

In light of science and innovation, Russia intends to continue the adoption of Clean Rivers of BRICS, and other priorities include the development of digital economy and artificial intelligence, the construction of comfortable and smart city, the realization of sustainable development and the introduction of innovation.

The current coronavirus infection has highlighted other priorities in BRICS Initiatives, one of which, is to create vaccine centers, put forward by BRICS. Given the tough health situation worldwide, the main issues in the field of health care have involved in ensuring the health and safety of people, the application of epidemic prevention measures and the cooperation of national health care system. Russia proposes to summarize the advanced epidemic prevention measures adopted by the BRICS countries, so that these experiences can be widely shared by not only the BRICS countries but professionals from other countries.[①]

Despite the fact that the outbreak has largely disrupted Russia's plans (For example, about 200 events at different levels are planned during the year of the presidency), the BRICS agenda has been still important, because in the complex situation where even the international relations paradigms are fast-changing, BRICS is still an important organization that contributes to global stability that other countries or integration alliances cannot.

[①] The Russian Ministry of Health held the BRICS Senior Health Officials Meeting/The official website of the Russian Federation in its BRICS Presidency of 2020. https: //BRICS -russia2020. ru/news/ 20200508/395195/Minzdrav-Rossii-provel-vstrechu-v-formate-videokonferentsii-starshikh-dolzhnostnykh-lits-stran-BRIKS-po. html.

Key Points of Cross-cultural Communication in the History of China-India Cultural and People-to-people Exchanges[*]

Duan Mengjie[**]

Abstract: The result of China-India exchanges depends on the people. The China-India cultural and people-to-people exchanges tradition in related to the history of the development of two countries' civilizations for over two thousand years, has been known for the inheritance and testimony of the friendship between the two countries. The foundation of the close people-to-people bond between the two countries in the future with depth and breadth far beyond our imagination. At the end of 2018, with the first meeting of the China-India high-

---

[*] This paper is the phased research result under the youth project of annual scientific research of Sichuan International Studies University, "The Image of China under the Mirror of Hindi Newspapers and Periodicals" (SISU202034), and non-universal language country regional research project for the construction of internationalized humanistic characteristics in Chongqing universities, "the Research on cultural and people-to-people exchanges in BRICS Countries under the Background of the Belt and Road Initiative" (CIISFTGB1903), and the research project of Chongqing international strategic research institute (CIISFTGB2005).

[**] Duan Mengjie, a Doctoral Student, is a Hindi Professional Teacher at Chongqing Non-Universal Language College of Sichuan International Studies University, mainly engaged in the Study of Indian Language and Culture, Sino-Indian Cultural and People-to-people Exchanges and Cross-cultural Communication.

level people-to-people exchanges mechanism achieving a complete success, China-India cultural and people-to-people exchanges entered a new stage, marking another key point in the history of exchanges. 2020 is the 70th anniversary of the establishment of China-India diplomatic relationship, and this paper aims to sort out the key cultural points in history of China-India cultural and people-to-people exchanges and pave the way for cross-cultural communication between Chinese and Indian civilizations.

Keywords: China-India Cultural and People-to-people Exchanges; China-India Relations; Cross-cultural Communication

Ⅰ. Introduction

China and India, as oriental civilizations boasting long history known as two dazzling pearls on the vast land of Asia, have been adjacent to each other for thousands of years. Nehru wrote in the book *Discovery of India*, "China and India 'are proud of the record of living in peace with each other for thousands of years... Their relationship is also of great significance for themselves and the world."[①] As an extremely important part of China-India relations throughout the history, cultural and people-to-people exchanges began long before the high-level visits, reaching its peak after Buddhism was introduced into China from India and the cultural key points in the China-India cross-cultural communication have continued to emerge, laying a solid foundation for the later cultural and people-to-people exchanges. In the process of China-India cultural and people-to-people exchanges, the questions about what the key points are and how we should make good use of these key points of culture in the process of China-India cross-cultural communication are what this paper tries to sort out and explore.

---

① [India] Nehru, Discovery of India, *World Knowledge Publishing House*, 1956, p. 1.

II. The Definition of China-India Cultural and People-to-people Exchanges

1. The Connotation of Cultural and People-to-people Exchanges

In "observe the laws of heaven and earth to understand the changes of the seasons, pay attention to cultural ethics to make people behave under civilized etiquette", the so-called "cultural ethics" in the *Book of Changes* originally refers to various phenomena in human society while *Cihai* defines "cultural ethics" as "various cultural phenomena of human society", so the connotation of "cultural ethics" has been embodied from various phenomena of human society in a broad sense to various cultural phenomena of human society in a narrow sense. Strategic mutual trust, economic and trade cooperation, and cultural and people-to-people exchanges are the three main components of China's foreign relations and three pillars of major-country diplomacy with Chinese characteristics in the new era, with cultural and people-to-people exchanges covering the most subjects and as the foundation of Sino-foreign relations proposed by Xi Jinping. The "cultural ethics" in the cultural and people-to-people exchanges between China and foreign countries in the context of today's globalization refers to "the advanced, scientific, excellent, and healthy parts of human culture, including advanced values and norms, valuing the role of people."[①]

When Du Kewei, director of the Chinese and Foreign cultural and People-to-people Exchanges Center of the Ministry of Education, gave a lecture at Si-

---

① On September 18, 2019, Du Kewei, director of the Chinese foreign cultural and people-to-people exchanges Center of the Ministry of Education, held a lecture on the theme of "adhering to the concept of cultural and people-to-people exchanges and furthering the cultural and people-to-people exchanges between China and foreign countries in colleges and universities" at Sichuan International Studies University. This is a record of a part of his speech at the lecture.

chuan International Studies University, where he made a clear definition of the connotation of cultural and people-to-people exchanges: "cultural and people-to-people exchanges refer to exchanges among people carried out by various subjects in various related fields in various forms."① Various related fields include education, science and technology, culture, health, sports, tourism, media, press and publishing, film and television art, youth, women, languages, archives, think tanks, etc., and can also be extended to ecological protection, poverty alleviation, disaster reduction, heritage protection, human resource development, military exchanges and other fields; various subjects include governments, schools, enterprises, social groups, individuals, etc. From this connotation, the cultural and people-to-people exchange, a person-to-person exchange and a culture-to-culture exchange, involve a wide range with a variety of levels in a flexible form. In July 2017, the "*Several Opinions on Strengthening and Improving Cultural and People-to-people Exchanges Work*" issued by the General Office of the Central Committee of the Communist Party of China and the General Office of the State Council, stated that the current purpose of strengthening and improving the work of cultural and people-to-people exchanges between China and foreign countries is to "promote the harmony between the people of China and foreign countries and mutual learning from civilizations"② and meanwhile, it is necessary to innovate high-level cultural and people-to-people exchanges mechanisms.

---

① On September 18, 2019, Du Kewei, director of the Chinese foreign cultural and people-to-people exchanges Center of the Ministry of Education, held a lecture on the theme of "adhering to the concept of cultural and people-to-people exchanges and furthering the cultural and people-to-people exchanges between China and foreign countries in colleges and universities" at Sichuan International Studies University. This is a record of a part of his speech at the lecture.

② Xinhua News Agency: "Document 'Several Opinions on Strengthening and Improving cultural and people-to-people exchanges'", the official website of the Information Office of the State Council of the People's Republic of China, December 22, 2017, http: //www. scio. gov. cn/tt/zdgz/ Document/1614051/1614051. htm. /1614051/1614051. htm.

2. The Connotation of China-India Cultural and People-to-people Exchanges

Historically, China-India cultural and people-to-people exchanges are a model of friendly exchanges among civilizations in the world[①]. At present, the establishment of a high-level cultural and people-to-people exchanges mechanism between China and India is on the right track. On December 21, 2018, the foreign ministers of China and India co-chaired the first meeting of the China-India high-level people-to-people exchanges mechanism in New Delhi, the capital of India, and identified eight key cooperation directions; on August 12, 2019, in the second meeting of the China-India high-level cultural and people-to-people exchanges mechanism held in Beijing, the foreign ministers of the two countries jointly signed the action plan for exchanges and cooperation between the Ministries of Foreign Affairs of China and India in 2020 and witnessed the signing of bilateral cooperation documents in people-to-people and cultural fields, such as culture, sports, traditional medicine, and museums,[②] showing the China-India cultural and people-to-people exchanges mechanism has been initially formed. At the 70th anniversary of the establishment of China-India diplomatic relationship, China-India relations usher in great development in 2020 and China-India cultural and people-to-people exchanges are about to play a key role in it. To answer the questions on how to establish a China-India high-level cultural and people-to-people exchanges mechanism and how to lay a good foundation for China-India relations, we should trace the origin from a historical perspective, look back on history, and explore more possibilities of China-India cultural and people-to-people exchanges.

[①] Yin Xinan, Sino-Indian cultural and people-to-people exchanges Research: History, Status Quo and Cognition, *Current Affairs Press*, 2015, p. 12.

[②] Ministry of Foreign Affairs: "The second meeting of the China-India High-level cultural and people-to-people exchanges Mechanism is held in Beijing, co-chaired by Wang Yi and Indian Foreign Minister Subrahmanyam Jaishankar", official website of Ministry of Foreign Affairs, August 12, 2019. https://www.mfa.gov.cn/web/wjbzhd/t1688111.shtml.

Ⅲ. Key Cultural Points in the History of China-India Cultural and People-to-people Exchanges

Many classic cases are in the history of China-India cultural and people-to-people exchanges, some widely known, and some not well known. Anyway, the key cultural points in China-India cultural and people-to-people exchanges are worthy of being summarized and used for references.

1. *Zhina* and Silk Clothes

"China" "Chine" in French with Sanskrit "Cina" as its source, once transliterated as *Zhina*, continuing into modern Hindi and used worldwide. The way the name *Zhina* was introduced to India may be closely related to China-India initial exchanges because the pronunciation of "Cina" is similar to "Qin" and is derived from the Chinese character "Qin", which was first proposed by French Sinologist Paul Pelliot (1878 - 1945). The earliest Indian documentary record that can be tested is in Kautilya's *Shastra* in the early Maurya Dynasty, written in the 4th century BC, coinciding with the time when Qin unified Shu, in which such phrases as "silk and silk clothing were produced in Cina"[1] existed. Besides, the word (Cina) is also reflected in the *Mahabharata*, one of the two major epics in India[2], respected by the Indian people as "a history book" with an extremely broad impact in India. The fact that the word (Cina) can be written into the epic poem shows that the Indian people had a preliminary understanding of China at that time, which is likely to be related to the nomadic tribes of the

---

[1] Xue Keqiao, A History of Sino-Indian Cultural Exchange, The Commercial Press, 1998, p. 6.

[2] The term "Cina (China)" appeared in Chapter 10 of Bhishma. When Chikuo asked Quansheng about the situation of both sides of the war, Quansheng introduced the situation of the supporters of the enemy to Chikuo. Section 64 of it mentioned "Cina" and the king of this country belongs to the Kshatriya caste. In this war, he supported the enemy, and finally the whole army was destroyed. This country called "Cina" is China.

Huns, Yuezhi, and Dawan that were active in northern and northwestern China at that time, referred to the Chinese as the "Qin people" for a long time and with the migration of tribes, this name was passed to ancient India. It can be inferred from the phrase "silk and silk clothing are produced in China" in *Shastra that* before the unification of Qin Dynasty, China and India had begun direct or indirect non-governmental trade with Chinese silk and silk clothing affirmed and promoted in some Indian regions and included in the Indian epic *Mahabharata* as a national image. The word (Cina) had also been widely spread, which had contributed to the initial understanding and communication between China and India.

Through the above research, we can see that the beginning of China-India cultural and people-to-people exchanges can be roughly before the Qin Dynasty unified China in the 3rd century BC, and the history of Sino-Indian cultural and people-to-people exchanges has exceeded two thousand years.

2. Moon Rabbit and Mansions

It is generally accepted that China-India cultural and people-to-people exchanges were after Buddhism was introduced to China and the spread of Buddhism to the east greatly promoted China-India cultural and people-to-people exchanges, but in fact, two-way China-India cultural and people-to-people exchanges had already begun before Buddhism was introduced. Here are two classic cases as examples.

In the story of moon rabbit, the ancient Chinese folklore, why not other animals in the moon in the imagination of the ancients instead of a rabbit? According to Mr. Ji Xianlin's research, the story of the origin of the Chinese so called "jade rabbit", closely related to India, circulated in both India and China, was recorded in Volume 7 of the *Traveling Notes of the Western Regions in Great Tang Dynasty*. Dishitian (Śakra) in the form of an old man, came to the martyrs' pool to test the three animals, fox, rabbit, and monkey, begging for food from them. The fox carried a carp and the monkey gathered fruits from the trees but the rabbit found nothing at all, so the old man complained, and the rabbit immediately asked the fox and monkey to collect firewood and make a fire, saying: "The benevolent! I am humble, and I can't do what I'm asked for. I'm willing to offer myself as your meal"①. After the rabbit threw himself into the fire, Dishitian (Śakra) revealed his true identity, lamented for a long time and drew the likeness of the rabbit on the Moon for all to see to make the rabbit immortal.

The beginning of this story reads: "Tathagata burned himself while practicing Bodhisattva in Stupa in the west of Martyr Pool."② The word "Stupa" is transliterated from Sanskrit (stupā), which is a form of a tower in India with a large number of applications in Hindu and Buddhist buildings. From the sentences "Tathagata burned himself while practicing Bodhisattva in Stupa" and "at that time, the Di Shitian wants to test the people who practice the Bodhisattva"③ and so on, it can be seen that this is the story of Buddha Jataka (Jātaka), formed no later than the third century BC according to the current archaeological research. The earliest record of the Moon Rabbit in China is in Qu Yuan's *Heavenly Questions* during the Warring States Period, which includes the sentence "what is the black spot in the moon? Is it a rabbit hiding in the belly of the moon"④, expressing doubt about the existence of the moon rabbit. The specific time of the poem is not available, but based on Qu Yuan's birth and death year (approximately 340 BC - 278 BC), it can be inferred that it was later than the story of Buddha Jataka (Jātaka). Regarding the origin of this story, Mr. Ji Xianlin also made a judgment, which is that "because this story is ancient in India and widely spread in India with many records in the ancient books, it is reasona-

---

① Original works of Xuanzang and Bianji, proofread by Ji Xianlin, etc. Collating notes on the western regions of Datang, Zhonghua Book Company, 2004, p. 579.
② Same as above.
③ Same as above.
④ Qu Yuan, Dong Chuping's translation and annotation, Translation and Annotation of the Song of Chu, Shanghai Ancient Books Publishing House, 2006, p. 80.

ble to say that it originated in India."[1]

The "coincidence" of moon rabbit is a testimony of China-India cultural and people-to-people exchanges, and an example of the influence of early Indian culture on Chinese culture, illustrating the attraction and interoperability of the cultures of China and India, and the transmission channels hidden behind the cultural and people-to-people exchanges are also worth exploring.

As mentioned above, the China-India cultural and people-to-people exchanges during this period were two-way. The "Moon Rabbit" came from India and similarly, Chinese culture also had a certain influence on India, especially in astronomy.

Since ancient times, the theory of Twenty-Eight Mansions in China is similar to that in ancient Indian astronomy, which is not a coincidence as the story of the moon rabbit. According to Mr. Zhu Kezhen's textual research, "it seems that there is no doubt that India's Twenty-Eight Mansions and China's have the same origin."[2] There are many similarities between China and India, enough to prove the theory of homology, while the question, which one comes first, argued by Chinese foreign scholars for nearly two hundred years. "In the three theories of originating from India, Babylon, and China, the Chinese origin theory provides the strongest evidence"[3]. The Japanese astronomer Shinzo Shinjo believes that the Twenty-Eight Mansions originated in China during the Zhou Dynasty, which is consistent with the current archaeological discoveries, in which, "Changsha Mawangdui Silk Book *Five Mansions* (168 BC), Hubei Shui Hu Di Qin Mu Zhu Jian *Rishu* (mid 2nd century BC), Anhui Shuanggudui disc lacquerware (165 BC), and Hubei Zenghouyi lacquer box cover (433 BC) all appeared with all the

---

[1] Ji Xianlin, A History of Sino-Indian cultural and people-to-people exchanges, Xinhua Press, 1991, p. 11.
[2] Zhu Kezhen, Collections of Zhu Kezhen, Science Press, 1979, p. 235.
[3] Zhao Yongheng, Li Yong, The Formation and Evolution of Twenty-Eight Mansions, Chinese Journal of History of Science and Technology, Issue 1, 2009, p. 110.

names of Twenty-Eight Mansions"[1].

The origin of the moon rabbit or the Twenty-Eight Mansions, the early result of China-India cultural and people-to-people exchanges, are both the collision and exchange between cultures, showing that the cultural and people-to-people exchanges between China and India were two-way.

3. Buddhism in the East

During the Han Dynasty, Buddhism began to spread to China and the China-India cultural and people-to-people exchanges reached a historical peak in the Sui and Tang Dynasties. The China-India cultural and people-to-people exchanges model has been greatly enriched in the process, which is reflected in many aspects:

a. Music Interoperability

According to legend, when Zhang Qian explored the Western Regions, he obtained two tunes in the Western Regions, called "Mahadur". Then, Li Yannian made 28 interpretations in Martial Music, which had a great influence on future military music.[2] In the title of the song, "Maha" means "great and vast" in Sanskrit, which can prove its origin in ancient India, and the music exchange between China and India has existed in ancient times.

With the spread of Buddhism in the East, Buddhist music with Chinese characteristics appeared under the influence of Indian Buddhist music. In teaching Buddhist scriptures, Indian Buddhists must not only memorize the scriptures, but also pay special attention to rhymes, chanting and singing with cadence, and fiction alternating with rhymed verses, which means chanting scriptures in prose style, and singing scriptures in rhyme style, making scriptures not boring and easy to remember. After Buddhism was introduced to China, people called chanting scriptures *Zhuandu* and singing *Jisong Fanbei*. The founder of Buddhist mu-

---

[1] Zhao Yongheng, Li Yong, The Formation and Evolution of Twenty-Eight Mansions, Chinese Journal of History of Science and Technology, Issue 1, 2009, p. 110.

[2] Wang Fuli, The meaning of the song name Mahadur and related issues, Historical Research, 2010, 3, p. 103.

sic and the creator of *Fanbei* is generally believed to be Cao Zhi, a famous writer and poet during the Three Kingdoms period,[①] the son of Wei Wu Emperor Cao Cao and the younger brother of Wei Wen Emperor Cao Pi, called King Chen Si by later generations because he was once named King Chen and his posthumous title was *Si* after his death. The story of his creation of Buddhist music, called *Yushan Fanbei* by later generations, is recorded in the Southern Dynasties Liang Sengyou's *Compilation of Notes on the Translation of the Tripitaka*, in Volume 12, *King Chen Si's notes on the Sanskrit sound system of Yushan*, but unfortunately only one title passed down, still making Cao Zhi a messenger of Indian music in China. This is a good story in the history of Chinese Buddhism, and it has promoted the China-India cultural and people-to-people exchanges.

b. Talent Exchanges

During the Three Kingdoms period, Buddhist culturehas its influence in China in the collision with Chinese traditional culture with the number of Buddhist followers gradually increased, and it is generally believed that the first climax of Indian Buddhists coming to China during the Wei, Jin, and Southern and Northern Dynasties when 30 or 40 Indian monks came to China, according to *Biographies of Eminent Monks*.

At the same time, people in China also began to travel westward to seek the Dharma, but they traveled westward entirely for religious beliefs, not sent by the government. During the Three Kingdoms period, Zhu Shixing went westward to Khotan (Hotan, Xinjiang) to seek Dharma, and sent his disciples to bring the original Sanskrit version of the *Prajna Sutra* back to the mainland. Although he could not reach India, he was the first person to seek Dharma in the west, and "he being a pioneer means a lot to the later generations"[②]. According to the records in the *Biographies of Eminent Monks*, the representatives of seeking

---

[①] Xue Keqiao, A History of Sino-Indian cultural and people-to-people exchanges, The Commercial Press, 1998, p. 25.

[②] Xue Keqiao, A History of Sino-Indian cultural and people-to-people exchanges, The Commercial Press, 1998, p. 25.

Dharma westward include Zhu Fahu in the Western Jin Dynasty, proficient in 36 languages, Kumarajiva, a Chinese and Indian Buddhist scholar and translator in the pre-Qin Dynasty, Faxian, the writer of *Record of The Buddhistic Kingdoms* in the Wei, Jin and Southern and Northern Dynasties, and Xuanzang who sought Dharma from the West in the Tang Dynasty. They not only obtained the Dharma, but also greatly promoted the China-India cultural and people-to-people exchanges to reach an unprecedented climax. The communication between Chinese and Indian eminent monks was, to a certain extent, the exchange of talents. Every eminent monk was a translator of Buddhist scriptures and they achieved the purpose of communication on the language level.

c. Literary Interoperability

Mr. Lu Xun once wrote in the inscription of *Chi Hua Man*: "I once heard that Tintu's fables are pretty rich, as the deep spring in the forest. The art and literature of other countries are often influenced by it."[①]. The "other countries" here includes China. Indian myths and fables have had a deep influence on Chinese literature, from the story of "Moon Rabbit" mentioned above to the ghost stories in the Six Dynasties and the legendary stories like *Bianwen* in the Tang Dynasty. This influence is mainly manifested in two aspects. One is the motif of the story. According to textual research, many widely-known Chinese stories were introduced from India, such as "all tricks have been exhausted" in Liu Zongyuan's article *Donkeys in Guizhou*, which is similar to the seventh story in the fourth volume of the *Panchatantra* of ancient Indian stories. Another example is "Cao Chong Weighs an Elephant" in the "Three Kingdoms: Wei", similar to the story of weighing an elephant in the *Miscellaneous Treasure*[②]. The second is the style. The "frame structure" or "continuous interspersed structure" began to manifest in the structure of the Tang legends. The organization of the story

---

① Lu Xun, Complete Works of Lu Xun, Volume Seven, People's Literature Publishing House. 2005, p. 103.

② Ji Xianlin, edited by Wang Shuying, Ji Xianlin on Sino-Indian cultural and people-to-people exchanges, New World Publishing House, 2006, pp. 279 - 286.

to manifest in the structure of the Tang legends. The organization of the story went from independent to interconnected, and the style was in line with *Mahabharata*, one of the two major epics in India, *Jātaka* in Pali and *Panchatantra*, a collection of stories.① For example, Wangdu's *Ancient Mirror* starts with a main story and connects many short stories through the mouth of different characters. It can be seen that the literary exchanges between China and India in ancient times were very rich and in-depth, which reflected the grand China-India cultural and people-to-people exchanges at that time.

4. Sugar-making Methods

The high-level cultural and people-to-people exchanges promoted by China and India have also existed since ancient times, and the representative case is sugar-making methods. Due to its unique climate factors, India has been producing sugarcane since ancient times and is familiar with sugar making methods, so China, relatively backward in sugar-making methods at the time, sent envoys on the official level to India to learn sugar-making methods in the early Tang Dynasty.② After learning and making improvements, the refined white sugar China produced surpassed India in terms of color and taste, and then India learned from China on how to make refined white sugar. Therefore, in modern Hindi, white sugar and white granulated sugar are called "cīnī", which also means "Chinese" in the Hindi language. The exchange of sugar-making methods is a typical example of the high-level cultural and people-to-people exchanges, which has great significance in the history of China-India cultural and people-to-people exchanges.

---

① Duan Mengjie, The Development of the Framework of Panchatantra in Eastern and Western Folk Literature, Literary Education (Part 2), Issue 6, 2019, p. 22.

② See the record in New History of the Tang Dynasty Volume 221, The Biography of the Western Regions · Mojieta Kingdom: Zhenguan 21... Tai Zong sent envoys to learn sugar-making methods, immediately asking Yangzhou for its sugar canes. The color and taste are much better than that in the Western Regions.

IV. The Possibility of Cross-cultural Communication between China and India

From the above analysis, the long and profound history of China-India cultural and people-to-people exchanges over two thousand years has laid a solid foundation for the establishment of a China-India high-level people-to-people exchanges mechanism between, offering lessons for the cross-cultural communication in the following areas:

1. Downplaying the "Clash of Civilizations" and Exploring Cultural Similarities

"Countries tend to follow countries with similar civilizations and resist countries that have no civilizational commonality with them"[①]. With Clash of Civilizations rampant nowadays, we should turn our attention from the West to the East to see that Chinese civilization and Indian civilization are both Eastern civilizations, and they are geographically and culturally close and extremely tolerant. Since ancient times, the China-India exchanges have never been interrupted, and greatly developed especially driven by the eastern spread of Buddhism. Exploiting cultural exchange points, such as the "Moon Rabbit" mentioned above, is conducive to enhancing mutual understanding, reducing the sense of estrangement and promoting mutual communication between the Chinese and Indian people.

2. Learning from the Experience of Buddhist Scripture Translation and Strengthening the Foreign Translation of Chinese Classics

A large number of Buddhist scriptures, translated and introduced during the Han, Sui, and Tang Dynasties, greatly promoted the spread of Buddhism in China

---

① Samuel Huntington, translated by Zhou Qi, etc., The Clash of Civilizations and the Reconstruction of World Order, Xinhua Publishing House, 2010, p. 135.

and introduced Indian culture into China, which has been prominently reflected in the field of Chinese storytelling. In ancient times, the intertranslation of classics was mainly on the translation of Buddhist scriptures. The eminent monks translated the scriptures retrieved from Tintu into Chinese and held lectures. This "only import, no export" situation led to an imbalance of the China-India cultural and people-to-people exchanges, and the Indian people lack a window to understand China, so we should strengthen the foreign translation of Chinese classics. Due to the use of many local languages in India, attention should also be paid to bilingualism in the process of multilingualism. The Chinese classics that have been translated into English should be greatly recommended in India, and the translation of Chinese classics into Hindi should be strengthened to enhance the understanding of China by the Indian grassroots.

3. High-level Support for Cultural and People-to-people Exchanges

The development of sugar-making methods has benefited from the high-level advancement of China and India. However, since ancient times, the China-India cultural and people-to-people exchanges have been dominated by non-governmental spontaneous exchanges, and no high-level cultural and people-to-people exchanges mechanism has been established. In recent years, after the first meeting of China-India high-level cultural and people-to-people exchanges, China-India cultural and people-to-people exchanges embarked on a "top-down" road, with frequent high-level exchanges activities and non-governmental exchanges not widely held. As a way of communication between people, cultural and people-to-people exchanges should learn from past to develop non-governmental cultural and people-to-people exchanges, and encourage people in China and India to organize spontaneous non-governmental activities. High-level cultural and people-to-people exchanges mechanisms should pave the way for non-governmental cultural and people-to-people exchanges activities and incline to non-governmental activities in high-level meetings and activities. The two tracks should be parallel to develop the communication between people.

Ⅴ. Conclusion

The China-India high-level cultural and people-to-people exchanges mechanism established in 2018 under the advocacy of General Secretary Xi Jinping and Prime Minister Modi is of great significance to the positive development of China-India relations. 2020 marks the 70th anniversary of the establishment of diplomatic relations between China and India. The leaders of China and India have determined 2020 to be "India-China Cultural and People-to-People Exchanges" year and agreed to celebrate the 70th anniversary of the establishment of China-India diplomatic relationship by hosting 70 events, which are greatly affected under the influence of the "black swan", the epidemic situation of COVID-19 and the recurring frictions due to historical border issues, one of the biggest obstacles to China-India cultural and people-to-people exchanges between since 1962.

Cultural and people-to-people exchanges depend on interpersonal communication. Although China-India relations are "constrained by major structural factors such as territorial disputes, Tibet issues, cross-border river issues, China-Pakistan relations issues and maritime strategic competition"[1], we should put aside the dispute and seek development by actively seeking the cultural commonalities between China and India, and using key cultural points as the starting point to promote the communication between the people of China and India.

---

[1] Zhang Jiadong, Problems and Transcendence in Sino-Indian Relations. Journal of China's Peripheral Diplomacy, No. 1, 2016, p. 164.

Disaster Management Capacity of South Africa and Its Challenges: An Analysis of South Africa's Response to the COVID-19 Epidemic

Meng Lijun[*]

Abstract: South Africa stresses disaster management, and has instituted a comprehensive disaster management system which has played an important role in South Africa's response to the COVID-19 epidemic. At the same time, the challenges faced by this system were revealed in this process. Those challenges mainly include emergency response resources shortage, the hardship to sustain people's livelihood and the pressure to maintain economic operation.

Keywords: South Africa; Disaster Management; COVID-19; Challenges

South Africa has contributed to disaster management since 1997 when it issued the *State of Emergency Act* to deal with various emergencies, later in 2002 the *Disaster Management Act* came out that has further improved the establishment of disaster management system with its crucial structure improved. This system, under the guidance of the *Disaster Management Framework* formulated

---

[*] Meng Lijun, the Lecturer from the Institute of International Relations of Sichuan International Study University.

in accordance with the Act, includes contents of establishment of disaster management institutions, personnel appointments, operating mechanisms, division of responsibilities and rights, department coordination, coordination central and local governments coordination, and actions in spheres of prevention, preparedness, response recovery.

The *Disaster Management Act* of South Africa was issued in 2002 and promulgated in 2003, as a particular law to cope with various disasters. Then on April 2004, it begun to be implemented officially, consisting of 8 chapters and 65 subsections with uniformly stipulated regulations on disaster definition, disaster prevention, disaster reduction, emergency preparedness, response measures, disaster recovery, and establishment of disaster management centre in all spheres of government (national, provincial, municipal), voluntary management and other matters. "Disaster", as the definition of the Act, refers to "progressive or sudden, widespread or localized, natural or human-induced occurrence which causes or threatens to cause: death, injury or disease; damage to property, infrastructure or environment; or disruption of the life of a community and is of a magnitude that exceeds the ability of those affected by the disaster to cope with its effects only using their own resources"[1]. And "disaster management" means a continuous and integrated multi-sectoral, multi-disciplinary process of planning and implementation of measures aimed at preventing or reducing disaster risks, emergency preparedness, mitigating the severity or consequences of disasters, a rapid and effective response to disasters, post-disaster recovery and rehabilitation.[2] It is clearly shown that disaster management in South Africa is a comprehensive system covering what we commonly refrred to as "urgency", "emergency", and "public incident". It involves all respects of disaster prevention, implementation, and recovery with uniformity in the approach taken by all levels of governments, departments and various social communities.

---

[1] Disaster Management Act. 2002, section 1, Chapter 1.
[2] Disaster Management Act. 2002, section 1, Chapter 1.

Ⅰ. Overview of South Africa's Disaster Management System

1. Institutions and Responsibilities

Intergovernmental Committee on Disaster Management (ICDM) is responsible for the coordination of disaster management in South Africa, established by the President in accordance with the Law, consisting of ministers of the central government involved in disaster management or the administration of legislation; MECs of each province involved in disasters management in their respective provinces selected by the Premier of the province concerned; members of municipal councils selected by the South Africa Local Government Association. The chairman of the committee is a minister of the cabinet whose department is most responsible for the manegement of a specific disaster. The responsibilities of the committee, include coordinating (according to section 3 of the Constitution) intergovernmental coorperation on disaster management matters, reporting such coorperation to the cabinet and making suggestions and recommendations to the Cabinet on developing a unified national framework for disaster management that could be implemented by all spheres of government, statutory functionaries, non-governmental institutions, the private sector, communities and individuals.

South Africa also established a consulting mechanism with the National Disaster Management Advisory Forum being the functional organization. It is organized by a minister of the cabinet whose department is most responsible for the manegement of a specific disaster, and the Head of National Disaster Management Centre serves as the chairman. The members include the Head of National Disaster Management Centre; a representative of each national department whose Minister is a member of ICDM, designated by that minister; a representative of each provincial department whose MEC is a member of ICDM, designated by that MEC; municipal officials selected by the South Africa Local Government Association; representatives of other role-players designated by the minister which may include commerce, mines, agriculture, health care, education, labor, insurance, religion and social welfare, science and technology; disaster management experts, and other personnel co-opted by the Forum for a specific period or discussions. The forum is a platform on which various executives involved in disaster management consult one another and coordinate their respective actions on matters relating to disaster management. At the same time, the forum should make recommendations to ICDM concerning the disaster management framework, and provide advice on disaster management related matters to any organ of state, statutory staff, non-governmental organizations, and communities, and private sector.

The Department of Cooperative Governance and Traditional Affairs in South Africa is responsible for the implementation of the *Disaster Management Act*, under which, National Disaster Management Centre is specifically responsible for coordinating governmental institutions at all levels, statutory staff, disaster management-related executors and communities to promote the construction of the integrated and coordinated disaster management framework to reduce and prevent disasters risk. The Head of National Disaster Management Centre is appointed by the Minister of Cooperative Governance and Traditional Affairs and is responsible for the overall affairs of the centre. Beside the head, the staff of the centre include persons in the service of the Department designated by the director of the Department, internal staff appointment in the Ministry of Cooperation Governance and Traditional Affairs, employees seconded from other organ of state or organizations if needed. The Head of the Centre may assign part of the duties to its staff or to the provincial or municipal disaster management centres in accordance to the Act. The National Disaster Management Centre must: specialize disaster management matters; monitor government of all levels and statutory to comply with the Act and the Disaster Management Framework; supervise the process of post-disaster recovery and reconstruction; communicate and preserve disasters and related information; provide disaster management consultation and advice for organs of state, statutory functionaries, communities and other institutions; make recommendations regarding disaster management funds and make the fund available; and make recommendations on draft legislation on national disaster management and the convergence of national, provincial and municipal disaster-related legislation, assist in the implementation of legislation related, provide opinions on the declaration of the national state of disaster, promote the recruitment, training and participation of volunteers, promote disaster management capacity building, training and education throughout the public, promote the development of disaster management research and cooperation with provincial and municipal disaster management centre. Meanwhile the National Disaster Management Centre should establish a smooth liaison mechanism to document information needed for disaster management, including the contact information, division of labor, and emergency service capabilities of various emergency response institutions involving governments at all levels, non-governmental organizations, private sectors, experts, voluntary organizations, international institutions, foreign non-governmental organizations. Besides, the National Disaster Management Centre should establish and maintain a disaster management information system to collect, organize and preserve information relating to disaster management including disaster warning, prevention, emergency response capabilities and resources, disaster management research and training facilities and other disaster-related information. In addition, the National Disaster Management Centre also has responsibility for formulating disaster management plans and strategies, monitoring and evaluating disaster management plans and disaster prevention, treatment and mitigation proposals put forward by spheres of governments; providing advice and guidance to executives on implementation relating to disaster management by means of issuing bulletins or taking actions, predicting and evaluating the type, degree of harm and impact of disasters that have occurred or will occur to determine the level of response. Finally, the National Disaster Management Centre also needs to yearly submit an annual report to the Minister of the department involved in disaster management, about the situation of disasters that occurs during the year in each province, the result of monitoring and mitigation initiatives, the effects and evaluation of emergency plans and strategies.

2. Operation of the Disaster Management System

The Disaster Management Framework in South Africa performs within national, provincial, and municipal spheres of government. This article mainly focuses on the performance at the national level. South Africa drafted the *Disaster Management Framework* under the *Disaster Management Act*, which clearly divided the process of disaster management into four performances: policy-making, implementation, recommendation, and international cooperation, as shown in Figure 8-1:

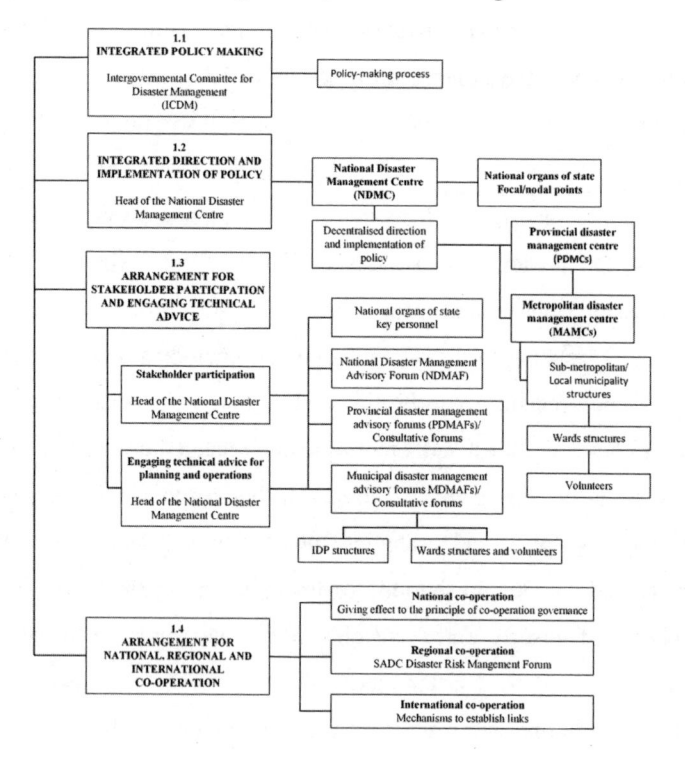

Figure 8-1 the Operation of South Africa's Disaster Management System

Source: *Disaster Management Framework*[①]

---

① *Disaster Management Framework*, section 1.1.1, chapter 1.

The first modulerefers to the decision-making of the central government, and the process is shown in Figure 8-2. First, the National Disaster Management Centre collects policy recommendations related to disaster risk management policy and submits them to the National Disaster Management Advisory Forum; then, recommendations should be submitted to the Relevant Cabinet cluster committees for assessment and further recommendations before being submitted to the ICDM and thereafter Cabinet for final decision, then it will be sent back to the National Disaster Management Centre for implementation and further improvement.

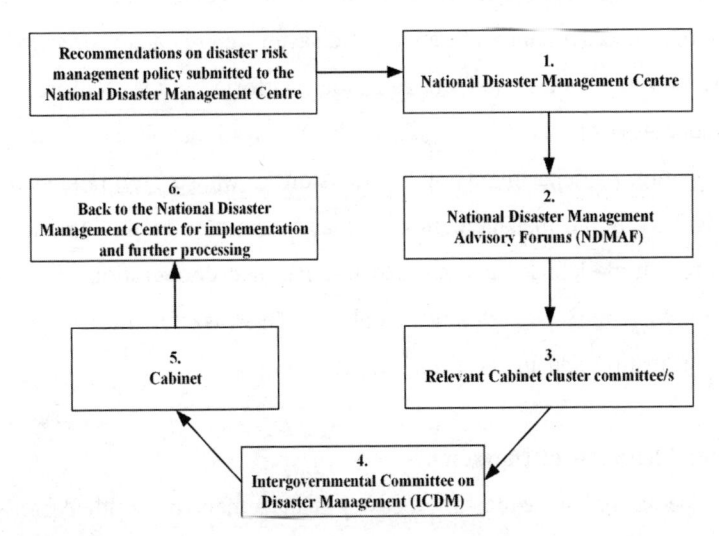

Figure 8-2 Decision-making Process of South African Government for Disaster Management

Source: *Disaster Management Framework*[①]

The second modulerefers to the implementation, which is coordinated by the National Disaster Management Centre through cooperation and discussion among disaster-related departments of the central government. The disaster man-

---

[①] *Disaster Management Framework*, section 1.1.2, chapter 1.

agement policies must be submitted to the ICDM for assessment, there after the Cabinet for final decision. Then they will be sent back to the National Disaster Management Centre for implementation. The National Disaster Management Centre is responsible for making detailed policies and guidelines according to concrete situations. Provincial and municipal disaster management centres will follow those guidelines and implement those polices engaging communities and other institutions and individuals involved in disaster management.

The third module is the recommendation, usually connected with the decision-making process with linkages with government decision-making. The main sources of opinions comes from the opinions of functional departments (including opinions of provincial and municipal disaster centre) and professional opinions. The communication and coordination platform is the National Disaster Management Advisory Forum, organized by the National Disaster Centre, with the participation of departments and professionals, whose recommendations will be summarized by the management centre and submitted to the superior.

The fourth module is regional and international cooperation that is subject to the Foreign Affairs Department, mainly involves disaster information sharing, policy coordination and international assistance.

3. Disaster Management Measures

The specialized measures of disaster management in South Africa can be divided into three stages: pre-disaster preparedness, emergency response, and post-disaster recovery and rehabilitation.

Disaster Management Framework requires all government departments involved in disaster management to formulate disaster management plans a part of their whole work plans and submit them to the National Disaster Management Centre. Each department's plan should clarify the department's work involved disaster management, the role and responsibilities of the department in the overall work of national disaster management, the role and responsibilities in emergency response, post-disaster recovery and rehabilitation, the performance capacity, and specific disaster management strategies, the disposal measures and procedures in face with disaster and the financial guarantee relating to disaster management In addition, each department should regularly evaluate and update its disaster management plan, and coordinate it with the plans of other departments and institutions.

In addition, South Africa attaches great importance to disaster warning, disaster education and research. Early warning mainly consists of the collection, monitoring and dissemination of disaster risk information. The South African National Disaster Management Centre has formulated corresponding risk information collection specifications and guidelines according to different types of disasters (geology, biology, climate, technology, environment), and requires governments at all levels and various government institutions to integrate disaster risk assessment with production development planning and submit a risk assessment report every year. Disaster risk monitoring mainly includes disaster hazard tracking, disaster event tracking and hazard monitoring. National and provincial government departments and relevant research institutions are responsible for monitoring, updating and reporting disaster risk information to the National Disaster Management Centre according to their respective business scopes. In addition, disaster management centres at all levels have established mechanisms to obtain and evaluate disaster risk information, and issue risk warnings.

Disaster education and research mainly involve disaster-related knowledge education, skills training, public awareness training and disaster management research. The South African National Disaster Management Centre is responsible for formulating a national disaster education, training and research framework, combining primary and secondary school curriculum, relevant professional qualifications, and government staff ability training to implement education and training projects so as to improve the capability of the public, professionals and government personnel to response to disaster event timely.

The emergency response to disasters involves a series of response measures that the country can take when entering a disaster state. When a national-level disaster occurs, the ministers of the departments involved in the disaster can declare the country into a state of disaster according to law. After that, the minister has the right to issue or authorize other departments to issue regulations or instructions to deal with disasters after consulting the ministers of other disaster-related departments. These regulations and instructions mainly involve: the opening of resources available to the central government, such as stores, equipment, vehicles, facilities, etc.; the dispatch of emergency service personnel from central government departments; the application of some or all of the provisions of the national disaster management plan; the evacuation of people in disaster-affected areas and evacuation; internal and external transportation links in the affected area; internal and external transportation of people and materials in the affected area; requisition of houses in the affected area; provision, control and use of temporary emergency accommodation; suspension or restriction of the sale, distribution or transportation of alcoholic beverages in the affected area; installation and maintenance of temporary communication lines inside and outside the disaster region; release of disaster information; emergency procurement procedures; measures to promote disaster response and post-disaster recovery and reconstruction; other measures to prevent disaster escalation or alleviate the impact of disasters; steps to obtain international assistance, etc. Each of the above-mentioned regulations and directives contains penalties for violations. The national disaster status can last for 3 months after the announcement, and the minister of the competent department may announce the end or extension of the disaster status in advance depending on the circumstances, and each extension shall not exceed 1 month.

South Africa's Disaster Management Framework only makes some principled provisions for post-disaster recovery and reconstruction. For example, the primary responsible department for disaster management should promote the establishment of post-disaster reconstruction teams, determine reconstruction tasks, ensure the smooth progress of reconstruction, supervise the reconstruction process, and ensure reconstruction work conducive to the follow-up development of the disaster-affected area.

II. South Africa's Management of the COVID-19 Epidemic

1. South Africa's Epidemic Management Measures

South Africa's response to the COVID-19 epidemic can be divided into two periods: "strict control" and "relaxed control" distinguished by whether to adopt strict isolation measures.

The chairman of the South African COVID-19 Epidemic Ministerial Advisory Committee divided the South African government's response to the COVID-19 epidemic into 8 stages[1], as shown in Figure 8-3. The first stage is

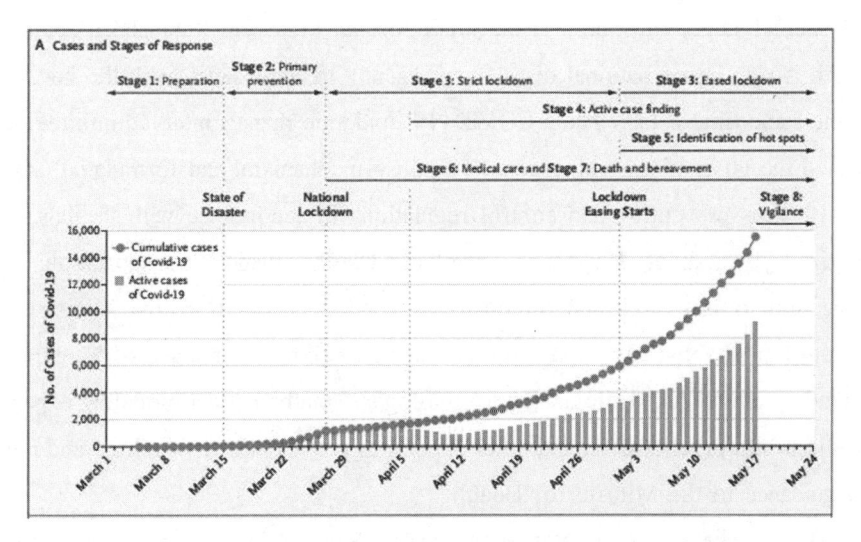

Figure 8-3 The Different Stages of South Africa's Response to the Epidemic and Its Development

Source: Salim S. Abdool Karim[2]

---

[1] Salim S. Abdool Karim, The South African Response to the Pandemic, The new england journal of medicine, 382 (24), June 11, 2020.

[2] Salim S. Abdool Karim, The South African Response to the Pandemic, The new england journal of medicine, 382 (24), June 11, 2020.

the preparation stage, that is, the establishment of virus detection capabilities. The South African Ministry of Health has been following up the development of the epidemic. On January 31, when the World Health Organization announced the COVID-19 virus as an "international public health emergency", the emergency operations centre was activated, and rapid performance groups were established in 9 national provinces, to ensure the managemant and control the suspected cases, timely warning, organization of a large number of staff to monitor and report on epidemic risk based on the established disaster risk information collection, monitoring machine. Until March 5, 2020, South Africa had its first confirmed case.

Ten days after the first case was discovered, the number of confirmed cases in South Africa reached 51, and the epidemic prevention and control entered the second stage. On March 15th, South African President Ramaphosa declared South Africa into a national disaster emergency in accordance with the law, and at the same time established a COVID-19 epidemic management committee, activated the government's emergency response mechanism, and formulated COVID-19 virus prevention and control regulations in accordance with the law, authorized government departments involving health, finance, transportation, and education to issue relevant directives as needed. In addition, the Ministry of Health has established a high-level advisory committee composed of 51 experts including clinicians, virologists, epidemiologists, mathematical modeling experts, public health practitioners, and other experts to provide strategic advice and policy guidance to the Minister of Health.

In this phase and the subsequent phases, South Africa has introduced a series of comprehensive measures to deal with the epidemic involving prevention and control, treatment, and people's livelihood. Prevention and control measures mainly include closing sea and land ports, canceling social activities, suspending store operations, closing schools and some nursing facilities, suspending visits to corrections and detention centres, launching epidemic prevention publicity campaigns, establishing isolation sites, and mobilizing the National Defense

Forces to assist the police in maintaining society order. Treatment measures include designating 11 public hospitals to treat patients with COVID-19 pneumonia free of charge; encouraging private laboratories to provide testing services, setting up "drive-through" testing stations and mobile testing vehicles to expand the scale of testing; rebuilding or expanding hospitals and implementing "emergency procurement procedures", doctors training and exchange treatment experience with China to improve treatment capabilities. In terms of people's livelihood protection, the South African government requires that basic goods and services must not be arbitrarily increased in price, suppliers must not hoard goods, and product sales must be distributed fairly; shelters that meet hygiene standards are provided for the homeless, quarantine places for residents who cannot be isolated at home; to pay wages to employees of troubled companies through the "employee temporary relief plan", and provide a monthly tax subsidy of 500 rand for more than 4 million private enterprise employees whose income is less than 6,500 rand. In addition, Ramaphosa also announced on April 21 that it will implement an economic support and social assistance program of about 26.3 billion U.S. dollars to fight the epidemic, help the poor and trapped enterprises, and resume work and production.

The fourth stage is mainly for a large-scale test, the stage of actively discovering infected patients. The South African government employs more than 28,000[1] community worker went to the high-risk community for case testing. The fifth stage focuses on controlling the local spread of the epidemic in hotspots regions; the sixth stage focuses on the treatment of patients including the establishment of temporary hospitals to provide medical services for patients with mild symptoms; the seventh stage focuses on the burial of died patients, the psychological assistance of cured patients and dead patients' relatives; the last stage mainly involves the monitoring of herd immunity and the prevention of

---

[1] Salim S. Abdool Karim, The South African Response to the Pandemic, The new england journal of medicine, 382 (24), June 11, 2020.

subsequent epidemics.

2. The Effect of Epidemic Management in South Africa

Throughout the process of the development of the COVID-19 epidemic in South Africa, especially in the period of strict control, the government has demonstrated good ability and leadership in responding to disaster events. Decisive leadership is indispensable in the response to the COVID-19 epidemic, and the common knowledge feature of decisive leadership is to clearly understand the consequences of danger and slow action, and to take quick action on this basis.[1] Studies have shown that the speed with which strict measures are taken against the COVID-19 epidemic can produce significantly different results.[2] The South African government has decisively declared that the country has entered a disaster from the early stage of the epidemic, issued prevention and control regulations, established an emergency management agency, and authorized government departments such as the Ministry of Transport, the Ministry of Trade and Industry, the Ministry of Health, and the Ministry of Education to quickly issue separate response regulations, and use the National Defense Force to assist the police to maintain social order and ensure the implementation of various measures. From decision-making, planning to implementation, it reflects the government's accurate judgment and thorough efficient execution in the face of emergencies. The effect of these measures is obvious. For example, research shows that the prohibition of alcohol alone has a positive effect on epidemic control[3]. Rapid quarantine measures and extensive screening are the key to dealing with the virus

---

[1] Ahmed Mohammed Obaid Al Saidi, Fowsiya Abikar Nur, Ahmed Salim Al-Mandhari, et al. Decisive leadership is a necessity in the COVID-19 response. *The Lancet*, Vol. 396, 295 - 298.

[2] Hale T, Angrist N, Kira B, et al. Variation in government responses to COVID-19 (version 6. 0). Blavatnik School of Government working paper. May 25, 2020. https: //www. bsg. ox. ac. uk/sites/default/files/2020 - 05/BSG - WP - 2020 - 032 - v6.0. pdf (accessed June 25, 2020).

[3] Reuter, H., Jenkins, L. S., De Jong, M., Reid, S., & Vonk, M. (2020). Prohibiting alcohol sales during the coronavirus disease 2019 pandemic has positive effects on health services in south africa. African Journal of Primary Health Care & Family Medicine, 12 (1).

and are also characteristics of South Africa's early success[1]. "The government's leadership in effectively controlling the spread of the COVID-19 virus using existing policy packages has achieved remarkable results."[2] As of the same time, the government's targeted relief measures for the poor and homeless people have also won the general support of the people.[3]

However, South Africa's strict "city lockdown" measures that began on March 26 have been gradually unblocked from May 1, and various prevention and control measures have been further released on June 1, and the epidemic has rebounded. As of the end of August, the total number of confirmed cases in South Africa has exceeded 620,000, with more than 11,000 confirmed cases per million people. Why did South Africa gradually relax its prevention and control efforts when the early prevention and control measures have achieved significant results, leading to a more serious follow-up epidemic? The reason is closely related to the challenges facing South Africa's Disaster Management Framework. "South Africa's response to the COVID-19 pandemic is like a big ship built while sailing."[4]

Ⅲ. Challenges to South Africa's Disaster Management Capacity Building

"Emergency management capabilities signify a country's comprehensive national power... it is practically shown that a country's level of public safety pro-

---

[1] Bibi-Aisha Wadvalla. (2020). COVID-19: Decisive action is the hallmark of south Africa's early success against coronavirus. Bmj, 369.

[2] Ataguba, J., Ayo-Yusuf, O., Greeff, M., Hofman, K., Lutge, E., Madhi, S., ... Wright, C. (2020). COVID-19 statement: The unanticipated costs of COVID-19 to south africa's quadruple disease burden. South African Journal of Science, 116 (7), 1-2.

[3] Marcus, T. S., Heese, J., Scheibe, A., Shelly, S., Lalla, S. X., & Hugo, J. F. (2020). Harm reduction in an emergency response to homelessness during south Africa's COVID-19 lockdown. Harm Reduction Journal, 17, 1-8.

[4] Salim S., Abdool Karim. The South African Response to the Pandemic, *The new england journal of medicine*, 382 (24), June 11, 2020.

tection depends on three dimensional elements: 1) the economic foundation and productivity level; 2) science and engineering capabilities; 3) the concept of governance, development model, value recognition, especially the macro policy orientation of local governments."[1] The emergency management capability of a country also relies on its own basic capabilities such as economy, resources, and technological level because "effective human, financial, and material resources is the basis for emergency response work."[2] The International Health Regulations require that each State party shall possess eight core responsibilities including national legislation, policies and financing, coordination and communication between national departments concerned, monitoring, response, preparation, risk communication, human resources and laboratories, among which, the financing, human resources, and laboratory capabilities are also requirements for a country's resource protection. Examining the emergency response capability (or disaster management capability) for the country depends on its institutional measures in the various aspects of prevention, preparation, response, and recovery and smooth and efficient system performance; besides, the operational guarantee capability is also indispensable to the realization of an emergency system. Emergency management short of implementation capability is impractical, just as software out of hardware support cannot run, just as surveys in Burundi and other countries have shown that whether to guarantee funds became the main stumbling block to the success of disaster risk reduction.[3]

Although South Africa is widely regarded as an international eugenic in disaster risk management, there are still a large number of studies showing that it

---

[1] 刘铁民：《构建新时代国家应急管理体系》，《中国党政干部论坛》2019 年第 7 期，第 6—11 页。

[2] 闪淳昌、周玲、秦绪坤、沈华、宿洁：《我国应急管理体系的现状、问题及解决路径》，《公共管理评论》2020 年第 2 期，第 5—20 页。

[3] Kellett, J. and Sparks, D. (2012), Disaster Risk Reduction: Spending Where it Should Count, *Global Humanitarian Assistance*, Somerset, pp. 1 - 40. Kellett, J. and Sweeney, H. (2011), Analysis of Financing Mechanisms and Funding Streams to Enhance Emergency Preparedness, *Development Initiatives*, Somerset, pp. 1 - 142.

has many shortcomings in the process of implementing disaster risk reduction measures as the lack of appropriate local skills and implementation capabilities.[1] The challenges facing South Africa's disaster management are largely due to its insufficient ability to guarantee the implementation of various disaster management plans and measures. South Africa has been facing a lot of pressure in the process of fighting the COVID‐19 epidemic, as a result, many of its measures to deal with the epidemic became unsustainable. These pressures include: shortages of hospital beds, doctors, medical equipment, protective material; limited production capacity of medical materials, insufficient material reserves, and limited social resources; unemployment of low-income groups, shortage of living materials for the poor; the industries of tourism, catering, transportation shocks, and the business difficulties for small and medium-sized enterprises; taxes reduction; heavier debt due to the anti-epidemic expenditure, and the government's financial pressure increasing. The above-mentioned pressures are the main reasons why South Africa's early effective anti-epidemic measures cannot be sustained. This article believes that South Africa's difficulties in emergency resources, livelihood security and economic operation are the main challenges facing its disaster management capacity building. These challenges restrict South Africa's disaster management framework from playing a better role.

1. Challenge to Emergency Response Resources

The first problem that South Africa faced in the response to the COVID‐19 epidemic was the shortage of medical materials. Like most countries, South Africa had serious shortages of masks, protective clothing and other materials, ventilators, monitors and other equipment when the epidemic broke out. Due to the lack of production capacity, the shortage of these supplies cannot be made

---

[1] Dewald, V. N. (2015). Disaster risk governance in africa. *Disaster Prevention and Management*, 24 (3), 397‐416.

up by domestic production in short term. Export bans and panic buying of medical supplies in other countries have made it more difficult for South Africa to obtain these substances. South African President Ramaphosa actively promoted the localized production of medical materials and led the establishment of the "African Medical Material Supply Platform"[①], and Minister of Trade, Industry and Competition also believes that Africa should increase its economic resilience and reduce its dependence on external supplies: "African countries are learning a painful lesson, that is, we can't just always stay in raw material exporting countries and medical supplies and food importing countries"[②]. However, a slow remedy can not meet an urgency. It is difficult to establish a perfect and sustainable medical material production system in a short time because, it is far from a day's work.

South Africa's emergency resource shortages in response to the COVID-19 epidemic are also reflected in its insufficient capacity for treatment. South Africa has long faced the threat of infectious diseases such as AIDS and tuberculosis, so that the public has a huge demand for medical services. According to a survey of 195 countries and regions released by The *Lancet* in May 2018, South Africa's medical accessibility and quality index score was 49.7, lower than the global average (54.4), ranked 127th among all survey respondents.[③] "Serious capacity shortages and structural problems have weakened the ability of

---

① South africa: President ramaphosa launches the africa medical supplies platform to help fight COVID-19 coronavirus pandemic. (2020). MENA Report, Retrieved from https: //search. proquest. com/docview/2415712921 · accountid = 13855.

② Coronavirus-south africa: Building african economic resilience is key for continental prosperity, says minister patel in briefing african union ministers: The disruptions caused by covid - 19 to global supply-chains has come at an enormous economic cost to countries across the world, including those in africa. (2020, Jul 28). African Press Organisation. Database of Press Releases Related to Africa Retrieved from https: //search. proquest. com/docview/2427496927 · accountid = 13855.

③ Measuring performance on the healthcare access and quality index for 195 countries and territories and selected subnational locations: A systematic analysis from the global burden of disease study 2016. (2018). The Lancet, 391 (10136), 2236 - 2271.

the South African health system and its staff to meet public service requirements."① In addition, due to limited medical resources being concentrated on responding to the COVID-19 epidemic, it is difficult for a large number of patients with other infectious and underlying diseases to obtain basic medical services. Similar deficiencies are also manifested in "the limited professional skills and research capabilities make it impossible to carry out research on disease transmission and vaccine and to conduct treatment research for local cases."② The insufficiency of medical resources clearly reveals the challenge of emergency resource guarantee faced by South Africa's disaster management capacity building.

2. Challenge to People's Livelihood

Another problem that the South African governmentis faced with in disaster management is to guarantee the living of the poor. About a quarter of South Africa's population lives in slums, most of whom do not have fixed jobs or incomes and cannot store food and daily necessities to prevent the epidemic or other disasters. They live in humble homes without running water, and their sanitary conditions are bad. In addition, South Africa has a large number of homeless people and refugees, and the COVID-19 epidemic has exposed their vulnerability. Strict isolation measures make them lose their source of livelihood, and the distressed living conditions make it impossible for them to maintain social distance or self-isolate. The "closure" measures implemented to control the epidemic have also led to the bankruptcy of many small and medium-sized enterpri-

---

① Richard Downie, Sahil Angelo. (2015). Assessing South Africa's Ability to Meet Its Health Needs, in Counting the Cost of South Africa s Health Burden, 4 - 18. Retrieved from http: //www. jstor. com/stable/resrep23948. 8, current as of day 1st September, 2020.

② Umviligihozo, G., Mupfumi, L., Sonela, N., Naicker, D., Obuku, E. A., Koofhethile, C., . . . Balinda, S. N. (2020). Sub-saharan africa preparedness and response to the COVID-19 pandemic: A perspective of early career african scientists [version 1; peer review: Awaiting peer review]. Wellcome Open Research.

ses, so that a large number of workers being unemployed and living in trouble. An assessment report assessing the impact of the COVID-19 epidemic on the economy and business of KwaZulu-Natal province showed that 45.7% of employees were severely affected by the epidemic and had to accept a pay cut; 29.7% of employees were required to take paid leave which relies on government subsidies; some employees have been temporarily dismissed.[①] It is extremely difficult for people with no resources to comply with strict prevention and control regulations. Therefore, ensuring the basic livelihood of the poor has become a key point in the fight against the epidemic. The South African government has adopted a series of measures such as distributing free food, providing clean drinking water, establishing temporary isolation places for homeless people, reducing taxes, and providing financial subsidies for small and medium-sized enterprises. However, due to successive droughts, capital outflows, increased debt, and slow economic development in South Africa in recent years, the government can use very limited funds for people's livelihood protection. Therefore, the lack of people's livelihood guarantee capacity constitutes a serious challenge for South Africa's disaster management capacity building.

3. Challenge to Economy Operation

Disaster events will hinder the normal operation of the economy, and which, will in turn restrict the effects of various efforts such as disaster reduction, disaster relief, and disaster recovery. Research by Marc Suhrcke et al. showed that the economic crisis will make the spread of community-borne diseases worse.[②] During the COVID-19 epidemic, strict "closure" measures

---

① South africa: MEC nomusa dube-ncube on coronavirus COVID-19 KwaZulu-natal economic and business impact assessment report. (2020). MENA Report, Retrieved from https: //search. proquest. com/docview/2415058531 · accountid = 13855.

② Suhrcke, M., Stuckler, D., Suk, J. E., Desai, M., Senek, M., McKee, M., . . . Semenza, J. C. (2011). The impact of economic crises on communicable disease transmission and control: A systematic review of the evidence. PLoS One, 6 (6), 1 - 12.

means partial stagnation of economic operations. In South Africa, where the economy lacks resilience, government has to consider how much and how long the economic operation can withstand the interference caused by strict anti-epidemic measures when making anti-epidemic decisions. In fact, South Africa's economy, which is highly dependent on commodity exports and consumption, has been hit hard by the epidemic. According to a report issued by the United Nations Development Programme, South Africa's GDP in 2020 may fall by 8%, and it may take 5 years to return to the level of 2019.[①] The economic collapse is a greater disaster than the disaster event itself. In order to avoid losing sight of the other, the South African government has to strike a dangerous balance between epidemic prevention and economic operations; that is, an important reason for its gradual relaxation of control measures when the epidemic situation has not improved fundamentally, and it also reflects the constraints it encountered in disaster management. It is not what the South African government wants to change the anti-epidemic strategy under the pressure of economic operation, but it deeply reveals the far-reaching impact of the economy's basic disaster management capacity building.

Ⅳ. Conclusion

South Africa has established a complete and effectivedisaster management framework, which played a key role in the early stage of the COVID-19 epidemic, delayed the arrival of the peak of the epidemic and avoided the collapse of the medical system. However, disaster management capabilities are closely related to a sound management system and strong protection capabilities, and neither is indispensable. After implementing the 35-day blockade measures, the

---

[①] U. N. development programme: South africa's GDP could plunge 8% this year because of pandemic. (2020, Sep 01). Targeted News Service Retrieved from https: //search. proquest. com/docview/ 2438960820 · accountid = 13855.

fact that South Africa had to gradually relax its epidemic control measures shows that its disaster management capacity building still faces severe challenges. These challenges mainly came from three fields: emergency supplies, people's livelihood and economic operation. Definitely, disaster management capacity building will inevitably be affected by social and cultural factors, so further research is needed.

Book Review

Review on Brazil and BRICS: Trade and Policy: Looking Back to the Past and Challenging the Future

Liu Mengru* Tong Xueying**

Abstract: This paper summarizes the views in the book *Brazil and BRICS: Trade and Policy*①, which, makes a comparative analysis of BRICS countries on the historical development, existing problems and suggestions on future development in light of various data and indicators in the economic and trade field. This paper aims to introduce the main contents of the book and the important points of view, and then makes comments on them. It is divided into four chapters: the first chapter summarizes the contents of the book; the second and the three conclude the main points of views with reviews to each chapter of the book; and the third draws inspiration from this book and the current world situation, further to provide suggestions to the development and win-win cooperation of the BRICS

---

* Liu Mengru, Lecturer on Portuguese Linguistic, Sichuan International Studies University, Member of Institute of BRICS Research of Sichuan International Studies University, engaged in Portuguese Teaching and Related Research in Portuguese Speaking Countries.

** Tong Xueying, student, Sichuan International Studies University, mainly studies on regional country research.

① O Brasil e os Demais BRICs: comércio e política, compiled by Brazilian economist Renato Baumann, which has been translated into English as Brazil and BRICS: Trade and Policy in this paper.

countries in the future.

Keywords: BRICS; Trade; Policy; Market Competition

Ⅰ. Introduction to Brazil and BRICS: Trade and Policy

In recent years, theBRICS countries①has received mcreasing attention from the academic due to its important strategic position and growing international influence in the world. Representing emerging market countries of the world, BRICS have made ajoint voice on major international and regional hotspot issues and promoted the reform of global economic governance for many years, so that emerging market countries and developing countries have greatly enhanced their status and got more say in international society. In this regard, BRICS is symbolic of a collective group on the international stage, which easily causes the ignorance to the differences between countries and their specific characteristics. Brazil, as one of the BRICS members, shall enhance its awareness of other BRICS countries, establish cooperative partnership, identify potential opportunities and engage in jointly coping with possible challenges. This book, against the background, was co-published by CEPAL② and IPEA③ aiming to discuss the characteristics of the BRICS countries and the possibility of deepening cooperation among them by comparatively analyzing Brazil and other BRICS members.

In light ofa large number of data analysis, this book aims to constitute a fundamental framework for commercial strategies with a more intuitive view to the specific national conditions of the BRICS countries. The book is divided into seven chapters as follows: a) analyze the trade relations between Brazil and other BRICS countries in comparative analysis of the trade structure and potential

---

① Comissão Econômica para a América Latina e o Caribe (CEPAL), Brazilian Economic Commission for Latin American.

② Comissão Econômica para a América Latina e o Caribe (CEPAL), Brazilian Economic Commission for Latin American.

③ Instituto de Pesquisa Econômica Aplicada (IPEA), Brazilian Institute of Applied Economics.

competition among BRICS countries; b) focus on the trade competition between Brazil and China in the North American market, and make recommendations in basis of the performance of China and Brazil on trade competition; c) analyze the international market openness of China, India and Brazil, and give corresponding suggestions; d) estimate the international trade participation rate of China, Brazil and India, in analysis of the policies and regulations adopted in the economic reform of the three countries; e) analyze the situation of China's direct foreign investment, especially in Latin America; f) analyze the issues faced by the BRICS countries and other emerging economies under current world situation and the hegemony of the United States. g) predict the possible cooperation patterns among Brazil and other emerging economies including BRICS countries from the perspective of Brazil.

Ⅱ. Chapters Review

This book makes a comparative analysis of BRICS which represents emerging economies; while given the different positions among the BRICS countries, involving China, Brazil, India and Russia, in the competition of global economic, their development undoubtedly lead to different orientations. Many factors cause their distinct features including geographical location, population and different national policies. Starting from these factors, by comparison of information as trade tariff, trade similarity index, comparative advantage index, market penetration rate, as well as the relevant indicators such as gross fixed capital formation, domestic savings, nominal exchange rate and international savings, this book analyzes the trade relations among BRICS members, concludes the similarities and differences of their development formations, and explores the composition of their trade flow. Through the data analysis of trade performance over the years, it is found that China is the most promising developing country among the BRICS countries, counting for a leading position in international trade competition. In the face of China's competitive advantage in trade, the authors analyze it from different aspects, compare the economic systems and historical policies of China, India, and Brazil, and offer suggestions for the future development of each country, taking into account its own "factor endowments". [1]Besides, this book focuses on the trade cooperation and competition between China and Brazil that it clarifies the recent competition status between China and Brazil in the North American market considering the trade performance of both countries, then predicts the possible future cooperation patterns and finally suggests that BRICS together with emerging economies should jointly explore the development potential and development direction in process of globalization.

1. Trade Relations between Brazil and other BRICS Countries

1.1 National Conditions of the BRICS Countries

This chapter reveals the influence and decisive role of population factor on domestic export products and production mode by analyzing the general population distribution of these countries. Both China and India have lower labor cost and larger market demand than that of Brazil and Russias due to their large population base and high population density. According to the GDP of the BRICS countries from 1990 to 2008 it is shown that China's GDP is three times over Brazil; India twice of Brazil, and Russia less than one tenth of China, which to some extent, reflects the influence of population factor on economic development.

Meanwhile, the proportion of the total GDP ofthe BRICS countries to the world GDP increased from 7.5% in 1990 to 11.7% in 2008; the total import

---

[1] Factor endowment, refers to the quantity of various factors of production in a country. The productive factors generally include three factors of land, labor and capital, and some also take productive technology and economic information into account. The factor endowment theory states that the export product from a country should be the comparative advantage products made of the relatively cheap and abundant productive factors in this country; while the import products should be those made of relatively scarce and expensive productive factors.

and export trade volume of the BRICS countries has doubled; and China still contributed the most to those achievement while Brazil's performance was not outstanding due to its multilateral trade opening policy at that time. In the 1990, having similar market openness, Brazil did not perform as well as India for their respective market policies.

This paper compares the trade performance of the BRICS countries by means of the import penetration rate and export propensity index. For Brazil, India and Russia, import rate is over export rate, while China fares vice versa, which is believed as a positive performance of participating in the international market.

Considering the reform of productive structure, the biggest difference among the BRICS countries lies in the fields of agriculture and industry. In terms of agriculture, early to the 1990s, Brazil's proportion of agriculture has decreased by 6%, while recently statistical data shows that other countries also have a proportion of comparative reduction as China and India by 10%. As for industrial sector, Brazil and Russia showed a significant decrease, while China and India still maintained an upward trend rather large-scale growth. To conclude, this book points out that Brazil's productive structure is similar to that of developed countries with high proportion of service industry, while China and India are still in their way to achieve industrialization.

1.2 Bilateral Trade Relations

This section analyzes the closeness and intensity of bilateral trade between Brazil and otherBRICS countries by means of trade partner importance index and trade intensity index. At the beginning of this century, China's import of bean food counted for half of the total import volume from Brazil, but the trade partner importance index has shown that, the trade closeness to Brazil hit a yearly increase until 2004 when the import and export relationship between China and Brazil has reversed, that is, Brazil, the once big trade export country, turned into an import country. Different from China-Brazil trade relation, the bilateral trade between Russia and Brazil keeps a relatively small and slow increase; while the bilateral trade between India and Brazil is beset with variable factors, where, Brazil's export to India is unstable and the import volume mcreases.

In addition to the trade partner index, the trade between China and Brazil can be measured by trade intensity index, which shows they have made a good performance and the bilateral trades between Brazil and other BRICS countries are also relatively positive. Indeed there is no absolutely optimistic to the trade among the BRICS countries: the trade intensity index of Brazil, India and Russia has declined; even China in its leading position, has turned down to economic recession in 2002 and 2008, having a bad impact on the trade sector.

The author points out that itis beneficial for Brazil and other countries to adjust their import and export trade policies in accordance with the trade partner index and trade intensity index .

1.3 Comparative Analysis of Trade Tariff

This chapter adopts the Herfindahl Hirschmannindex (HHI)①, export diversity index and relative entropy②to the analysis of the bilateral trade of Brazil with China, India and Russia, concluding that the structure of products exported to China tends to be more concentrated, while the concentration rate of import structure tends to be smaller and more diversified; besides, the import index for Brazil in Brazil-China relation is nearly close to the world standard index. In terms of the trade relationship of Brazil, India and Russia, they have the similar HHI index and relative entropy index in some degree.

1.4 Similarity of Trade Composition

Trade similarity index refers to the proportion of the same product exported by two countries to the third country, counting to the total export volume of the country. This chapter points out that Brazil has the import structure similar to other BRICS countries to a certain extent, especially to China, despite of

---

① Reflecting the concentration of trade structure, the higher the HHI value, the higher the market concentration indicating the higher the degree of monopoly.

② The closer the relative entropy is to '1', the lower the concentration of trade tax.

trade composition similarity index, intra-industry trade index, referring to the lower the index, the lower the competition risk, should also be considered into trade competition to maximize the interests and avoid vicious competition. The book points out that that countries should strengthen their own advantages when engaging in trade activities.

1.5 Comparative Advantages

Based on therevealed comparative advantage Index, Lafay index, export comparative performance index and export specialization index[1], this chapters analyzes the trade situation of the BRICS countries and enumerates their corresponding advantageous areas, among which, China has the largest number of advantageous areas, followed by India and Brazil. Amang these countries, manufacturing is the dominant sector for China and India with a large population; in Brazil over 200 categories of advantageous products mostly belong to categories 0, 2, 5, 6 and 7;[2] while in Russia the categories of superior products decreased.

The analysis above can draw conclusions as follow: China is a large economy with more advantageous industries that concentrated in the manufacturing industry; India ranks second and also sets manufacturing as the advantage fild; while Russia, as an European country, has relatively weak competitiveness in this field.

1.6 Gain and Loss Under Market Competition

This section compares the market occupancy of China and Brazil in Latin America and other trading regions. Although Brazil's market share in competition with China has been on the decline in Mexico and the United States, and countries of MERCOSUR, Central and South America, it has maintained profita-

---

[1] The two indexes are: Índice de Desempenho Exportado Comparado and índice de especializa 6 o das exporta à es.

[2] Standard international trade classification (SITC) is used for statistics and comparison. The categories mentioned in this paper are: 0: Food and live animals; 2: non-edible raw materials; 5: chemical products and related products; 6: finished products classified by raw materials; 7: machinery and transportation equipment.

ble in other regions. But this profitability still has gap with that of China, especially in major trade regions.

1.7 Suggestions

This chapterbriefly introduces the basic information of BRICS countries with their characteristics of bilateral trade by comparative analysis of trade tariffs, trade similarity index, comparative advantage index and market penetration rate. Indicators of total fixed capital formation, domestic savings, nominal exchange rate and international savings are also analyzed to clarify the relationship among Brazil and other BRICS countries, so that the differences lied in their developing patterns can be measured, which help deepen the understanding of the composition of trade flows among countries, and further to explore more possibilities for future trade cooperation. Generally, the BRICS have gradually increased their proportion in the world economy as a whole group rather "than hegemonic group". while the bilateral relations between Brazil and other BRICS countries are not actually the same; compared with China, Brazil and India do not have an advantage in product quantity. On the other hand, Brazil mainly benefits from the Latin American market but this situation has been reversed in recent years due to China's market expansion. By analyzing the similarities and differences of the BRICS countries, this chapter puts forward suggestions that Brazil should focus on certain development areas, so as to strengthen trade linkage with other BRICS countries and improve the competitiveness of Brazil's own products.

2. The Competition between China and Brazil in North America

This chapter takes the quantity, quality, product types and the similarity of export trade structure between China and Brazil from 2000 to 2008 as the comparative analysis object to explore their trade competition mode. From 2000 to 2005, the export similarity of China and Brazil gradually increased, while then, since 2005, due to the increasing market competitiveness of Chinese products, Brazil's exports to the North American market showed a decrease, which led to the decline of export similarity between the two countries. Previously, during the end of the last century and the beginning of this century, China's export products quickly occupied the market with the advantages of "low profits and high sales" and "large quantity products with guaranteed quality". Statistically, in 1992-2004 Brazil lost one-third of its North American market to China. Then from 2000 to 2008, to cope with the competition crisis, Brazil adopted measures to improve the quality of export products to compete with China, reflecting that Brazilian exporters must make changes to improve their competitiveness under this pressure.

Generally compared with Brazil, China is more competitive in exporting to North America with the obvious growth tendency. According to the Herschel Orin mode[1], in the competition between China and Brazil, natural resources is the most competitive category for Brazil, and shoes are the one with declining competitiveness; while for China, except for mineral products, almost all categories have increasingly grown, of which, machinery, leather, textile and clothing are more prominent. Meanwhile, in the U. S. market, although the total number of export categories has increased, Brazil has lost its export monopoly position in some fields where it comes up against China; some products even completely lost competitiveness that might be replaced by China anytime. In this context, Brazil is about to faced with the dilemma of reducing market share or even completely losing the product market. For this case, the author points out that to deal with the competition with China, Brazil should actively explore to enlarge the export products fields, increase the diversification of export products, and drop the similarity of export structure down, so as to avoid the direct competition with China.

---

[1] According to the theory of Herschel Orin mode, a country should export the products produced by using its relatively abundant production factors, and import the products produced by using its relatively scarce production factors.

3. Trade Openness of China, India and Brazil

China, India and Brazil had not had the relatively open market until the 1980s. And it was only in latest 20 years that the reform has obviously carried out. The rupee was made convertible in 1994 when India became an Article Ⅷ country; the Chinese RMB and the Brazilian real were made convertible in 1996 and 1999, respectively. ① Countries with free currency convertibility can gain many benefits, including but not limited to: the government can gain more from seigniorage that indeed speed up the establishment of international trade partnership; the transportation cost in the private sector turns lower because, the currency convertibility reduces the impact of exchange rate evaporation on domestic production and foreign trade. Krugman once stated that hysteresis phenomenon② acts especially on countries where currencies are free to convert. So that foreign exchange legislation is not enough to guarantee currency convertibility and customs protection in regional integration is essential as well.

To conclude, Brazil is better than China and India in foreign exchange legislation, but the trade policies of China and India are more reasonable than Brazil. Different countries have different technical standards and factor endowments, forming their distinct development advantages and balance points, which points the way to China, India and Brazil on improving the trade openness, as Krugman believes that "the best way to understand the operation of the world economy is to dig out the internal situation of each country".

---

① According to the International Monetary Fund, if a country realizes the free convertibility in the current account, this country's currency can be defined as a convertible currency. Since the free convertibility clauses lists the eighth Article of the IMF Agreement, the country that was usually called as 'the Eighth Article Country'.

② "Hysteresis" is originally a physical concept and which is applied to economics research late, meaning that an initial equilibrium of economy can not be recovered with the external impacts, which will reach to another kind of equilibrium with the economic variables inconsistent to the original one. (source: Hysteresis Phenomenon and Its Application in Western Economics) HTTPS: www. 1xuezhe. exuezh. com-mqkkart221277 · Dbcode = 1 & Flag = 2).

4. China and Brazil: Participating in International Trade

In recent years, emerging countries have made great achievements in international society with stronger economy and growing political influence that specifically refers to the increasing influence on global multilateral relationships. However, from a internal point of view of China, Brazil and India, both the economic growth and political influence for the three countries have not yet kept pace with each other synchronously, among which, China has the best performance. Since 1999 when financial crisis broke out, Brazil had to make certain adjustments to its strategic plans as adding export economic incentives, while, India adopted a more conservative reform strategy until 2002.

In the 1970s, Chinaintroduced reform and opening up policy that has reformed the domestic production structure. And it is noticeable that China's export volume has risen up from less than 1% in 1980 to 9% by 2007, and the import volume has also increased from 1% to 7%.

For Brazil, bulk commodities account for the main proportion of import and export. And Brazil mainly imports medium and high-strength technology products. From 1991 to 1999 Brazil has experienced a period of large-scale import liberalization, then, although Brazil still maintains the mechanism of import liberalization, it still tries to change the strategy for trade opening by changing the exchange rate mechanism and implementing export incentives.

For India the export structure totally stays still, and the trade distribution has not changed significantly since 2002 when India achieved international trade freedom. India has reduced tariffs and taken some quantitative restrictions, in addition, it has changed some plans for import control as the expansion of concession import licenses and restriction of import licenses. India implemented the slow import liberalization and marginal export incentive at the early stage; later, it deepened the reform of liberalization, reduced the tariff and non-tariff barriers of import, raised price, and implemented the export promotion program so as to improve the country's foreign competitiveness. Directorate General of Foreign

Trade affiliated with the India Ministry of Commerce and Industry has released *The 2009 - 2014 Foreign Trade and Industry Policy Report* on August 27,[①] which clarifies India's foreign trade policy objectives and specific measures in the next five years. The report states that:

At present, the global economy is facing the most serious challenge after World War II, and WTO has predicted that global trade will shrink by 9%. Although India's economy has performed relatively well in the crisis, its export volume has shrunk sharply for 10 consecutive months. The report summarizes the foreign trade in 2004 - 2009, and points out that India has achieved two major goals in five years: one is that India's share of global trade in goods has doubled; the other is that foreign trade has played an important role in economic growth and employment promotion.

The overall goal of the new foreign trade policy is to tap export potential, improve export performance, encourage foreign trade and promote trade balance. The report points out that the government will reverse the downward trend of exports by means of fiscal stimulus, institutions reform, procedures simplification, strengthening global market access, diversification of export markets, improvement of export related infrastructure construction, transaction costs reduction and full refund of export indirect tax. By March 2011, the export will grow by 15% and the export volume will reach 200 billion US dollars; exports will rise up by 25% from 2011 to 2014, and India's share of global trade will doubled by 2020.

5. China's Foreign Investment in Latin America

5.1 China's Economic Strength

Started in 1978, the reform and opening up[②] in China has achieved the sustained and rapid economic development with an average annual growth of nearly

---

① Directorate General of Foreign Trade affiliated The India Ministry of Commerce and Industry: The 2009 - 2014 Foreign Trade and Industry Policy Report http: //in. mofcom. gov. cn/article/ddfg/waimao/20090920090906513018. shtml.

② It has been only 30 years since China's reform and opening up.

10%, which is a historical miracle. And in 2009, China became the world's largest exporter. In 1980, when the economic reform started, China mainly exported products with low value-added tax (such as textiles and clothing), and then gradually exported high-tech products. Nowadays, China has been able to compete with the United States. From 2004 to 2008, China's foreign investment has created a tenfold increase from US $5.5 billion to US $52.1 billion. According to the 2003 global economic report of Goldman Sachs[1], it is predicted that China will surpass the United States in 2041 and become the world's largest economic power.

5.2 China's Foreign Direct Investment

In the early days, China was an ideal investment target country rather than the big foreign investment country. Developing countries has the market with more investment potential where the investment aims to gain superior resources; while investment in developed countries pursues higher efficiency. China as the "world factory" with a a large population, naturally attracts a large number of foreign investment. At the beginning of 1990, China ranged the largest foreign direct investment target country among developing countries that by 2007, leaped the second largest foreign direct investment target country after the United States in the world. In 1999, the "going out" strategy put forward by the Chinese government promoted the pace of China's globalization. Then in 2001 China joined the WTO and gradually stepped onto the world stage. In this chapter, three reasons for China's vigorous development of foreign investment was concluded, that is, first to maintain China's average annual GDP growth at 8% - 10% because the rapid economic development needs the import of natural resources; second to enhance the competitiveness of Chinese enterprises in the international market; final to apply the technology earned from the investment target industrial countries to their own industries, for example, Lenovo, Huawei and

---

[1] Refers to the Global Economic Report entitled Dreaming with BRICS: The Path to 2050 released by Goldman Sachs in October 2003 https: //world. huanqiu. com/article/9CaKrnJngEX).

TCL that all have once adopted this way to their own development.

5.3 China's Direct Investment in Latin America

In Latin America, the region's foreign direct investment was once dominated mainly by European countries and the United States, where the proportion of investment from Asian countries including China was very small; until 2000, the direct investment of China began to increased. On the one hand, the cooperation patterns among China and Latin America countries include the sales relationship, meaning that China imports mineral resources, oil and natural gas from Latin American countries to support domestic rapid economic development by means of ways including but not limited direct purchase and merger of companies; on the other hand, the cooperation model can be connect with local merchants as well, such as sending auto parts made in China to Argentina for assembly that greatly reduces the transportation cost. In addition, recently China and Latin American countries start the relationship of loan creditors, that is, some enterprises export raw materials to China as loan guarantee, and others, such as ZTE, supplies financing for capital turnover.

According to a study of the Asia Pacific Foundation of Canada, it is no doubt that China's foreign investment will achieve increasing growth in the future, but at that time, only 27% of the enterprises achieved foreign investment, most of which relied on the strategy of "going out"; and no more than 6% of the foreign investment reached US $10 million. In view of this, the author suggests that for Chinese enterprises to go abroad and to build up domestic brands in the world stage, they should set up their own industrial plans or look for joint ventures rather taking the route of acquisition and merger.

The authorsuggests that the direct investment of China in Latin America should be oriented in three ways: 1) search for raw materials, energy and food resources for the domestic development of China; 2) upgrade the industries to level the competitiveness in international trade; 3) diverse the investment model at the currency disadvantage inferior to dollar.

6. BRICS and the Change of Hegemony

The term of "BRICS" is controversial. To response it, the author said that the concept of BRICS referring to a group of countries was initially proposed by an economist according to various date analysis, which would not have a huge impact on the world structure. Nevertheless, the author holds a positive attitude towards China's development, believing that China is the country likely to leap to the world's top economies list, and may be able to surpass the United States in 2040.

Compared with the performance of the BRICS countries in other fields, which country among China, Brazil, India and Russia can take over the "lender of last resort" shall be decided by their national development and international status. However, none of these countries is better able to develop this capability despite of China that has the most potential. The Chinese government is making efforts to push it forward, which at present still under a slow growth, indicating that there is still a long-turn development to achieve this goal. In this regard, China should prepare in two respects: first the fiscal deficit; then to turn China's yuan into a freely convertible currency and to provide fund support for cooperative countries or organizations.

This book tends to compared China with India for both country have a large population, and holds that China and India are more likely to become potential countries to lead the development of BRICS. The development of India comes up against the negative factors including poor infrastructure conditions, low happiness index of residents and high illiteracy rate, which however, have not brought India's "globalization" to a standstill. On the contrary, too many norms in India will hold back the business. For China, the development lies in the large population base, and nowadays the effect of scientific and technological innovation has been growing. In recent years, the development of China's own technology has achieved a lot, leaping to a leading position in many fields that has caused certain effects on other countries. On the one hand, it will promote some developed countries to carry out technological innovation, on the other hand, it will also cause growing unemployment in other developed countries and developing countries like Brazil.

The author states that just by the quantitative analysis of the economic effects of BRICS can only partly reflects the influence on diplomatic economy and international economy. Considering the population, economy and military situation as well as the current technological development of BRICS, it can be concluded that in the future BRICS will scale up the export in the international market and increase the GDP on the current basis. And the author believes that it is unreasonable to discuss the importance of the G7 and BRICS separately for both have played the essential role in achieving worldwide integration. The population base of the G7 and BRICS together account for one half of the world's population and the volume of economy aggregates for two-thirds of the world's economy, meaning that both two groups have surpassed the G20 to some extent. Brazil's foreign minister Celso Amorim publicly stated on the Sao Paulo State Newspaper that "it will be very difficult for G7 to make decisions without consultation from BRICS. Although it has not yet taken place, it does not mean that it will not happen in the future."

It is pointed outin the book that presently China has provide the best development mode of "globalization" reflected in actively seeking new markets, introducing technology, ensuring domestic raw materials and energy supply. In the first half of the 20th century, China made great efforts to develop domestic enterprises to improve their international competitiveness; by contrast, Brazil, Russia and India, as the countries with large population, did not take strong measures in market competition. Under the global financial crisis in 2008, China's economy also suffered heavy losses with exports plummeting by 40%, but it soon recovered in early 2010 after a short-term adjustment.

Finally, the author believes that to enhance their international status, the BRICS countries should focus on not merely their own development but the development of other countries and existing problems; and consider the imbalance of development caused by environmental or long-term impact of public health emergencies in some areas. In terms of current economic statistics, the name "Bric" would put China first in terms of importance, as "Cirb".

7. Brazil and the Emerging Countries in the World

In this paper, emerging countries are divided into the first generation of emerging countries and the second generation of emerging countries. The newly industrialized countries belong to the first generation of emerging countries. Different from developing countries, the newly industrialized countries pay more attention to export after experiencing import growth. According to the book, the concept of "BRICS" was put forward at the end of the cold war when the second generation of emerging economies sprang out along with the profound evolution of the global economic structure. In 1990s, Under the concept of hegemony in the Washington consensus[1], there is no real political meaning or internal cooperation between emerging countries. The author states that the alliance of five countries in BRICS is quite different from that of the third world alliance, which, even has things in with South South cooperation in many ways but not in the same.

As for the relationship between Brazil and emerging countries, the author believes that the government's existing economic policies create conditions for the country to participate in the second generation of emerging markets; meanwhile the country's foreign policies aim at making closely linkage with these emerging powers politically. In this regard, the author points out two directions for Brazil: first to strengthen globalization and deepen the interdependence of the global economies, then to create a consumer market, such as the "Family Fund Project, raising the national minimum wage and other income related projects" advocated by the Lula government. The fact is mentioned that Brazil is in-

---

[1] Washington Consensus is a set of neoliberal political and economic theories that emerged in 1989 for Latin American countries and transitional countries in Eastern Europe.

creasingly close to other emerging countries in foreign policy that still closer to China in trade relations. At the same time, its trade with India has become increasingly frequent since 2005. Compared to the trade with China and Brazil, the trade between Brazil and India is influenced by political factors; while the trade between China and Brazil with rapid growth and large volume is due to the strength of China's trade itself. Except the considerable trade with Brazil, China also became an important trade partner of South Africa and India in 2009.

This paper discusses the BRICS in the fields of finance, trade, environment, foreign policy, among which the most urgent issues are environment protection, energy conservation and emission reduction. For the BRICS countries, Russia shows less interest in the Kyoto Protocol due to domestic production requirements. Although China also pursues the high-intensity economic development, it has a positive attitude towards the signing of the Kyoto agreement. However, India created the most increase of total carbon emissions by 10%, which is contrary to the reduction content of the agreement. In contrast, Brazil has the best balance between environmental protection and its own development, and its carbon emissions have remained basically unchanged in the past two decades.

III. Enlightenment

There have beenchallenges on the existence of "BRICS" in international community, claiming that BRICS is only a temporary group based on the statistical data analysis. The fact is since the first summit in Yekaterinburg, BRICS have repeatedly contributed to the international financial crisis, and actual contributions made by BRICS in the international arena can not be ignored. People. cn commented that "the BRICS has exchanged views on major international hotspot issues such as the reform of international financial institutions, food security, climate changing in the past 10 sessions, then the BRICS is gradually realizing the transformation from concept to practice."① It is believed that the BRICS is a representative group to promote the diplomatic and trade exchanges among BRICS countries, whith is formed on basis of this concept and has great strategic significance.

As there presentative of emerging economies, BRICS develop so rapidly endowed with their own advantages. China and India rank first and second in the world in terms of population; Russia has vast land; and Brazil enjoys unique natural resources and environment. China and India profit from "demographic dividend", known as the "world factory" and "world office" respectively. Russia and Brazil take the natural resource advantages known as "world gas station" and "world raw material base". Compared with other BRICS countries, China has the largest scale and trade increment contribution, more than the other four countries combined. With the development of technology, it is an indisputable fact that China has take the leader not only in the BRICS but in the world with an increasing influence.

In this book, the author fully affirms China's economic performance and international status, and recognizes the influence of population base on national economic development. However, this paper believes that there are certain limitations in analyzing GDP simply from the factor of population base and the book mainly focuses on the volume of trade between China and India but neglects Russia. However, if the cutting-edge technology and military strength are taken into account, Russia's relative importance shall be enhanced. Besides the analysis of the influence factors on GDP by means of econometric model shows that GDP growth will also be affected by money supply, import and export balance, fiscal revenue etc. .

Among the BRICS countries, Brazil has the closest trade relations with China. Through the comparative analysis of the advantages and trade similarity in the book, as well as the research on the competition and complementarity of bi-

---

① http: //theory. people. com. cn/nl/2017/1012/c40531 - 29583869. html.

lateral trade between China and Brazil, the enlightenment can be drawn as following: both countries should strengthen the export of products with distinct advantages according to their own resource endowment, at the same time, the two countries can use the complementarity of both sides to strengthen trade exchanges, so as to find more opportunities for trade cooperation. In addition, this paper views the author's opinion that China did not invest heavily in the domestic market in the early stage but increased the intensity of foreign direct investment as not comprehensive. Looking back on the development of China's foreign investment in the past 40 years, it can be concluded that China's foreign direct investment has experienced four stages since 1979: since the founding of the People's Republic of China, China focused on internal adjustment to achieve economic recovery; in the 1980s, China began to have a good momentum for foreign development; to the end of the 20th century, China made adjustments on specific matters such as foreign exchange management and international economic cooperation. Facts show that China has been in a state of steady development in line with its national conditions.

Despite the rapid development of emerging economies, the world is still dominated by the hegemony of United States that none of emerging economies is able to defend or replace. It is generally believed that the decline of one country must lead to the rise of another, this theory of the Rise and Fall of Great Powers however, in the face of such a hegemonic power as the United States, can hardly give a strong explanation. The United States is far from reaching the decline period of hegemony, and the emerging powers are far from rising to the extent to replace the US hegemony.

The book mentioned Brazil's commitment to maintain the same carbon emissions as in 2007 by 2020, and China has announced a 40%-45% reduction in carbon emissions by 2020. However, according to the Emission Gap Report of the United Nations Environment Programme in 2019, it is pointed out that "efforts to reduce emissions in recent years have failed."[1] For BRICS countries, the promotion of their international influence and status should not merely focus on their own economic development, and it is essential to participate in international affairs, such as environmental protection, combating terrorism, solving the problem of world poverty.

BRICS countries have taken the lead in recovery after the financial crisis and achieved rapid economic growth. There exist similarities and complementarities among BRICS countries. Therefore, how to balance the relationship between competition and cooperation will be a common problem for BRICS countries. Nowadays, under the pressure of US hegemony, China is in increasingly difficult situation. How to maintain good relations with BRICS countries and realize trade growth is a new challenge for China.

The outbreak of COVID-19 pandemic in early 2020 has a great impact on the global economy. As the fastest and most efficient country to prevent and control the epidemic, China can not only provide support to BRICS countries in epidemic prevention and control, but actively strengthen ties with BRICS countries in the field of trade and seek opportunities for cooperation. Opportunities and challenges coexist, the best opportunity hides in the face of challenges. On the other hand, it is helpful for China to further grasp the opportunity for further strengthening the economic ties, as the so-called "prosperity makes friends" and to relieve the economic downturn risk and seek more cooperation opportunities to get through tough together.

---

[1] The status and role of BRICS in global governance. http::: theory. people. com. cnnnl12017 710122c40531-29583869. html//www. unenvironment. org/interactive/emissions-gap-report/2019/report_zh-hans. php.

图书在版编目（CIP）数据

金砖国家国别与合作研究.第二辑/蒲公英，游涵主编.
—北京：时事出版社，2021.10
ISBN 978-7-5195-0435-9

Ⅰ.①金… Ⅱ.①蒲…②游… Ⅲ.①国际合作—研究 Ⅳ.①D812

中国版本图书馆 CIP 数据核字（2021）第 162438 号

出版发行：	时事出版社
地　　址：	北京市海淀区彰化路 138 号西荣阁 B 座 G2 层
邮　　编：	100097
发行热线：	（010）88869831　88869832
传　　真：	（010）88869875
电子邮箱：	shishichubanshe@ sina. com
网　　址：	www. shishishe. com
印　　刷：	北京良义印刷科技有限公司

开本：787×1092　1/16　印张：18.5　字数：290 千字
2021 年 9 月第 1 版　2021 年 9 月第 1 次印刷
定价：98.00 元
（如有印装质量问题，请与本社发行部联系调换）